New Casebooks

THE TURN OF THE SCREW
and
WHAT MAISIE KNEW

New Casebooks

PUBLISHED

Antony and Cleopatra
Hamlet
King Lear
Macbeth
A Midsummer Night's
    Dream
Shakespeare's History Plays:
    Richard II to Henry V
Shakespeare's Tragedies
Twelfth Night
_____

Feminist Theatre and Theory
Waiting for Godot and
Endgame
_____

Bleak House
Wilkie Collins
Joseph Conrad
David Copperfield and
    Hard Times
Emma
E. M. Forster
Frankenstein
Great Expectations
Jane Eyre

Mansfield Park and
    Persuasion
Middlemarch
Toni Morrison
Mrs Dalloway and To the
    Lighthouse
Sense and Sensibility and
    Pride and Prejudice
Sons and Lovers
Tess of the d'Urbervilles
Tristram Shandy
The Turn of the Screw and
    What Maisie Knew
Villette
Wuthering Heights
_____

William Blake
Chaucer
Coleridge, Keats and Shelley
Seamus Heaney
Philip Larkin
Victorian Women Poets
Wordsworth
_____

Postcolonial Literatures

Further titles are in preparation

New Casebooks Series
Series Standing Order
ISBN 0–333–71702–3 hardcover
ISBN 0–333–69345–0 paperback
(outside North America only)

You can receive future titles in this series as they are published by placing a standing order. Please contact your bookseller or, in case of difficulty, write to us at the address below with your name and address, the title of the series and the ISBN quoted above.

Customer Services Department, Macmillan Distribution Ltd
Houndmills, Basingstoke, Hampshire RG21 6XS, England

New Casebooks

THE TURN OF THE
SCREW
and
WHAT MAISIE KNEW

EDITED BY
NEIL CORNWELL AND MAGGIE MALONE

First published 1998 by
MACMILLAN PRESS LTD
Houndmills, Basingstoke, Hampshire RG21 6XS
and London
Companies and representatives throughout the world

ISBN 0–333–68479–6 hardcover
ISBN 0–333–68480–X paperback

A catalogue record for this book is available from the British Library.

This book is printed on paper suitable for recycling and made from
fully managed and sustained forest sources.

10   9   8   7   6   5   4   3   2   1
07   06   05   04   03   02   01   00   99   98

Typeset by Expo

Printed in Hong Kong

First published in the United States of America 1998 by
ST. MARTIN'S PRESS, INC.,
Scholarly and Reference Division,
175 Fifth Avenue, New York, N.Y. 10010

ISBN 0–312–21466–9

Contents

Acknowledgements

The editors and publishers wish to thank the following for permission to use copyright material:

Marianne DeKoven, for material from *Rich and Strange: Gender, History, Modernism* (1991), pp. 47–63, 227–9. Copyright © 1991 Princeton University Press, by permission of Princeton University Press; Barbara Eckstein, 'Unsquaring the Squared Route in *What Maisie Knew*', *The Henry James Review*, 9:3 (1988). Copyright © 1988 the Johns Hopkins University Press, by permission of the Johns Hopkins University Press; Shoshana Felman, for edited material from 'Turning the Screw of Interpretation', *Yale French Studies* (1977) published as 'The Scene of Writing: Purloined Letters' in *Literature and Psychoanalysis: The Question of Reading: Otherwise*, ed. Shoshana Felman, the Johns Hopkins University Press (1982), by permission of Yale French Studies; Ronald Knowles, for 'The Hideous Obscure: *The Turn of the Screw* and Oscar Wilde' by permission of the author; T. J. Lustig, for material from *Henry James and the Ghostly* (1994), pp. 115–25, 271–2, by permission of Cambridge University Press; Beth Newman, for 'Getting Fixed: Feminine Identity and Scopic Crisis in *The Turn of the Screw*', *Novel: A Forum on Fiction*, 26:1 (1992). Copyright © NOVEL Corp. 1992, by permission of Novel; John H. Pearson, for 'Repetition and Subversion in Henry James's *The Turn of the Screw*', *The Henry James Review*, 13 (1992). Copyright © 1992 the Johns Hopkins University Press, by permission of the Johns Hopkins University Press; Julie Rivkin, for material from *False Positions: The Representational Logics of Henry James's Fiction* (1996), pp. 123–45, 160–2, 209–11. Copyright © 1996 by the Board of Trustees of Leland Stanford Junior University, by permission of Stanford University

Press; John Carlos Rowe, for material from *The Theoretical Dimensions of Henry James* (1984) Methuen & Co., pp. 123–46, 271–3, by permission of Routledge and the University of Wisconsin Press; Ronald Schleifer, 'The Trap of the Imagination: The Gothic Tradition, Fiction and the "Turn of the Screw"', *Criticism*, 22:4 (1980), by permission of Wayne State University Press; Sheila Teahan, for '*What Maisie Knew* and the Improper Third Person', *Studies in American Fiction*, 21:2 (1993), by permission of Studies in American Fiction.

Every effort has been made to trace the copyright holders but if any have been inadvertently overlooked the publisher will be pleased to make the necessary arrangement at the first opportunity.

General Editors' Preface

The purpose of this series of New Casebooks is to reveal some of the ways in which contemporary criticism has changed our understanding of commonly studied texts and writers and, indeed, of the nature of criticism itself. Central to the series is a concern with modern critical theory and its effect on current approaches to the study of literature. Each New Casebook editor has been asked to select a sequence of essays which will introduce the reader to the new critical approaches to the text or texts being discussed in the volume and also illuminate the rich interchange between critical theory and critical practice that characterises so much current writing about literature.

In this focus on modern critical thinking and practice New Casebooks aim not only to inform but also to stimulate, with volumes seeking to reflect both the controversy and the excitement of current criticism. Because much of this criticism is difficult and often employs an unfamiliar critical language, editors have been asked to give the reader as much help as they feel is appropriate, but without simplifying the essays or the issues they raise. Again, editors have been asked to supply a list of further reading which will enable readers to follow up issues raised by the essays in the volume.

The project of New Casebooks, then, is to bring together in an illuminating way those critics who best illustrate the ways in which contemporary criticism has established new methods of analysing texts and who have reinvigorated the important debate about how we 'read' literature. The hope is, of course, that New Casebooks will not only open up this debate to a wider audience, but will also encourage students to extend their own ideas, and think afresh about their responses to the texts they are studying.

John Peck and Martin Coyle
University of Wales, Cardiff

Introduction

NEIL CORNWELL AND MAGGIE MALONE

Why couple *The Turn of the Screw* with *What Maisie Knew*? The spectral horror of *The Turn of the Screw* (1898) may seem an extreme and unlikely fictional progression from the educational ripening of *What Maisie Knew* (published the previous year). One recent commentator, however, reads *What Maisie Knew* as, in effect, a reversal of the succeeding work, arguing that Maisie's assorted guardians in the early chapters 'are as bizarre as the ghosts in *The Turn of the Screw*'; *What Maisie Knew* thus 'begins as a ghost story, its eerie "turn of the screw" being that Maisie cannot even see the ghosts that haunt her existence'.[1] The connection between the two texts does, indeed, lie in the difficulties they both pose concerning the uncertainties of what can be known. By the end of the nineteenth century, it is widely accepted, many of the categories and ideas that had seemed established and certain over so much of the Victorian period were beginning to appear in a more tenuous light. The change is particularly clear in James's career. It was in this decade, for most of the nineties and until he had concluded *The Sacred Fount* in 1900, that Henry James chose temporarily to leave aside his renowned international theme of Americans in Europe and to concentrate instead on the elusive, at times virtually intangible, nuances of English society. *The Turn of the Screw* and *What Maisie Knew* are his two most successful works in this context.

I

James seemed to dismiss *The Turn of the Screw* in letters of 1898 as 'rather a shameless pot-boiler' and 'that wanton little Tale'.[2]

However depreciative of this work he may then really have felt, it does appear that he subsequently came to value it more highly – as well he might. The tone of *The Turn of the Screw* is something that he later sought to recapture, especially for his unfinished novel, *The Sense of the Past*, which he worked on in 1900 and again in 1914–15. According to William James, Jr, moreover, when asked by his sister-in-law in 1910, '... "Henry, why don't you write *another* story like 'The Turn of the Screw'?", Uncle Henry replied, "My God Alice, I wish I could!"'.[3] Criticism has endorsed such a wish by paying more attention to *The Turn of the Screw* than to any other of James's, in a number of cases, more lavishly acclaimed works.

The critical literature on *The Turn of the Screw* has indeed been voluminous and continues to snowball as newer critical approaches are brought to bear. Detailed surveys of this body of criticism are available elsewhere, but a brief outline here is still necessary, to sketch a background to the more recent period.[4] Early readings took the novella largely at face value, as a ghost story (an unnamed governess is seemingly confronted by two former employees – the master's valet and the previous governess – who, she comes to believe, have returned from the dead to reclaim the two children now in her charge), with critics expressing subjective evaluations as to taste and merit.[5] From the 1920s, however, more intricate responses began to emerge. Rather than accept the ghosts as spectral apparitions, critics began to read other answers from the puzzles posed by the text: perhaps a hysterical governess had hallucinated Peter Quint and Miss Jessel. A dichotomy between 'apparitionist' and 'non-apparitionist' (or, conversely, 'hallucinationist' and 'non-hallucinationist') interpretations first developed and then raged, fostered largely under the aegis of the American school of New Criticism (basically a less rigorous version of the close textual reading practised by Russian Formalism and often tinged with a New England puritanism). The question of the 'reality' or otherwise of the ghosts consequently dominated critical discourse for some decades.

Edna Kenton, in an essay of 1924, first seriously challenged the reliability of the governess's account. This stance was developed, impressively for its time, by Harold C. Goddard, in a lecture dating from the early 1920s but first published only in 1957. Edmund Wilson pioneered a Freudian analysis in 1934, in a celebrated essay that, when revisited now, however, seems remarkably thin on textual detail. The apparitionist backlash was led by Robert Heilman who, in an article of 1948, argues for a biblical allegory of corruption in the Garden of Eden.[6] The plethora of articles apart, copious critical editions were produced, as well as full monographs promoting both the hallucinationist and non-hallucinationist tendencies.[7]

In many of these early readings, supposed authorial intention was all too frequently invoked as evidence for the arguments made, some critics placing notebook entries, letters and the subsequent preface (written a decade later) on an equal textual footing with the prose fiction itself, notwithstanding Goddard's sage warning that 'in these matters it is always the work itself and not the author that is the ultimate authority'.[8] Theoretical objections apart, such testimony as may be gathered from these particular sources is, as far as *The Turn of the Screw* is concerned, at best conflicting. Furthermore, and as if the text did not raise enough vexed questions from within, critical problems were not infrequently compounded by selective presentation of evidence (often arising from questionable readings or downright misreadings), special pleadings and excursions beyond the text.[9] Older readings, lacking clear methods of analysis, provided contradictory interpretations and the novella remained puzzlingly obscure.

II

By the end of the 1960s, however, argument of an either/or nature over the 'reality' of the ghosts began to give way to a stress on ambiguity: the issue was now held by many, though by no means all, critics to be undecidable. Early advocates of this powerful line of argument included John J. Enck, Paul N. Siegel and Charles Thomas Samuels.[10] What might be called the 'old' ambiguity was based on an admissibility of simultaneous readings: equal cases being tenable both for and against the existence of the ghosts. Such an approach was strongly reinforced by the advent of Tzvetan Todorov's theory of the fantastic, based on a more genuinely textual ambiguity. This was applied to texts in which the supernatural was posited in such a way as to give rise to narratorial and consequently reader hesitation, with *The Turn of the Screw* seen as a prime example.[11] What we have called the old ambiguity, that of a dualistic story, as Peter G. Beidler states, 'at once *both* ghost story *and* a psychological study',[12] thus gave way to the new ambiguity, one based in language and demonstrable through techniques of de-construction. The 'new criticism' of *The Turn of the Screw* was ad-vanced by a critical position not only recognising but valorising fabulaic puzzle and textual indeterminacy as narrative principles. In a word, where previously critics had sought – ineffectively – to unravel the text, more recent commentaries have revelled in its uncertainties.

If Todorov's structuralist approach to ambiguity and the fantastic may be seen as one godfather of modern criticism of *The Turn of the Screw*, another – and older – godfather undoubtedly must be Freud. Freudian theory stimulated not only the earlier type of psy-chological exegesis commencing with Edmund Wilson; it also sup-plied the concept of the 'uncanny', which itself contributed to Todorovian methodology.[13] Freud's concept of the uncanny (*Das Unheimliche*) is seen as something at the same time unfathomable, yet 'uncannily' familiar. For present purposes it may be considered as close to the Todorovian 'fantastic', lurking somewhere between the areas explicable by, on the one hand, realistic (or psychological) criteria and, on the other, supernatural causes. The uncanny was clearly a concept in waiting for the Jamesian ghostly text.

Aspects of Freudianism and post-Freudianism, as may be expected, have permeated a range of contemporary critical ap-proaches to James. These developments, with particular regard to *The Turn of the Screw*, date from 1976–7, when three seminal ex-tended critical essays appeared. Christine Brooke-Rose's structural-ist analysis argues for 'two clear, simple, but mutually exclusive fabulas', while Shlomith Rimmon detects a 'double-directedness' (deriving 'from an interaction between the reader's hypothesis and a character's statement' and suggestive of conflicting inferences) in key details encoded in the text.[14] Shoshana Felman employs post-Freudian deconstructionist techniques, again to illustrate an appar-ently definitive inconclusiveness.[15] This vital stage in criticism of *The Turn of the Screw* is here represented by an excerpt from Felman (see essay 2). Felman, like Brooke-Rose and Rimmon, em-phasises the text's dualities, while bringing to bear a plurality of modern theoretical strategies and exposing the failings of much of the earlier criticism.

As Beidler has remarked, the published scholarship on *The Turn of the Screw*, particularly since the 1970s, 'has taken on a life of its own'.[16] This has been the case not only in quantity, but in breadth. *The Turn of the Screw* has attracted, and continues to attract, at very least its fair share of eccentric, or in some way aberrant, readings. Mrs Grose has been proposed as the evil arch-manipulator; or as the real mother of the children with their 'uncle' as father; Quint has emerged as a living prowler, guarding a demented Miss Jessel;[17] Douglas has been claimed as the real Miles, while a homoerotic relationship between Quint and Miles has been suggested as being somehow attributable to a similar relationship between Douglas and the narrator.[18] Miles has also been claimed as a hoaxer, dressing up as the ghosts.[19] Appealing as such theories may be, their sustainability by reference to the text remains, to put it mildly, doubtful. Acceptance of the identification of Douglas with Miles, for instance, would necessitate disbelieving Douglas's denial that this is the case (*TS*, p. 23);[20] If Douglas, and by implication the narrator, *are* disbelieved here, why should we believe anything at all? The suggestion, made by a number of critics (see Beth Newman's comments, essay 6), that the primary narrator (of the framing prologue) might be female is in a different category: interesting it may be and there may be nothing in the text to refute it, but it still seems to us, on balance, unlikely.[21] Recent readings perhaps also classifiable as eccentric include one entertaining interpretation finding all answers in the rabid bisexual activity of just about every character; and another which untenably premises its otherwise interesting gender-based discussion on a quest for revenge on the governess's part for having been literally seduced by the uncle in Harley Street.[22] *The Turn of the Screw* has indeed given rise to such a scholarly farrago that essays have been devoted to that very phenomenon itself: either as hermeneutic paradigm, or as critical scandal.[23] At times we almost seem to be reaching the position claimed by Fred Botting for Mary Shelley's most famous novel: '*Frankenstein* is a product of criticism, not a work of literature'.[24]

III

However, if we return to recent critical trends somewhere nearer the mainstream of James criticism, we can discern several determinate ways of reading, or lines of enquiry, the more prominent of which are represented in the present collection. It should be mentioned, however, that the contributions of critics are not always confinable within whatever category to which, for the sake of convenient labelling, they may tend to be consigned.

Felman (essay 2) uses Lacan and Derrida to deconstruct not only *The Turn of the Screw* but also the older, cruder Freudian interpretations, seen as onesidedly and inadequately ignoring the inconclusiveness of the text. Modern psychoanalytical readings may be found in essays by Ned Lukacher and Stanley Renner.[25] Such an approach now offers a more sophisticated grounding of image and plot in psychosexual fantasy while, in common with many other recent modes of reading, situating the whole in a fuller cultural context. An interesting psychological variant is provided by Karen Halttunen, who brings to bear psychology contemporary to the story, in particular that of Henry's brother, the American psychologist and philosopher William James.[26]

Felman's deconstruction inevitably stems from her close scrutiny of the text's language, a trend here pursued also by T. J. Lustig (essay 5); convincing linguistic analyses, confirming the inherence of textual ambiguity, are furnished too by Darrel Mansell and Norman Macleod (the latter demonstrating that James's revisions for the New York edition even reinforced the ambiguity).[27] Sigrid Renaux, in her 1993 monograph, sees *The Turn of the Screw* as 'an iconic/symbolic writing' and 'a long spiral' from beginning to end, encoded in the very 'T' and 'S' of the title words.[28] A number of commentators have concentrated on the structure of the tale and, more recently, the nature of the framing device.[29] In each case, the emphasis has fallen on framing, in various senses, on the uncertainty of the text, and on how language, by its very nature, cannot provide a single clear perspective.

Several additional newer slants on *The Turn of the Screw* require at least a brief mention. Fairy-tale motifs have recently been noted, most comprehensively by Lisa G. Chinitz (1994).[30] A longer established generic approach, situating the tale within the Gothic tradition (and noting its contemporaneity with *Dracula*), is supplied by Ronald Schleifer (see essay 1). Film criticism makes its contribution in an essay in which Andrew Higson reads Jack Clayton's cinematic adaptation, *The Innocents* (1961), against the original tale.[31] In the 1990s child abuse has become a near-ubiquitous issue and its potential for *The Turn of the Screw* has been explored by Allan Lloyd Smith and by Albaraq Mahbobah.[32] Camille Paglia, in terms of her grand narrative of art and decadence, sees the tale as 'a great rebirth of the archaic' and the governess as 'a Decadent artist, joining moral and aesthetic extremes, evil with beauty, a Beardsleyesque black and white'.[33] Sexual politics is now a growing theme in James criticism and is represented here in a new essay by Ronald Knowles (essay 8).[34] These readings add new dimensions or give prominence to areas previously unnoticed; what has been achieved is a sense of the rich variety of readings stimulated by the text.

Two further major critical strands demand particular emphasis. Following that of Felman, the work of John Carlos Rowe stands as a central piece of *The Turn of the Screw* criticism (see essay 3), following largely from its switch of emphasis to social issues and the discourse of power.[35] John Pearson, for instance (essay 4), builds on both Felman and Rowe in his examination of framing in *The Turn of the Screw* from the perspectives of gender and power relations. Historical materialist, or Marxist, readings deal with the economic and class relations underlying the novella and in several cases discern a colonial subtext of India (the place of residence of the uncle's relatives: see *TS*: p. 25).[36] Materialist readings of *The Turn of the Screw* only caught on, it would seem, as the obsession with the 'reality' of the ghosts declined, but also as criticism itself came (or returned) to look at the historical conditions that surround the text.

Feminism and gender studies, often informed by ideas from cultural materialism or psychoanalysis, began to contribute strongly in the 1980s; this provided both a development of 'governess studies' (see Beth Newman, essay 6) and an exploration of the treatment of gender in a modernist context (Marianne DeKoven, essay 7). David McWhirter (1993) considers *The Turn of the Screw* a text in which 'the suspense of genre coincides with a simultaneously threatening and liberating suspense of gender'.[37] In such a reading the frame of the text, and its language, are joined with the representation of gender in an extensive and uncanny dissolving of boundaries, so that the novella effects an undoing of the rigid limits that hold together social ideas and rationality.

Interest in the ghosts as ghosts does, however, continue to survive. Peter Beidler's survey essay (of 1995) claims to detect 'a nostalgia' for more decisive readings and, in his somewhat revisionist monograph (of 1989), he had reargued the apparitionist case, this time laced with historical and cultural material, on the basis of comparisons with case histories drawn from contemporary psychic research. It may however be countered that, if this proves anything, it is merely that James maximised the plausibility of his ghostly depictions in accordance with perceptions familiar at the time: hardly a new or startling argument.[38]

IV

Finally, in terms of recent approaches to the text, mention should be made of the phenomenon of intertextuality (which, for present purposes at least, may be seen as a more sophisticated approach to older notions of antecedents, influence, quotation and allusion) with regard to *The Turn of the Screw*: that is, the use of texts both anterior to Henry James and from within his *oeuvre*. Camille Paglia, in her compendious study of decadence, has an expansive sentence covering predecessors to James's protagonist: 'Charlotte Brontë's governess invades the Arcadia of a Jane Austen country house, which she disorders with Poe's obsessive eroticism'.[39] The significance of the governess's reading of Fielding's *Amelia* has been noted, as has the impact of *Jane Eyre*; governesses in general and in particular have been much discussed, as we have already seen, while Hawthorne is frequently quoted as a father-figure to James's fiction and Leon Edel has unearthed a probable pre-text in Tom Taylor's story 'Temptation' (1855).[40] Such evidence underlines the extent to which *The Turn of the Screw* constantly fictionalises (or metafictionalises) itself as a story.

Children feature strongly in James's compositions of this period; moreover, biographers and certain other commentators remain keen to bring childhood and family influences to bear on his fiction. James's earlier stories in the spectral mould have been revisited in depth in Lustig's *Henry James and the Ghostly* (1994). There are, in addition, non-ghostly tales which anticipate details of *The Turn of the Screw*. 'Gabrielle de Bergerac' (1869), 'Master Eustace' (1871) and the mildly homoerotic 'The Pupil' (1891) can all be seen in this light.[41] A still earlier story, 'A Landscape Painter' (1866), has a framing structure comparable to *The Turn of the Screw*, plus a number of anticipatory images.[42] Fascinating though the particulars of any of these works may be, we would do well to heed Lustig's warning that: '[t]o read a later work in terms of an earlier one is ... almost always to simplify both and often to use the original text as an improvised key to pick the lock of the later'.[43]

A wide range of intertextual elements may thus be added to the resurgence of historical, social and cultural preoccupations which, along with close attention to language and structure, have served to emphasise the multiple meanings, the gaps and the incoherencies embedded within, and flaunted by, the Jamesian text. Criticism of the recent period (which we here date from Felman's essay of 1977), a good representation of which is offered in the present volume, demonstrates by its vibrancy and its variety of approach the continuing fascination, a hundred years on, of *The Turn of the Screw*.

V

Children, governesses and knowledge haunted James, in the 1890s in particular, in what now seems an uncanny preview of our own fascination, in the 1990s, with children, sex, and the adults who care for, or abuse, them. Earlier *A London Life* (1888) had included features anticipating *What Maisie Knew*, while, as far back as his first novel, *Watch and Ward* (1871), James had attempted a female *Bildungsroman*. He subsequently placed *What Maisie Knew* in volume XI of the New York edition of his works, with *In the Cage* (1898) and 'The Pupil' (1891). In effect, the former tale literalises Maisie's verbal messages between adults in the telegrams spinning out from the centre of her web at the telegraph office: the telegraphiste is a sort of Maisie under the influence of a Mrs Wix-type romantic vision. 'The Pupil' is the tale of a young boy, who fails to escape from his awful family with his tutor, dying just at the moment when flight is possible. *What Maisie Knew* (1897) follows *The Other House* (1896), a 'dramatic' novel in which yet another Jamesian child dies, a child who by her mere existence got in the way of adult passions. *What Maisie Knew* precedes both *The Turn of the Screw* and *The Awkward Age* (1899), the latter a novel concerned with an older version of Maisie and what she did or did not know about the goings on in her mother's racy set.[44]

The reception of *What Maisie Knew*, with its story of Maisie caught between adults and their unstable relationships, seems a pale reflection of the history of *The Turn of the Screw* criticism. From F. R. Leavis (1950) to Charles Thomas Samuels (1971) critics took sides – Maisie seen as innocent or corrupt, Mrs Wix as saint or sinner – and were once again caught in a Jamesian textual trap.[45] How much do the children (does the child) know? Marking a significant departure from this interminable moral debate, Juliet Mitchell's essay (which Barbara Eckstein takes issue with: see essay 9), 'Portrait of the Artist as a Young Girl' (1972) charts Maisie's progress – the progress of the novel – as the development of an artistic vision, the vision of James and Maisie at the end coinciding.[46] Mitchell also isolates Mrs Wix as an ultra-possessive mother, suitable mother-figures for Maisie being a preoccupation of a number of later critics (Merla Wolk, Sheila Teahan), and bisects the novel into the two viewpoints: the straight, innocent one of Maisie and the crooked, pornographic one of Mrs Wix; Mitchell thus points the way for later narrative theorists to separate Maisie from her creator and narrator (Wolk, J. Hillis Miller, and the three essays in this volume).[47]

If Mitchell saw Maisie's knowledge as vision, others focusing on a phenomenological approach (i.e. the philosophical investigation of phenomena as apprehended by consciousness) to *What Maisie Knew* end up wondering if she can know anything at all. Paul B. Armstrong (1978) wants us to ask 'how can Maisie know?'[48] In her excess of seeing over understanding, Maisie is imprisoned in a world of ambiguity, a surplus of her unreflective experience over what she can appropriate in reflection (in other words she cannot 'know' anything; she hasn't got the words for it). M. A. Williams (1980) takes issue with Armstrong's insistence on Maisie's epistemological confusion.[49] Comparing Merleau Ponty's phenomenological reduction (i.e. a return to the immediacy of experience before it has been overlaid and categorised by the range of neatly interpretative schemes: a 'wonder' in the face of the world) and Maisie's wonder, he links this in with morality; reduction lays the foundation for a fresh vision, a new creative morality, distinct from the moralism of a Mrs Wix. In effect, therefore, Maisie's decision to give up Sir Claude is an existential moral decision.

Whether Maisie is seen as an artist or as an existential moralist, her decision is ultimately to give up Sir Claude, her 'stepfather'. Miller draws our attention to the fact that Maisie is one of a long line of Jamesian heroines whose morality involves 'giving up' someone (Maggie Verver: *The Golden Bowl*; Millie Theale: *The Wings of the Dove*).[50] In his examination of James's ethical law of abnegation, Miller comes to the conclusion that the ethical import of Maisie's decision is undecidable. Is it made with the idealism of an innocent child, or with an adult's knowledge of sexual desire (the either/or of Maisie's innocence or corruption)?[51] Miller, unlike earlier critics who were content to settle for either/or, considers how the text brings us to this inconclusion. The undecidability is located in the doubling of phrases in the last chapter: 'I love Sir Claude – I love *him*'.[52] Exploring the implications of free indirect discourse in the novel, Miller posits Maisie to James as Galatea is to Pygmalion: in James's case a Galatea who escapes her creator.

Teahan (essay 11) further develops this line of inquiry, to the extent that we may question whether the project itself, the telling of Maisie's knowledge, is not an impossibility.

Exploiting the techniques of reader-response theory, Randall Craig (1981) sees Maisie as at once a reader of her circumstances, a mirror of the contemporary reading public and a model for all readers of the text.[53] Nicola Bradbury (1979) reads the silences in the text in opposition to its 'social languages', drawing attention to the link between what she calls the 'dramatic period' of James's writing, during which *What Maisie Knew* and *The Awkward Age* were written, and James's extension of the scope of silence.[54] The link between Maisie and dramatic method is frequently explored by critics, some (see Eckstein, essay 9) connecting it with James's abandonment of writing in favour of dictation, a move made in the very middle of the *Maisie* novel-writing process.

Regarding (like Mitchell) Maisie ultimately as an observer, an artist looking in on life, Jonathan Havey (1991) reaches this conclusion by way of Melanie Klein's psychoanalytical method of development theory.[55] Thus the child splits off the negative from the ideal aspects of experience, as a defence against anxiety in the early stages of life (the good and bad breast), later to reintegrate these idealised and persecutory fragments into the same source: the now whole perception of the mother. Havey reads the parental figures in the novel as the idealised and persecutory splits of Kleinian theory, gradually coming to resemble one another, as do Maisie's step-parents (the ideal) and her parents (the persecutory). Havey thus brings together psychoanalysis and narration in an analysis that throws into relief Julie Rivkin's reversal of the process (essay 10): namely the use of a fictional text to interrogate psychoanalytical theory.

Barbara Eckstein, the first of the three essayists on the novel included in this volume, more conventionally uses psychoanalysis, in her case a post-Freudian feminist variety with a dash of Derrida, to interrogate the text. Can a male writer articulate the growing knowledge of a young girl? For our three contributors, though in quite separate ways, it would appear not. All three make metatextual reference to James's preface statements about *Maisie* and his notebook entries (as with *The Turn of the Screw*: arguably though, in the case of *Maisie*, with less contentious results). The text alone, it seems, won't tell. For Eckstein, James comes up against the limits of his own narratorial and moral rules in this novel; the project collapses. Rivkin sees the abandonment of the oedipal narrative structure and resultant choice of the ironic distance between narrator and delegate as unbridgeable; Maisie escapes her paternal creator. For Teahan, the articulation of knowledge itself is impossible; ironic centres cannot hold; the Maisie narrative self-destructs, chronicle of a childhood death foretold by the James of the preface.

Perhaps it is not surprising that our three chosen essays on *What Maisie Knew* thread together the most stimulating recent trends in feminist, psychoanalytical and narrative critical thought to examine what is, after all, the tale of the growing awareness of a girl child. Texts choose their own most apposite critical theories in the circulation of discourses known as text and theory. As the link between story and knowledge is further broken down by those working at the cutting edge of critical theory (perhaps most clearly foreshadowed here by Julie Rivkin's undoing of the Oedipus story), who knows what surprises James's *Maisie* holds unknowingly? We have come a long way from those readers who were convinced that they could tell us what Maisie knew.

NOTES

1. Paul G. Beidler, *Frames in James* (Victoria, BC, 1993), p. 57.

2. *Henry James Letters*, Vol. IV, 1895–1916, ed. Leon Edel (Cambridge, MA, 1984), pp. 88, 84.

3. Cited by Jean Frantz Blackall, 'Cruickshank's *Oliver* and "The Turn of the Screw"', *American Literature*, 51 (1979–90), 178.

4. See in particular Peter G. Beidler, 'A Critical History of *The Turn of the Screw*', in Henry James, *The Turn of the Screw*, ed. Peter G. Beidler (Boston, 1995), pp. 127–51 (hereafter Beidler [1995]); and T. J. Lustig, *Henry James and the Ghostly* (Cambridge, 1994), pp. 111–15 and passim.

5. A selection of 'early reactions' (1898–1923) is included in the Norton Critical Edition, Henry James, *The Turn of the Screw*, ed. Robert Kimbrough (New York, 1966), pp. 169–80 (hereafter Kimbrough [1966]).

6. These four fundamental essays of the old criticism are reprinted in *A Casebook on Henry James's 'The Turn of the Screw'*, ed. Gerald Willen (New York, 1959; 2nd edn, 1969; hereafter Willen [1969]); Goddard, Heilman and an extract from Kenton are also included in Kimbrough (1966).

7. Willen (1959/69), and Kimbrough (1966), are both editions with copious additional materials (that by Willen is entitled 'A Casebook', but is not in the Macmillan series). See also Thomas Mabry Cranfill and Robert Lanier Clark, Jr, *An Anatomy of 'The Turn of the Screw'* (Austin, TX, 1965), which relentlessly presses the arguments raised by Goddard and Wilson; and E. A. Sheppard, *Henry James and 'The Turn of the Screw'* (Auckland, 1974), who is more sympathetic to the apparitionist cause and exercised by what she considers to be authorial intention.

8. Harold C. Goddard, 'A Pre-Freudian Reading of *The Turn of the Screw*', cited from Kimbrough (1966), p. 209. Such perspicacity, remarkable perhaps for its time, is not matched by many a subsequent commentator: see for example Wayne C. Booth, *The Rhetoric of Fiction* (Chicago, 1961), pp. 311–16; Booth's later *Critical Understanding: The Powers and Limits of Pluralism* (Chicago, 1979), pp. 284–301; and Dorothea Krook, 'Intentions and Intentions: The Problem of Intention and Henry James's *The Turn of the Screw*', in *The Theory of the Novel: New Essays*, ed. John Halperin (New York, 1974), pp. 353–72.

9. See Christine Brooke-Rose's devastating critique of the essays contained in Willen (1959/69), and Kimbrough (1966), 'The Squirm of the True: I, An Essay in Non-Methodology', *PTL*, 1 (1976), 265–94; revised in her book *A Rhetoric of the Unreal: Studies in Narrative and Structure, Especially of the Fantastic* (Cambridge, 1983), pp. 128–57.

10. John J. Enck, '*The Turn of the Screw* & The Turn of the Century', Kimbrough (1966), pp. 259–69; Paul N. Siegel, '"Miss Jessel": Mirror Image of the Governess', *Literature and Psychology*, 18 (1968), 30–8; Charles Thomas Samuels, *The Ambiguity of Henry James* (Urbana, IL, 1971).

11. Tzvetan Todorov, *The Fantastic: A Structural Approach to a Literary Genre* (Cleveland and London, 1973), p. 43; for further elaborations of this theory, see Brooke-Rose, *A Rhetoric of the Unreal*; and Neil Cornwell, *The Literary Fantastic: From Gothic to Postmodernism* (New York and London, 1990).

12. Peter G. Beidler, 'A Critical History of *The Turn of the Screw*', in Beidler (1995), pp. 127–8.

13. See 'The "Uncanny" (1919)', in Sigmund Freud, *Art and Literature*, The Penguin Freud Library, 14 (Harmondsworth, 1990).

14. Brooke-Rose, *A Rhetoric of the Unreal*, p. 229; Shlomith Rimmon, '*The Turn of the Screw*' in her *The Concept of Ambiguity – the Example of James* (Chicago, 1977), pp. 116–66 (138).

15. Shoshana Felman, 'Turning the Screw of Interpretation', *Yale French Studies*, 55/56 (1977), 94–207.

16. Beidler (1995), p. 128.

17. See Eric Solomon, 'The Return of the Screw', in Kimbrough (1966), pp. 237–45 (first published 1964); C. Knight Aldrich, MD, 'Another Twist to *The Turn of the Screw*', *Modern Fiction Studies*, 13 (1967), 167–78; reprinted in Willen (1969), pp. 367–78; and John A. Clair, *The Ironic Dimension in the Fiction of Henry James* (Pittsburg, PA, 1965), pp. 37–58.

18. Louis D. Rubin, Jr, 'One More Turn of the Screw', *Modern Fiction Studies*, 9 (1964), 314–28; reprinted in Willen (1969), pp. 350–66 (according to Kimbrough [1966], p. 275, this idea had been put forward in Carvel Collins, 'James's "The Turn of the Screw"', *Explicator*, 13, June 1955, item 49); Anthony J. Mazzella, 'An Answer to the Mystery of *The Turn of the Screw*', *Studies in Short Fiction*, 17 (1980), 327–33.

19. James B. Scott, 'How the Screw is Turned: James's *Amusette*', *University of Mississippi Studies in English*, 4 (1983), 112–31.

20. References to the text of *The Turn of the Screw* here are to Beidler (1995; page numbers noted as *TS*).

21. Two critics who put this case are Michael J. H. Taylor, 'A Note on the First Narrator of *The Turn of the Screw*', *American Literature*, 4 (1982), 717–22; Linda S. Kauffman, 'The Author of Our Woe: Virtue Recorded in *The Turn of the Screw*', *Nineteenth-Century Fiction*, 36, 2 (1981), 176–92. Also sympathetic to the idea is Terry Heller, *'The Turn of the Screw': Bewildered Vision* (Boston, 1989), p. 21. The nearest thing to a refutation within the text is the narrator's remark (p. 25): 'The departing ladies who had said they would stay didn't, of course, thank heaven, stay', which smacks to us of misogyny and a preference for male bonding (with Douglas, Griffin and whoever else).

22. Helen Killoran, 'The Governess, Mrs Grose and "The Poison of an Influence" in *The Turn of the Screw*', *Modern Language Studies*, 23 (1993), 13–24; Albaraq Mahbobah, 'Hysteria, Rhetoric, and the Politics of Reversal in Henry James's *The Turn of the Screw*', *Henry James Review* 17 (1996), 149–61.

23. See for instance Viti Elgar, 'The Origin and Validation of Interpretive Hypotheses or "The Turn of the Screw": Whose Screws Need Tightening?', *Essays in Poetics*, 4:2 (1979), 37–58; Dieter Freundlieb, 'Explaining Interpretation: The Case of Henry James's *The Turn of the Screw*', *Poetics Today*, 5 (1984), 79–95; Don Anderson, '"A Fury of Intention": The Scandal of Henry James's *The Turn of the Screw*', *Sydney Studies in English*, 15 (1989–90), 140–52.

24. Introduction to *Mary Shelley: Frankenstein*, ed. Fred Botting, New Casebook (Basingstoke and London, 1995), p. 1.

25. Ned Lukacher, '"Hanging Fire": The Primal Scene of *The Turn of the Screw*', in his *Primal Scenes: Literature, Philosophy, Psychoanalysis* (Ithaca, NY, 1986), reprinted in *Henry James's Daisy Miller, The Turn of the Screw and Other Tales*, ed. Harold Bloom (New York, 1987), pp. 117–32; Stanley Renner, '"Red hair, very red, close-curling": Sexual Hysteria, Physiognomical Bogeymen, and the "Ghosts" in *The Turn of the Screw*', *Nineteenth-Century Literature*, 43 (1988); revised and reprinted in Beidler (1995) pp. 223–41.

26. Karen Halttunen, '"Through the Cracked and Fragmented Self": William James and *The Turn of the Screw*', *American Quarterly*, 40 (1988), 472–90. Earlier essays using a similar approach include Francis X. Roellinger, 'Physical Research and *The Turn of the Screw*' (1949), reprinted in Kimbrough (1966), pp. 132–42; Oscar Cargill '*The Turn of the Screw* and Alice James' (1956, revised 1963), reprinted in Kimbrough (1966), pp. 145–65; and Paula Marantz Cohen, 'Freud's *Dora* and James's *Turn of the Screw*: Two Treatments of the Female "Case"', *Criticism*, 28 (1986), 73–87.

27. Darrel Mansell, 'The Ghost of Language in *The Turn of the Screw*', *Modern Language Quarterly*, 46 (1985), 48–63; Norman Macleod, 'Stylistics and the Ghost Story: Punctuation, Revisions, and Meaning in *The Turn of the Screw*', in *Edinburgh Studies in the English Language*, ed. John M. Anderson and Norman Macleod (Edinburgh, 1988), pp. 133–55.

28. Sigrid Renaux, '*The Turn of the Screw*': A Semiotic Reading* (New York, 1993), pp. 47, 35.

29. See, for instance, Donald P. Costello, 'The Structure of *The Turn of the Screw*', *Modern Language Notes*, 75 (1960), 312–21; David A. Cook and Timothy J. Corrigan, 'Narrative Structure in *The Turn of the Screw*: A New Approach to Meaning', *Studies in Short Fiction*, 17 (1980), 55–65. Terry Heller, in his '*The Turn of the Screw*': Bewildered Vision* (Boston, 1989), pays particular attention to the Prologue; Adrian Poole examines Griffin's story in 'Hauntings', a chapter of his *Henry James* (New York and London, 1991), pp. 140–59. See also Paul G. Beidler, *Frames in James: 'The Tragic Muse', 'The Turn of the Screw', 'What Maisie Knew' and 'The Ambassadors'* (Victoria, BC, 1993), pp. 47–56.

30. Lisa G. Chinitz, 'Fairy Tale Turned Ghost Story: James's *The Turn of the Screw*', *The Henry James Review*, 15 (1994), 264–85; see also Mary Hallab, 'The Governess and the Demon Lover: The Return of a Fairy Tale', *The Henry James Review*, 8 (1987), 104–15; and Renaux, '*The Turn of the Screw*'.

31. Andrew Higson, 'Gothic Fantasy as Art Cinema: The Secret of Female Desire in *The Innocents*', in *Gothick Origins and Innovations*, ed. Allan Lloyd Smith and Victor Sage (Amsterdam, 1994), pp. 204–17.

32. Allan Lloyd Smith, 'A Word Kept Back in *The Turn of the Screw*', in *Creepers: British Horror and Fantasy in the Twentieth Century*, ed. Clive Bloom (London, 1993), pp. 47–63; Mahbobah, 'Hysteria, Rhetoric ...'.

33. Camille Paglia, *Sexual Personae: Art and Decadence from Nefertiti to Emily Dickinson* (Harmondsworth, 1992), pp. 615, 613.

34. With regard to wider James studies, see Eve Kosofsky Sedgwick's analysis of 'The Beast in the Jungle', in her *Epistemology of the Closet* (Harmondsworth, 1994), pp. 182–212; and the controversial new biography by Sheldon M. Novick, *Henry James: The Young Master* (New York, 1996) and the ensuing correspondence it generated in *TLS* (1996–97) – this first volume does not, of course, reach the 1890s.

35. John Carlos Rowe, *The Theoretical Dimensions of Henry James* (Madison, WI, 1984).

36. For further materialist readings, see Bruce Robbins, 'Shooting Off James's Blanks: Theory, Politics, and *The Turn of the Screw*', *The Henry James Review*, 5 (1984), 192–9, effectively revised as '"They don't much count, do they?": The Unfinished History of *The Turn of the Screw*', in Beidler (1995), pp. 183–96; Paul B. Armstrong, 'History and Epistemology: The Example of *The Turn of the Screw*', *New Literary History*, 19 (1987–8), 693–712; Vincent P. Pecora, *Self and Form in Modern Narrative* (Baltimore, MD, 1989), pp. 176–213; and Graham McMaster, 'Henry James and India: A Historical Reading of *The Turn of the Screw*', *Clio*, 18 (1988), 23–40.

37. David McWhirter, 'In the "Other House" of Fiction: Writing, Authority and Femininity in *The Turn of the Screw*, in *New Essays on Daisy Miller and the Turn of the Screw*', ed. Vivian R. Pollak (Cambridge, 1993), pp. 121–48; in the same volume (pp. 91–119), see Millicent Bell, 'Class, Sex and the Victorian Governess: James's *The Turn of the Screw*' (Bell also includes a note on the evolution of her critical attitude to this text towards 'class and sex definition', p. 119). Another useful feminist analysis is Priscilla L. Walton, '"What then on earth was I?": Feminine Subjectivity and *The Turn of the Screw*', in Beidler (1995), pp. 253–67.

38. Beidler, 'A Critical History ...', in Beidler (1995), p. 140; Peter G. Beidler, *Ghosts, Demons and Henry James: 'The Turn of the Screw' at the Turn of the Century* (Columbia, 1989).

39. Paglia, *Sexual Personae*, 1992, p. 611.

40. May L. Ryburn, '*The Turn of the Screw* and *Amelia*: A Source for Quint?', *Studies in Short Fiction*, 16 (1979), 235–7; Alice Hall Petry, 'Jamesian Parody, *Jane Eyre* and "The Turn of the Screw"', *Modern Language Studies*, 13 (1983), 61–78; Lustig, *Henry James and the Ghostly* (1994), discusses other governesses and Victorian sexuality (pp. 146–62), James and Hawthorne (pp. 162–9), and various other sources (pp. 136–46); Leon Edel, *Henry James: A Life* (London, 1996), pp. 465–6, first published 1985; for a fuller account of 'Temptation', see Leon Edel and Adeline Tintner, 'The Private Life of Peter Quin[t]: Origins of "The Turn of the Screw"', *The Henry James Review*, 7 (1985), 2–4. See also Renner, '"Red hair"', on the red-haired tradition in negative or diabolical figures.

41. See Lustig, *Henry James and the Ghostly*, pp. 109–11, on 'Gabrielle de Bergerac'. Fred Kaplan, *Henry James: The Imagination of Genius* (London, 1993), on 'Master Eustace', claims that it 'sensationalises the less dramatic oedipal conflicts of the James household' (p. 131). Kaplan comments too on 'The Pupil', p. 414.

42. For a limited comparison of this story with *The Turn of the Screw*, see John Bayley, *The Short Story: Henry James to Elizabeth Bowen* (New York and London, 1988), pp. 40–59.

43. Lustig, *Henry James and the Ghostly*, p. 111.

44. This novel, incidentally, mentions Vamderbank's 'awfully clever' brother Miles, who had died aged seventeen: Henry James, *The Awkward Age*, ed. Vivien Jones (Oxford, 1984), p. 14.

45. See F. R. Leavis, 'What Maisie Knew', reprinted (from *Scrutiny*, 1950), *Anna Karenina and Other Essays* (London, 1967); Charles Thomas Samuels, *The Ambiguity of Henry James* (Urbana, IL, 1971). Among the many further essays preoccupied with moral sense, see Edward Wasiolek, 'Maisie: Pure or Corrupt?', *College English* (1960), 167–72; James W. Gargano, '*What Maisie Knew*: The Evolution of a Moral Sense', *Nineteenth-Century Fiction*, 16 (1961), 33–46; down to Jean Frantz Blackall, 'Moral Geography in *What Maisie Knew*', *University of Toronto Quarterly*, 48 (1978), 130–48.

46. Juliet Mitchell, '*What Maisie Knew*: Portrait of the Artist as a Young Girl', *The Air of Reality: New Essays on Henry James*, ed. John Goode (London, 1972), pp. 168–89.

47. Merla Wolk, 'Narration and Nurture in *What Maisie Knew*', *The Henry James Review*, 4, 3 (1983), 196–206; Sheila Teahan, see essay 11; J. Hillis Miller, *Versions of Pygmalion* (Cambridge, MA, 1990), pp. 23–81.

48. Paul B. Armstrong, 'The Phenomenology of James's Moral Vision', *Texas Studies in Literature and Language*, 20, 4 (1978), 517–37 (518).

49. M. A. Williams, 'The Drama of Maisie's Vision', *The Henry James Review*, 2, 1 (1980), 36–48.

50. Miller, *Versions of Pygmalion*, pp. 24–5, 56.

51. Miller, *Reading Narrative: Form, Ethics, Ideology*, ed. James Phelan (Columbus, OH, 1989), pp. 79–101.

52. Henry James, *What Maisie Knew*, ed. Adrian Poole (Oxford, 1996), p. 272; Miller, *Versions of Pygmalion*, pp. 59–60.

53. Randall Craig, '"Read[ing] the Unspoken into the Spoken": Interpreting *What Maisie Knew*', *The Henry James Review*, 2, 3 (1981), 204–12; see also Craig, 'Reader-Response Criticism and Literary Realism', *Essays in Literature*, 11, 1 (1984), 113–26.

54. Nicola Bradbury, *Henry James: The Later Novels* (Oxford, 1979), p. 17.

55. Jonathan Havey, 'Kleinian Developmental Narrative and James' *What Maisie Knew*', *University of Hartford Studies in Literature*, 23, 1 (1991), 34–47.

1

The Trap of the Imagination: The Gothic Tradition, Fiction and *The Turn of the Screw*

RONALD SCHLEIFER

In the last years of the nineteenth century two Gothic novels, *Dracula* and *The Turn of the Screw*, were published. Taken together they delimit, to some extent, the boundaries of Gothic fiction. Moreover, in so doing they define a sense of the modern. *Dracula* looks back to the tradition of Gothic fiction, asserting the numinous in the world. It locates itself simultaneously in the tradition of the explained supernatural, a tradition begun in Anne Radcliffe and culminating in the detective fiction of Poe, and in that other, occult tradition that uses supernatural horror as an assertion of the Sacred in the quotidian, a tradition begun in Monk Lewis and culminating in the arabesque of Poe. Both of these 'traditions' assert some sort of 'sense' in and for the world, whether it be horror or otherwise; they assert the significance of things, residing on the surface of things as they do for the detective, or in their depths, as they do for the magician (psychologist, priest, etc.). *Dracula* combines these in its very epistolary form which presents Dracula's double, the pseudo-priest Dr Van Helsing, who knows through arcane study what has happened (and like the initiate, refuses to tell); and the detective Dr Van Helsing (and Mina), who can discover the meaning of the mystery simply by marshalling facts and compiling the various manuscripts that form the story. In *Dracula* the reader knows – he sees things and into things – before the characters do because the texts are already compiled, the hints already marshalled. Never does he doubt the veracity of Harker's story – his written journal – in the way Harker doubts his own experience.

The Turn of the Screw also utilises these Gothic traditions – as commentators have demonstrated, it too locates itself between natural (i.e. the governess is hysterical) and supernatural (the ghosts are *there*, real corrupting forces) explanations.[1] Yet while *Dracula* looks back to the tradition of Gothic fiction, asserting the numinous in an apparently godless world, *The Turn of the Screw* looks forward to the irony, and even the laughter, of the self-conscious fictional enterprise of the twentieth-century Gothic of Borges and Kafka, Dinesen and even Thomas Mann. That is, the Gothic tradition culminates in Stoker's remarkable power to convey a sense of *presence*: a sense of power, meaning, understanding that explains and naturalises the horror of the past – the terror of temporality – by discovering the Sacred within (or at least behind) the fullness of moving time, the Profane. And the modern tradition, soon to become the lesson of laughter – 'I have lived long enough by now', one of Isak Dinesen's characters says, 'to have learned, when the devil grins at me, to grin back'[2] – begins with James's ability to base his novel on *absence*, on the fact that there is nothing, that nothing happens.

I

Stoker's world is presided over by Count Dracula, the past walking the earth, governing even dreams, and it is articulated by a host of narrators. Moreover, the book, *Dracula*, is presided over by writing, the *transcription* of living speech, itself metaphorically Undead: as Mina says to Seward, 'I think that the cylinders which you gave me contained more than you intended me to know'; 'no one must hear [your passionate words] spoken again. ... I have copied out the words on my typewriter and none other need now hear your heart beat, as I did' (p. 229).[3] And at the very end of the novel Jonathan notes that no 'authentic document' remains, only the transcription – one might call it the 'transfusion' – of the experience. This is a far cry from the governess's world in *The Turn of the Screw* which is presided over by the absent master, who lives elsewhere, and articulated by narrators who, like living speech itself, like purloined letters, never return.[4] Everyone returns in *Dracula*: the grave is opened, the dead return, the secret is revealed, so that *presence* – the voice and heart behind writing, the monster of evil and the sacraments of God behind the world, ubiquitous sexuality behind the story itself – is made manifest.

The central metaphor of *Dracula* is the grave, the crypt, and the space of the novel, despite all its continental movements, is defined by closings-in and confinements. The 'mystery' of *Dracula* is to find what already is there, hidden within the grave or simply spelled out, to be deciphered, in the diaries and records of the participants or on the gravestone itself: 'on it was but one word: DRACULA. ... Its emptiness spoke eloquent to make certain what I knew' (p. 374). The eloquence of the empty grave is the fact that Dracula walks the earth and needs only to be followed and trapped, discovered, spelled out, the meaning of his name made manifest. That is, the world of *Dracula* is a world already too full, where the dead walk and leave no room, even in dreams, for the living. The land of the past, Transylvania, co-exists with the modern world and threatens to engulf it. From Jonathan's first diary entry on his trip east there is an uncanny sense there is more to know than possibly can be known (a plenitude not unlike Poe's *Eureka*); and his first vision of the castle is oppressive because the building, the remnant of the past, is so imposing:

> I think I must have fallen asleep and kept dreaming of the incident, for it seemed to be repeated endlessly, and now looking back, it is like a sort of awful nightmare. ...
>
> When I could see again the driver was climbing into the calèche, and the wolves had disappeared. This was all so strange and uncanny that a dreadful fear came upon me, and I was afraid to speak or move. The time seemed interminable as we swept on our way, now in almost complete darkness, for the rolling clouds obscured the moon. We kept on ascending, with occasional periods of quick descent, but in the main always ascending. Suddenly, I became conscious of the fact that the driver was in the act of pulling up the horses in the courtyard of a vast ruined castle, from whose tall black windows came no ray of light, and whose broken battlements showed a jagged line against the moonlit sky.
>
> (pp. 22, 23)

This is the language of waking, waking onto a world so full of sentient creatures that the very darkness of the landscape seems to contain almost everything, to portend the larger significance of the places transversed. There is something, or seems to be, beyond, behind the landscape, locked there as Jonathan's 'dream' (later he doesn't remember the experience described in his journal) seems locked behind (within) his transcription of his experience. That there is something behind (within) the narrative of *Dracula* – something behind even the banal language of Lucy's letters – is given at the beginning in Jonathan's unremembered dream-journey; it stands at the beginning of the novel as Dracula's gravestone stands at the end, both serving to define and spell-out the mystery of the empty grave, to explain the absent corpse. The corpse, after all, is not absent; it is simply displaced, and the 'plot' of the novel – as Dracula's many crypts indicate – is to return the corpse to its proper place, its proper 'rest'.

The passage describing Jonathan's arrival at Castle Dracula demonstrates the importance of movement and rest in the novel: consciousness itself seems tied up with its environment; it begins when movement stops, just as Dracula himself – and especially his face (like that of Victor Frankenstein's monster) – stops the narrative whenever he (it) appears. This is important because Dracula's face, like the images of a dream and like Seward's heartbeat, can only be immediately apprehended; his face cannot be reflected. Dracula is an 'unmediated vision' – a *presence* – that is locked in experience; experience (narration) must be broken to release him. Meaning in *Dracula* is against time: like Count Dracula (who rarely 'appears' in the novel – or the grave – that bears his name), significance is a presence *behind* what happens in those charged moments when appearances are breached and the narrative halted.

Thus, waking is salvation: to become conscious, even of evil, is the repeated goal of the heroes of *Dracula*. This is why 'nightmare' – Jonathan Harker's metaphor that is also strangely literal – is the best and most common description of this and other Gothic novels. Dracula controls his victims by taking away their consciousness – dream (or trance: experience remembered as dream) is the meeting place of the vampires and their victims – and the heroes pit day against night in resisting this evil. The space of *Dracula* is defined by confinements, yet its action – the 'action' of Jonathan's consciousness – is a recurrent breaking-open of these confinements, breaching them as it were, until the dead walk the earth with the living. The end of *Dracula* is the violation of the crypt; it is not the ingestion of blood but its *transfusion* which is the mark of life against death.

For the novel does assert life against death. Even its portrayal of death – living death – is rendered in terms of repressed sexuality which commentators on the novel invariably describe.[5] Dracula is a sexual being – so are those 'voluptuous' vampires the novel recurrently describes – and what the narrative seeks to 'hide' under its metaphors of the dead is transfused with a sense of living sexuality which is unmistakable. After all, *Dracula* is the novel of marriages, 'polygamous' marriages as Van Helsing says (p. 182), but governed by a sexual presence that it barely conceals. This is the significance of the most striking breaching of confinement – a breaching of the movement of the narrative itself in the novel's longest paragraph, its longest 'set-piece':

> We threw ourselves against [the door]; with a crash it burst open. ...
> The moonlight was so bright that through the thick yellow blind the room was light enough to see. On the bed beside the window lay Jonathan Harker, his face flushed and breathing heavily as though in a stupor. Kneeling on the near edge of the bed facing outwards was the white-clad figure of his wife. By her side stood a tall, thin man, clad in black. His face was turned from us, but the instant we saw all recognised the Count – in every way, even to the scar on his forehead. With his left hand he held both Mrs Harker's hands, keeping them away with her arms at full tension; his right hand gripped her by the back of the neck, forcing her face down on his bosom. Her white nightdress was smeared with blood, and a thin stream trickled down the man's bare breast which was shown by his torn-open dress. The attitude of the two had a terrible resemblance to a child forcing a kitten's nose into a saucer of milk to compel it to drink. As we burst into the room, the Count turned his face, and the hellish look that I had heard described seemed to leap into it. ...
> (pp. 287–8)

This sudden interruption, like that of Jonathan's consciousness in the carriage, signals the halt of narrative movement: from the first 'burst' until the second a picture is provided, significant relationships are arranged, and narrative action stops. Yet in its stead – in the narrative gap – is offered the fullness of life, the presence of sexuality that hovers behind the narrative throughout the novel. Consciousness of such fullness is tied to such gaps; it begins when the narrative stops, revealing Dracula, and especially his physiognomy of 'devilish passion', in a picture. That is, Stoker is participating in what Paul de Man calls 'classical eighteenth-century theories of representation [which] persistently strive to reduce music and poetry to the status of painting ... [and in which] the possibility of making the invisible visible, of giving presence to what can only be imagined, is repeatedly stated as the main function of art.' Thus, de Man says,

> it confirms rather than undermines the plenitude of the represented entity. It functions as a mnemotechnic sign that brings back something that happened not to be there at the moment, but whose existence in another place, at another time, or in a different mode of consciousness is not challenged.[6]

Such 'pictures' or 'set-pieces' that halt action is the constant device of early Gothic novels: *Frankenstein*, Mary Shelley tells us, began with a dream of such a significant fact that haunted her until she 'wished to exchange the ghastly image of my fancy for the realities around' and thus turned to writing her 'ghost story'.[7] This is the method, too, of *The Monk*, whose subplot literally interrupts the (supernaturally) sexual night of Ambrosio and Matilda with a hundred-page diversion. The recurrent action of the heroes of *Dracula* is to write: to interrupt the action of the novel and transfuse, as quickly as possible, experience to the page, to overlay experience with writing, thus discovering the underlay of meaning, of the Sacred or its opposite. Finally, at the end after the monster is exorcised, writing is continued and fulfilled in Jonathan's and Mina's son, Arthur John Quincy Van Helsing Harker, into whom, in Mina's secret belief, Quincy's 'spirit had passed', underlay and overlay, like the Count's presence, horrible and sexual, upon which the heroes burst in the long set-piece of the novel. Arthur John Quincy Van Helsing Harker is the novel's final 'text', symbolical, occult, containing the presence of secret belief, in whom everything 'returns'. Like Dracula himself, he literally stops the narrative.

II

Yet life, as James says elsewhere, never really stops. The governess in *The Turn of the Screw* expects in Bly a vision such as Jonathan Harker has had: 'I suppose I had expected, or had dreaded, something so dreary that what greeted me was a good surprise' (p. 7).[8] What greets the governess is an experience she has never had, the possibility of movement, a sense of spaciousness – full-length mirrors, the broad fresh front of the house, expansive parks – 'the dazzle of ... possible ways' to encounter experience (p. 42). 'It was the first time, in a manner', the governess writes,

> that I have ever known space and air and freedom, all the music of summer and the mystery of nature. And then there was consideration – and consideration was sweet. Oh it was a trap – not designed but deep – to my imagination, to my delicacy, perhaps to my vanity; to whatever in me was most excitable.
>
> (p. 14)

The trap, for the governess, like her 'good surprise', is the trap of plenty, a world and 'a time so full that as I recall the way it went it reminds me of all the art I now need to make it a little distinct' (p. 14). This recalls the title of the novel itself, alluded to on the first page where it is suggested that a ghost story using a child 'gives the effect another turn of the screw', and that 'two children give two turns!' (p. 1). With these turns, something seemingly extra – something *supplemental* – is given, necessary only for the 'effect', a fullness, a plethora.[9] James called his short novel a trap for the unwary reader, 'a piece of ingenuity ... to catch those not easily caught' (p. 120, 'Preface'), and, as I will argue later, there is a trap lurking in the book's title itself. But the greatest trap, I think, is the governess's freedom and the fact that the novel proceeds, as her terror does, by the apprehension of possibility, spaciousness, and the ground of these, ultimately nothing at all.

For unlike *Dracula*, in *The Turn of the Screw* the breach of sleep does not 'dissipate' the terror, but rather enlarges it: waking, consciousness itself, is the terror. The story that 'holds' the Christmas revellers at the beginning of the novel is the story not of the terror of nightmare but of the terror of waking. An apparition, the story-teller tells us, 'of a dreadful kind' appears

> to a little boy sleeping in the room with his mother and waking her up in the terror of it; waking her not to dissipate his dread and soothe him to sleep again, but to encounter also herself, before she had succeeded in doing so, the same sight that had shocked him.
>
> (p. 1)

In *Dracula* terror and dream are never far apart; Jonathan's carriage ride, Mina's trances, Lucy's nightwalks, Renfield's madness, Van Helsing's midnight graveyard vigils, the vampires' night-time powers, all mark the borderline between waking and sleeping. For the governess, however, this terror is in waking, in consciousness itself: her constant terror is of what the children *know* beyond her; her sleep is lost, 'haunted', as she says at one point, 'with the shadow of something' she was not told (p. 27), but of which, nevertheless, she was strangely, uncannily conscious.

Soon after her establishment at Bly, the governess becomes convinced of the presence of ghosts. She 'sees' the figure of Quint as she walks through the park one day while she half expected to see the master of Bly himself. What is most remarkable about this encounter is that it is accompanied by an intense silence, as if all the world had stopped:

> The place moreover, in the strangest way in the world, had on the instant and by the very fact of its appearance became a solitude. To me at least, making my statement here with a deliberation with which I have never made it, the whole feeling of the moment returns. It was as if, while I took in, what I did take in, all the rest of the scene had been stricken with death. I can hear again, as I write, the intense hush in which the sounds of evening dropped. The rooks stopped cawing in the golden sky and the friendly hour lost for the unspeakable minute all its voice. But there was no other change in nature, unless indeed it were a change that I saw with a stranger sharpness.
>
> (p. 16)

Later the governess encounters this phenomenon again, referring to it as a 'ministering moment' felt when the 'summer had turned, the summer had gone; the autumn had dropped upon Bly and had blown out half our lights' (p. 52). In this second account of this 'strange' experience – one which alludes directly to the atmosphere of the 'first sight of Quint' – the metaphor of the world stricken by death is repeated, literally, in the autumn landscape. The second scene, however, like the scene of writing itself when the governess 'hears' 'again ... the intense hush', remains 'unaccompanied and empty', and the governess remains 'unmolested' – 'if unmolested one could call a young woman whose sensibility had, in the most extraordinary fashion, not declined but deepened' (p. 52) into increased perception, increased vision.

The vision is not of Quint – he figures neither in the autumnal scene nor in the scene of writing. Rather, it is a vision of what the governess calls a page later 'our prodigious palpable hushes ... – I can call them nothing else – the strange dizzy lift or swim (I try for terms!) into a stillness, a pause of all life, ... that I could hear through any intensified mirth or quickened recitation or louder strum of piano' (p. 53). What the governess apprehends is a silence *behind* the world, the recurrent 'chill' she mentions, heard and felt 'through' whatever momentary noise there is. She seems, for a moment, face to face with consciousness itself – empty, void, silent before the plethora of *its* objects – so that its only expression ('while I took in, what I did take in') is repetition which recurrently 'tries' for terms. The moment is transfixed in an 'unspeakable' apprehension, 'named' by pronouns without antecedents, as silence and death govern consciousness. Whether or not Quint's ghost is really on the battlement – the great question for Mrs Radcliffe, the question of 'eternal significance' for Lewis's Monk, the question of literal and psychosexual interpreters of *Dracula* – is really of no moment here. For the ghosts manifest themselves in *The Turn of the Screw* in absence, a sort of blank page upon which meaning is inscribed: with the 'apparition' – the governess's 'sharper' consciousness – the narrative and the world stop so that the silence, not meaning, behind them is 'heard' through them. In *The Turn* the dead do not prey on the living: when Mrs Grose asks the governess what can the ghosts do, the governess answers by repeating and echoing the question: '"Do?" I echoed ... "Don't they do enough?"' (p. 49). What they do is simply strike the living world dead and still its moving voices. The evidence of apprehension in *The Turn* – of 'waking', of consciousness, of horror – is absence, silence.

That this is a confrontation with the possibilities and spaciousness of consciousness can be seen in James's use of Stoker's central metaphor of confinement, 'the inner chamber of my dread'. When the governess finally 'sees' that the children are the objects of the ghosts' 'horrors', she feels exhilarated that Mrs Grose and herself 'might bear things together'.

> It was the idea, the second movement, that led me straight out, as I may say, of the inner chamber of my dread. I could take air in the court, at least, and there Mrs Grose could join me. ...
> '[Quint] was looking for little Miles.' A portentous clearness now possessed me. '*That's* whom he was looking for.'
> 'But how do you know?'
> 'I know, I know, I know!' My exaltation grew. 'And *you* know, my dear!'
>
> (p. 25)

Proof here is just the *repeated* assertion of knowledge, 'I know, I know, I know!', intransitive, a state of mind. The syntax of the

opening sentence of this section – one which began a weekly instal-
ment, and consequently was distanced from the preceding 'passage'
to which it refers – directs attention away from the object of vision,
seemingly designated by the pronoun 'what' (a pronoun without a
clear antecedent) to the governess's consciousness, 'her liability to
impressions', the ultimate referent of the pronoun:

> It took of course more than that particular passage to place us to-
> gether in the presence of what we had to live with as we could, my
> dreadful liability to impressions of the order so vividly exemplified,
> and my companion's knowledge henceforth – a knowledge half
> consternation and half compassion – of that liability.
>
> (p. 25)

The elements of this sentence that seem to refer outside the story
and the governess's discourse – 'what we had to live with', 'the
order so vividly exemplified', 'my companion's knowledge' – all
turn back to her 'liability', the impressions of consciousness. Even
the subject governing 'exemplified' is the story itself, the order
'exemplified [by what I said to Mrs Grose, by what I write here]'.
The inner chamber of dread is replaced with knowledge, but it is
knowledge without an object, without a 'referent', knowledge of
'nothing', which, as we shall see, can never be 'justified'.

This is why the major characters of *The Turn of the Screw* –
Quint, Jessel, the master of Bly – are literally not 'there'. The governess's characteristic experience – the object of the 'stranger sharpness' of her vision – is not, like Van Helsing's, to see 'into' and
'behind' things, but is to 'see' what is not there, to 'hear' the silence,
the hush. Her first observation about Mrs Grose is that she 'felt
within half an hour that she was so glad [to see me] ... as to be positively on her guard against showing it too much' (p. 7); later she
says, after her second encounter with Quint, that the 'terrace and
the whole place, ... all I could see of the park, were empty with a
great emptiness' (p. 21); and in the third 'interview' 'it was the dead
silence of our long gaze ... that gave the whole horror ... its only
note of the unnatural' until 'the silence ... became the element into
which I saw the figure disappear' (p. 41). Even her wakefulness, as
we have seen, is 'haunted with the shadow of something' not said
(p. 27).

Yet the crucial moment, I believe, is when the governess directs
her attention to the children in section xii, the centre of James's
tale. In discussing with Mrs Grose the children's 'systematic silence'

concerning the ghosts she has 'seen', the governess first wonders if she is mad and then realises 'my lucidity must have seemed awful'. Like the ghostly silence, her lucidity is apprehended in the act of speech, made 'palpable' in language: *because* of the 'systematic silence' she 'makes it out' that the children are in league with Quint and Jessel, that 'they're talking of *them* – they're talking horrors!' (p. 48). The governess realises – she 'sees' – in the process of talking to Mrs Grose that the children's 'unnatural goodness' was a fraud:

> The very act of bringing it out really helped me to trace it – follow it all up and piece it all together. 'They [the children] haven't been good – they've only been absent. It has been easy to live with them because they're simply leading a life of their own. They're not mine – they're not ours. They're his and they're hers!'
> 'Quint's and that woman's?'
> 'Quint's and that woman's. ...'
>
> (pp. 48–9)

Thus the unnatural goodness of the children convinces the governess that they know of the ghosts' existences; it convinces her of its opposite, the presence of evil. Time and again in the novel the *absence* of evidence is the surest proof: Flora's lack of response on the lakeshore is proof that 'she was perfectly aware' of the ghost (p. 31), and the governess herself, a moment before in this encounter with Miss Jessel, says that she 'was conscious – still without looking – ' of their 'visitor' (p. 29). Later she sums up her method of 'proof' when she says of the boat that Flora took that 'Our not seeing it is the strongest of proofs' (p. 69).

The void stands behind the world – behind nature and behind language – ready to expose itself in the intensity of silence, in the forceful arguments of absence. Here is the significance of James's title for his novel: it is not simply Douglas's remark that the presence of two children turns the screw of a ghost story about one. (This, I suspect, is for the unwary.) Rather, its significance lies in the governess's explanation of her strange and unnatural experience:

> ... my equilibrium depended on the success of my rigid will, the will to shut my eyes as tight as possible to the truth that what I had to deal with was, revoltingly, against nature. I could only get on at all by taking 'nature' into my confidence and my account, by treating my monstrous ordeal as a push in a direction unusual, of course, and unpleasant, but demanding after all, for a fair front, only another

turn of the screw of ordinary human virtue. No attempt, none the less, could well require more tact than just this attempt to supply, one's self, *all* the nature.

(p. 80)

The trap of the imagination turns the screw of experience, *supplements* it with nature, a fair front, the ordinary.[10] The unusual and unpleasant experience of which the governess is conscious is the experience governing consciousness itself, the dazzle and play of possibilities, of turning the screw, before the void. The governess 'turns' her monstrous ordeal into something ordinary – she supplements it – simply by narrating it, making (and taking) an 'account' of it. The important fact is that she *names* the ghosts, speaks to them and even speaks *for* them.[11] The conversation with Miss Jessel she reports to Mrs Grose (section xvi) never took place in the encounter itself (she had only 'looked at me long enough to appear to say that [she had a] right to sit at my table', p. 59). She also speaks for Miles (his 'exhibition of tact, of magnanimity [was] quite tantamount to his saying outright ...', p. 66), and for Flora ('"I'll be hanged", [the frank look she launched at me] said, "if *I'll* speak!"' p. 70). It all seems as if, as the governess says, her 'imagination had, in a flash, turned real' (p. 16).

Yet this 'turn', this 'reality' of the imagination is a far cry from the 'reality' that manifests itself in *Dracula*. The name of the Harkers' child is never spoken in *Dracula*, yet it contains a secret; the governess in *The Turn* constantly 'speaks' for significant silences in which seems to be no articulate secret. Thus, in another place she says, 'I somehow measured the importance of what I have seen by my thus finding myself hesitate to mention it' (p. 18). The unspoken (*unspeaking*) things she narrates somehow gain and measure their importance in their silence; the speech that gives them voices (*natural* voices which are not 'revoltingly, against nature') seems, like the governess's deepened awareness, a molestation. Chief among these is the silent awareness that governs her relations with the children. That silence was not vulgar, the governess says, not simply silent allusion to her 'predicament'. Rather, it was 'the element of the unnamed and untouched' in their relationship, 'as if, at moments, we were perpetually coming into sight of subjects before which we must stop short, turning suddenly out of alleys we perceived to be blind' (pp. 50–1). Stopping short is an apt image for the aim of Gothic novels in general which, as in the set-piece of

Dracula, elevate reactions over causes, the imagination over the world. What is most important, here and elsewhere in James, is the reaction – 'stopping short' – rather than those things before which one stops. That is, James's characters do not 'stop short' before a revelation of more than they are aware of – of what they are 'unconscious' of. Rather, they stop short before an occasion for discourse. Thus the first 'reaction' we see in this passage is the governess's articulation of her experience; experience is immediately translated ('turned') to metaphor, silence is immediately *narrated* in a hypothesised walk, 'as if we were perpetually coming into sight. …' That is, what is uncanny about her relation to the children is naturalised and humanised to a stroll, and even while it remains shocking – unusual and unpleasant – it gains a human face.

This is why people talk the way they do in James, and especially in *The Turn*: people are constantly 'anticipating' one another, completing one another's (unspoken? uncompleted? absent?) thoughts: 'Douglas completed my thought', the narrator says (p. 5). These anticipations take two forms in the dialogue of *The Turn*: characters speak by *repeating* what they heard ('"Quint's and that woman's?"/"Quint's and that woman's …"'); and by *completing* what they heard ('"I say … she was perfectly aware."/"Do you mean aware of *him*?"/"No – of *her*"', p. 31). This is the language of James's characters, filling the silence of spaces between words, supplying, as the governess says, *all* the nature, attempting to find a plethora of meaning where there is really very little.

Yet supplying the meaning through repetition and anticipation often becomes supplanting the meaning in these dialogues. Thus when Mrs Grose asks the governess if the ghost of Miss Jessel spoke in the schoolroom, the governess answers:

> 'It came to that. I found her, on my return, in the schoolroom.'
> 'And what did she say?' I can hear the good woman still, and the candour of her stupefaction.
> 'That she suffers the torments – !'
> It was this, of a truth, that made her, as she filled out my picture, gape. 'Do you mean', she faltered, ' – of the lost?'
> 'Of the lost. Of the damned. And that's why, to share them – ' I faltered myself with the horror of it.
> But my companion, with less imagination, kept me up. 'To share them – ?'
> 'She wants Flora.'
> (pp. 60–1)

But it doesn't matter, the governess continues, because she's made up her mind 'to everything', to write a letter to the master of Bly. This dialogue combines repetition and anticipation: it renders the governess's encounter with Miss Jessel a conversation while it makes the conversation itself an almost silent encounter. At the scene of writing the governess can 'still' hear Mrs Grose, but what she 'hears', once again, is silence: the most important parts of conversation are James's ubiquitous dashes – the signs of hesitation, 'faltering', hushes. Whenever the governess recounts encounters with the ghost she 'hears' again the hush, the faltering voice of nature, the silence. The recurring 'hearing' as she writes repeats the false 're-occurrence' of Miss Jessel's silent discourse in the schoolroom as she talks to Mrs Grose. She supplies the most natural of things, conversation, to that unnatural encounter. Such a supplement lies while it creates discourse, just as the constant anticipations – finding reasons 'why', filling out the picture – ultimately destroy discourse through repetition, interruption, confusion. When characters repeat one another they do so to question the meaning of discourse ('Quint's and that woman's?') and the answer they get is what they said; when they anticipate – a form of 'repeating' forward – they are usually mistaken.

The confusion of James's speakers is confusion of antecedents, of what has come before. They are always seeking origins to ground meaning and significance and make communication possible – origins, sexual and cultural, that literally haunt *Dracula* and the Gothic tradition itself.[12] 'I remember feeling with Miles in especial', the governess says, 'as if he had had, as it were, nothing to call even an infinitesmal history ... [and] scant enough "antecedents"' (p. 19). This is the most 'unnatural' aspect of Miles, that which the governess constantly wants to get 'behind', as she tries to get 'behind' his words (p. 47). In experience effects always *precede* causes – causes are defined always and already in retrospect. Thus to confuse antecedents, as the speakers of *The Turn* do, as Miles in his person seems to do, is to dislocate the speaker, to place him, like Kasper Hauser, momentarily in a causeless world. (One need only know Count Dracula's 'history' – a history in its fullness the antithesis of Miles' – to know him and his 'secret'.) This is what the silences of James, the governess's 'intense hush', do: they offer experience without cause that immediately demands the mediation and antecedents of language.

The governess's written account, after all, is her attempt to supply Miles with a history, with antecedents. That she does so by using her own antecedent, 'my vile predecessor' (p. 59), is charac-teristic of her discourse. But the question of Miles' 'history' is the question of *The Turn of the Screw*, the mystery to be detected and solved. And, as in *Dracula*, it is articulated in the written docu-ments of *The Turn*, the various letters that circulate throughout the novel. The governess's account begins with one such letter, one that literally precedes Miles home (as her reading of Gothic novels pre-ceded her visit to Bly), and announces the mystery of *The Turn*: Miles is dismissed from school without an explanation, without a 'history'. In a brilliant essay describing and contrasting letters and gossip in fiction Homer Brown suggests that 'the letter stands in the novel for what is connected with the past, origin, genealogical source, parent'.[13] Yet Miles has no past, no genealogy, no parent; that is the mystery 'his' letter announces. Moreover, this letter – like all the other letters in *The Turn* – is received by the wrong person; it is misdirected. Brown notes that 'it is always important that what the letter says can't be *said* in any other way, can't be spoken. Instead of the endless round of speculation that is gossip, the letter gives answers (information); its emphasis is *revelation*. The letter is a message to be delivered, gossip is *received*.'[14] What is revealed in *The Turn of the Screw* is precisely what cannot be spoken, what the governess cannot articulate or even 'see'. Like Miles' history, his antecedents, it is a revelation of absence, of 'nothing'. It is not the documentary hints of an infernal monster which, as in *Dracula* (or 'The Murders in the Rue Morgue'), only have to be compiled to reveal the horror. Nothing – absence, words without explanations, without antecedent referents – is the 'content' of all the letters to and from Bly.

'To play a role in the novel', Brown continues, '... letters must be read by someone other than the one to whom they are addressed. They must be Purloined.'[15] This is the situation of *The Turn*: the governess receives letters addressed to the master, both from the headmaster of Miles' school and the 'charming literary exercises' of the children (p. 54); Mrs Grose has the bailiff write her letters (p. 61); the governess writes to the master but doesn't tell Mrs Grose 'that my letter, sealed and directed, was still in my pocket' (p. 65); and Miles steals – purloins and destroys – this letter (p. 78). The letters of *The Turn of the Screw* are all misdirected. But why does Brown say that letters in novels 'must' be purloined? They 'must' be, I suspect, because when they are not misdelivered, there can be no plot, no 'narration'. Even the 'plot' of *Dracula* is the marshalling of letters, getting them 'straight'. When they are delivered there is only precisely what *The Turn of the Screw* lacks, '*revelation*'.[16]

Revelation, after all, is the problem of *The Turn*; its *problem* is its revealed ghosts and what the governess is to make of them. Revelation is more than a turn of the screw; it is revoltingly against nature. It destroys discourse, it creates a solitude, it strikes the world with silence, with death. Like Dracula, revelation is Un-dead, an absence, a *hiatus* in nature. The only response to it, as the governess shows – as the experience of Count Dracula, which time after time demands a written response, shows – is discourse, the *narrated* discourse that covers and denies (supplements and supplants) the lapse and asserts, against the silence, the ordinary and the human. As *Dracula* asserts, there can be no 'authentic document' (p. 382); and *The Turn* goes on to assert that even the 'transfusion' of the secret to the transcription is impossible. Letters 'must' be misdelivered because, like the governess's discourse, they supplement and supplant the revelation they 'contain': what the letter from the headmaster cannot *say* is that Miles 'said things' (p. 86). '"It was too bad"', Miles finally confesses, '... "What I suppose I sometimes said. To write home"' (p. 87). Instead of what he said, we have what the headmaster says (or really what the governess says: like Mrs Grose, we cannot read the letter); instead of to the uncle (himself a surrogate parent) the letter is delivered to the governess. The letter doesn't reveal, after all; it gives something else, more or less. It gives more *and* less. 'See him, Miss, first', says Mrs Grose, '*Then* believe [the letter]' (p. 11).

Yet the letters also give 'more'; they 'reveal'. The letters in *The Turn of the Screw* are constantly conflated with the ghosts. At the end Miles confesses that he stole and opened the governess's letter 'to see what you said about me':

> 'I opened it.'
> My eyes were now ... on Miles' own face. ... What was prodigious was that at last, by my success, his sense was sealed and his communication [with Quint] stopped: he knew that he was in presence, but knew not of what, and knew still less that I also was and that I did know. And what did this strain of trouble matter when my eyes went back to the window only to see that the air was clear again and – by my personal triumph – the influence quenched? There was nothing there. I felt that the cause was mine and I should surely get *all*. 'And you found nothing!' – I let my elation out.

He gave the most mournful, thoughtful little headshake.
'Nothing.'
'Nothing, nothing!' I almost shouted in my joy.
'Nothing, nothing', he sadly repeated.

(pp. 85–6)

The window and the letter both contain 'nothing' – the governess's letter was simply a request for an interview, for speech (p. 78). In this passage the governess conflates the letter and the ghost; she offers two narratives mirroring one another, the languages of life and of death. Quint and the letter 'disappear' at the same moment, in the same movement. The governess here is like and unlike the characters of *Dracula*, she both says and doesn't say more than she means, more *and* less than Miles understands. The 'presence' Miles is and isn't aware of, I believe, is the 'presence' of the governess's ambiguous speech, referring to the letter requesting discourse and to the ghost that stills the world's voices and strikes it with death. Her speech itself is 'misdirected', speaking to Quint's 'through' Miles, conflating emptiness and fullness. It is simultaneously full and empty, full of Quint, yet 'speaking' of a letter which means 'nothing'. Yet the conflation is more complete than this: Quint's ghost, like most of the 'objects' of the governess's sharper sensibility, is itself empty, a hush, absence; and the letter that 'contains' nothing promises the revelation of the interview – with the *absent* master, as this dizzying conflation continues. 'Which is why', Jacques Lacan writes, 'we cannot say of the purloined letter that, like other objects, it must be *or* not be in a particular place but that unlike them it will be *and* not be where it is, wherever it goes.'[17] 'Horrible as it was', the governess said earlier, 'his lies made up my truth' (p. 84).

The confusion of ghosts and letters is the confusion of writing and death (a situation suggested by Dinesen's preoccupation with Scheherazade in *Seven Gothic Tales*). Writing wards off silence, but it also creates its own silence. This is why, I suspect, the governess 'hears' better while she writes the text we read. When the governess discovers Miss Jessel in the schoolroom, 'at first blush' she imagines she sees 'some housemaid ... availing herself ... of my pens, inks and paper, ... [making] the considerable effort of a letter to her sweetheart' (p. 59). And of her first encounter with Quint she says, 'I saw him as I see the letters I form on this page' (p. 17). Writing confuses itself with death because it leaves so much out and doing so, it creates the double, 'mirroring' discourse I mentioned before, leaving too much in; it is inscribed in the face of loss.[18] Writing, like the letters formed on the page and the letter to the sweetheart, *has to be read*; it has *yet* to be read: this is what Brown means when he says 'the letter is a message to be delivered, gossip [speech] is *received*'. That delivery passes through and carries with it the intense hush, absence, death. The governess's whole narrative, itself making 'the considerable effort of a letter to [a] sweetheart' (yet, as Douglas says, it does so silently, 'not in any literal vulgar way' – p. 3), is misdirected to Douglas who, after 'a long silence' for which he 'had had his reasons' (p. 2), read it 'to our hushed little circle' (p. 4), and later, as a sort of death-bed statement 'committed' it to the narrator who offers it to us (p. 4).

This brings us to a final question of *The Turn*, the question of the governess's letter. For whom was it written? This question can only be asked of writing; speech, like gossip, is always directed, 'received'. (And yet this too is problematic: who, after all, 'receives' the governess's last speech to Miles/Quint? Or is it 'written' as well?) In a sense it is a misdirected letter to Harley Street, written *not to be delivered*, a letter to a sweetheart that 'speaks' – as Miss Jessel does – through silence, not in any literal, vulgar way. Yet in another sense the governess's writing is a letter that 'justifies', written in answer to the governess's own question in response to her experience: 'it was for the instant confounding and bottomless, for if he [Miles] *were* innocent, what then on earth was I?' (p. 87). At crucial moments the governess speaks of her justification – when she sees Miss Jessel the last time (p. 71), and when Mrs Grose informs her that Flora too 'says things' (p. 77). But the two motives come together in the governess's description of her daily 'hour' of peace she felt *before* the ghosts appear at Bly:

> It was a pleasure at these moments to feel myself tranquil and justified; doubtless perhaps, also to reflect that by my discretion, my quiet good sense and general high propriety, I was giving pleasure – if he ever thought of it! – to the person to whose pressure I had responded.
>
> (p. 15)

Her letter (*The Turn of the Screw*) justifies her – both in relation to the master and in relation to Miles, in relation to love *and* death – *only* if it is not delivered. If delivered it becomes literal and vulgar: in relation to the master it betrays his charges, in relation to Miles it betrays the unspoken possibility that her 'strange sharpness' in 'hearing' silences is madness.

Her letter covers 'confounding and bottomless' experience of guilt and, beneath this, of not being thought of – guilty or not – at all. Undelivered and unread, it supplements her guilt with 'justification' and supplants her absence – her 'ghostliness' – in relation to the master with the narrative altogether. Like the children, like the ghost of Miss Jessel, the governess has no one to write to, just as the letters she reads are meant for someone else. Her final attempt at justification is her final attempt to read the headmaster's letter (a letter not meant for her): 'He stole *letters*!' she says (p. 78). Yet this letter, finally, like the one she tries to write, says nothing; it marks the absence – the misdirection – of all the letters of *The Turn of the Screw*.

III

The trap of the imagination, then, is the fact that it responds to nothing – to empty letters, to ghosts, to its own unnatural power – the nothing that is not there and the nothing that is. Its language is Kierkegaard's irony, grinning at the devil with a language that wilfully misunderstands, that turns the screw, the language of fiction. Much as the ancient Athenians called the Furies the Eumenides and gave them human form, so James's narrative falsely names the unnatural horror of indifference the human horror of ghosts: it makes justification seemingly possible by discovering and humanising, as the Greeks had done, the chthonic origins of life, inarticulately expressed in the hush of silence. This takes place in and by means of language: Jacques Lacan has noted that in psychoanalysis the operative 'cure' of hysterics is not memory but verbalisation, and the same is true in James.[19] Value, that is, is created (supplementally, supplantingly) and *remains* in the misdirected, mistaking language which points it out – even in the Gothic language of horrible 'ghosts' that seem to speak out of the hush of nature.

The horror of ghosts in James's story is what Lacan calls the Symbolic, a shadow or unreal fiction without which we cannot live; they are what Derrida calls the *supplement* which both supplants and adds to an inarticulate, inhuman experience human images and values. Thus the action of fiction discovers value in the face of an indifferent world simply by articulating it. This is the strength of Kierkegaard's irony: to say something and to mean nothing, yet a nothing upon which to base human life. James's governess humanises the enigma of the children with ghostly antecedents which make their 'unnatural' goodness, their uncanny Otherness, humanly and verbally, if supernaturally, comprehensible. This action – the creation of human origins and antecedents, which is a return and an anticipation at once – is the business of language and the trap of the imagination.

From *Criticism*, 22 (1980), 298–319.

NOTES

[Ronald Schleifer situates *The Turn of the Screw* in a pivotal position between 'old' and 'new' Gothic. Beginning as a genre essay, Schleifer's study reads James's tale against the near contemporaneous *Dracula* (1897). Bram Stoker's novel is seen as looking back to the Gothic tradition of the turn of the nineteenth century, while *The Turn* looks forward to the self-conscious fiction of the twentieth. The primacy of the imagination over the 'real world' and the elevation of reactions over causes are seen as Gothic features within both texts, symptomised by 'stopping short' in repetitious and anticipatory speech, leading to supplanted or dislocated meaning. Schleifer uses Shoshana Felman (see essay 2) and Lacan on letters to underpin a discussion of misdelivery and non-delivery, amid an interweaving of ghosts and letters, writing and death, with *The Turn* itself ultimately viewed as 'letter'. The problem of unnatural revelation, or the terror beneath language, is here linked to Kierkegaard's conception of irony, as saying something yet meaning nothing, and yielding a sense simultaneously of return and anticipation. Ed.]

1. The 'natural' explanation is best exemplified by Edmund Wilson's famous essay, 'The Ambiguity of Henry James', in *The Triple Thinkers* (New York, 1938), pp. 122–64, in which he argues a psychoanalytic interpretation; the 'supernatural' explanation is best exemplified by Dorothea Krook, *The Ordeal of Consciousness in Henry James* (Cambridge, 1962), pp. 106–34, in which she argues a theological struggle of good and evil. Tzvetan Todorov argues that the Gothic – what he calls 'the fantastic – situates itself in the 'uncertainty', the 'hesitation' *between* natural and supernatural understandings of experience; see *The Fantastic: A Structural Approach to a Literary Genre*, trans. Richard Howard (Ithaca, NY, 1975).

2. Isak Dinesen, 'The Deluge at Nordeney', in *Seven Gothic Tales* (New York, 1934), p. 77.

3. Bram Stoker, *Dracula* (New York, 1965, Signet edition). All page references will be given in the text.

4. Roland Barthes argues that speech is distinguished from writing absolutely by the 'expendability of words' in speech; see especially *Writing Degree Zero* in *Writing Degree Zero and Elements of Semiology*, trans. Annette Lavers and Colin Smith (Boston, 1968). As I will argue, by not 'returning', the narrators of *The Turn* are never able to give up – to 'reveal' – the 'secret' of the novel.

5. The finest and most complete discussion of sexuality and *Dracula* is Leonard Wolf, *A Dream of Dracula* (New York, 1972), especially ch. 6.

6. Paul de Man, 'The Rhetoric of Blindness: Jacques Derrida's Reading of Rousseau', in *Blindness and Insight: Essays in the Rhetoric of Contemporary Criticism* (New York, 1971), pp. 124, 123.

7. 'Author's Introduction', to *Frankenstein*, in *Three Gothic Novels*, ed. Peter Fairclough (Baltimore, 1968), p. 264.

8. Henry James, *The Turn of the Screw*, ed. Robert Kimbrough (New York, 1966, the Norton Critical Edition). All page references will be given in the text.

9. The term *'supplement'* is found throughout the work of Jacques Derrida: see especially *Of Grammatology*, trans G. C. Spivak (Baltimore, 1976). Derrida uses the word in a double sense, as both a 'supplement' (an addition) and a 'substitute' (a replacement); the terms I use here are 'supplement' and 'supplant'. See also Avron Fleishman, 'Fiction as Supplement', in *Fiction and the Ways of Knowing* (Austin, TX, 1978), for a use of the term somewhat different from that which I am presenting.

   For an extended analysis of *The Turn of the Screw* that shares many of the terms and focuses of this study, see Shoshana Felman, 'Turning the Screw of Interpretation', in *Literature and Psychoanalysis, Yale French Studies*, 55/56 (1977), 94–207. Felman attempts, in a psychoanalytical examination of *The Turn*, 'not so much to *capture* the mystery's solution, but to follow, rather, the significance of its flight; not so much to solve or *answer* the enigmatic question of the text, but to investigate its structure' (p. 119). Felman's aim, however, is as much to explore the relation between literature and recent developments in psychoanalysis as it is to explore James's text.

10. The extent of these supplements can be gleaned from Felman's extended discussion of the title and its metaphors, pp. 126, 170f., 178, 180, passim.

11. One of the important controversies over *The Turn* revolves around the naming of the ghosts; see, for instance, Harold C. Goddard's elaborate discussion of their naming in 'A Pre-Freudian Reading of *The Turn of the Screw*', in the Norton Critical Edition, especially pp. 190–3. If, in fact, the governess doesn't 'name' the ghosts, it is clear from her report of Miss Jessel that she speaks *for* them.

12. For the place of the past in the Gothic tradition, see Leslie A. Fiedler, *Love and Death in the American Novel* (New York, 1966), especially ch. 6.

13. Homer Brown, 'The Errant Letter and the Whispering Gallery', *Genre*, 10 (1977), 590. Felman (pp. 139–48) has an extended discussion of the letters in *The Turn* that anticipates my own [see essay 2, Ed.].

14. Brown, p. 581.

15. Ibid., p. 583. Behind Brown's (and Felman's) discussion of letters is Jacques Lacan, 'Seminar on "The Purloined Letter"', trans. Jeffrey Mehlman, in *French Freud: Structural Studies in Psychoanalysis, Yale French Studies*, 48 (1972), 38–72. One should also see Derrida's reading of Lacan's reading, 'The Purveyor of Truth', trans. Willis Domingo et al., in *Graphesis, Yale French Studies*, 52 (1975); and Barbara Johnson's discussion of them all, 'The Frame of Reference: Poe, Lacan, Derrida', in *Literature and Psychoanalysis*, pp. 457–505.

16. Thus Felman notes, 'it is precisely *because* the letters *fail* to narrate, to construct a coherent, transparent story, that there is a story at all: there is a story *because* there is an unreadable, an unconscious' (p. 143) [see p. 48 below, Ed.]

17. Lacan, 'Seminar on "The Purloined Letter"' (p. 54). Felman also describes in a more extended theoretical discussion the conflation of letters and ghosts (pp. 149–61).

18. For a short discussion of the relation between writing and death, see Joseph N. Riddel's examination of Poe in 'A Somewhat Polemical Introduction: The Elliptical Poem', *Genre*, 11 (1978). Concerning 'The Raven' he notes, 'it is not a lost presence, the maiden Lenore, that is remembered, but "mournful remembrance" itself, remembrance as an emblem that is marked through and through as death. That is, utterance itself is death ...' (p. 465). See also Felman's argument that the manuscript of the story provides, much as Count Dracula *literally* does, 'a *return* of the dead *within the text*' (p. 128).

19. Of the importance of verbalisation in analysis, Lacan notes that the patient 'has made its passage into the *verbe* or more precisely into the *epos* by which he brings back into present time the origins of his own person', so that it is verbalisation, not memory, that humanises origins: see *The Language of the Self*, trans. Anthony Wilden (New York, 1975), p. 17. Why this should be so is an issue outside the scope of this essay. Nevertheless, I would like to make a tentative suggestion here. If, as I have argued, 'revelation' precludes narration and implies solitude and isolation, then narration would create at least some sense of community. Such a community is what I am calling the 'human' realm and what Lacan calls the Symbolic: it is the realm of language providing that Saussurian community of a 'system

of differences' which makes meaning possible. For a brilliant analysis of Lacan's terms, see Fredric Jameson, 'Imaginary and Symbolic in Lacan: Marxism, Psychoanalytic Criticism, and the Problem of Subject', in *Literature and Psychoanalysis*, pp. 338–95.

2

The Scene of Writing:
Purloined Letters

SHOSHANA FELMAN

The actual story of *The Turn of the Screw* (that of the governess and the ghosts) is preceded by a prologue which is both posterior and exterior to it, and which places it *as* a story, as a speech event, in the context of the 'reality' in which the story comes to be told. With respect to the story's *content*, then, the prologue constitutes a sort of *frame*, whose function is to situate the *story's origin*.

The narrated story is thus presented as the *centre* of the *frame* – the focal point of a narrative space which designates and circumscribes it from the outside as *its inside*. Placed *around* the story which becomes its centre the narrative frame, however, frames *another* centre within its *literal* space:

> The story had held us, *round the fire*, sufficiently breathless (...) He began to read to our hushed *little circle*, (...) kept it, *round the hearth*, subject to a common thrill.[1]
>
> (pp. 1 and 4)

Since the narrative space of the prologue organises both a *frame around the story* and a *circle around the fire*, since the fire and the story are both placed at the very *centre* of the *narration*, the question could arise as to whether they could be, in any way, considered *metaphors of each other* in the rhetorical constellation of the text. This hypothesis in turn opens up another question: if the content of the story and the fire in the hearth *are* metaphors of each other, how does this metaphorical relation affect the centrality of the two terms? [...]

> He turned round to the fire, gave a kick to a log, watched it an instant. Then as he faced us again: 'I can't begin. I shall have to send to town. ... *The story's written.* It's in a locked drawer – it has not been out for years.'
>
> (Prologue, p. 2)

> Sans ce qui fait que le dire, ça vient à s'écrire, il n'y a pas moyen de faire sentir la dimension du savoir inconscient.
>
> (J. Lacan, 1974 Seminar)

> ... l'histoire nous laisse ignorer à peu près tout de l'expéditeur, non moins que du contenu de la lettre ... nous n'en pouvons retenir qu'une chose, c'est que la Reine ne saurait la porter à la connaissance de son seigneur et maître.
>
> (J. Lacan, *Séminaire sur la lettre volée*)

The fact that 'the story's written', underlined by the narrative suspense that that fact creates, has two important implications:

(1) The story is a *text* and not just a series of events: it has its own *materiality* and its own *place;* it exists as a material object;

(2) As a material object, the manuscript is independent of the narrator, who is, rather, himself dependent on *it:* the narrator is dependent on the place and materiality of the written word.

This double implication will in turn have three immediate consequences:

(1) It is *impossible* for the narrator to *begin;* there seems to be a problem inherent in the beginning as such, since it is first *postponed*, and then *replaced* by a 'prologue': 'I can't begin. I shall have to send to town. ... The story's written', says Douglas. However, when the manuscript has arrived, Douglas explains the need for 'a few words of prologue' (p. 4) which will substitute for the beginning, since 'the written statement took up the tale at a point after it had, in a manner, begun' (p. 4).

(2) The manuscript's place is a 'locked drawer' – a closed, secret place: for the story to be told, the lock has to be forced, the hideout

opened up: a seal of silence must be broken, and the story's 'opening' is thus literally and figuratively an *outbreak:*

> 'The story ... has not been out for years. I could write to my man and enclose the key; he could send down the packet as he finds it.' ... he had *broken* a thickness of ice, the formation of many a winter; had had his reasons for a long silence.
>
> (Prologue, p. 2)

> Mrs Griffin spoke. ...
> '... It's rather nice, his long reticence.'
> 'Forty years!' Griffin put in.
> 'With this *outbreak* at last.'
> 'The *outbreak*', I returned, 'will make a tremendous occasion of Thursday night.'
>
> (Prologue, p. 3)

(3) In order for there to be a narrative at all, Douglas must have the manuscript *sent* to him through the mail. There is thus an *address* on the text: *the story is a letter*. Indeed, it is triply so: sent first by the governess to Douglas, then by Douglas to himself, then by Douglas to the narrator. As a letter, the narrative entails both a *change of location* and a *change of address*.

In fact, the manuscript-letter is itself a story about letters: the first narrative event of the governess's story is the cryptic letter announcing Miles's dismissal from school; then the governess mentions that she intercepts the children's letters to the Master; then there is the troubling question for the governess of the letter Mrs Grose wants sent to the Master about the goings-on at Bly, which the governess promises to write herself; and finally, the governess's letter to the Master is intercepted and destroyed by Miles.

What is striking about these letters is that they all bear a curious resemblance to the letter of the manuscript itself. They are addressed and sealed:

> ... my letter, *sealed and directed*, was still in my pocket.
>
> (ch. 18, p. 65)

To open them requires that a seal be broken, that violence be done; the letters' opening instigates a sort of crisis:

> The postbag, that evening ... contained a letter for me, which, however, in the hand of my employer, I found to be composed but of

a few words enclosing another, addressed to himself, with a *seal still unbroken*. 'This, I recognise, is from the head-master, and the head-master's an awful bore. Read him, please; deal with him; but mind you don't report...' *I broke the seal with a great effort* – so great a one that I was a long time coming to it; took the unopened missive at last up to my room and only *attacked it* just before going to bed. I had better have let it wait till morning, for it gave me a second sleepless night.

(ch. 2, p. 10)

In the story as in the prologue, the materiality of writing, as the materiality of the manuscript, seems to create a problem of beginnings. Like Douglas, the governess finds it difficult to begin:

I went so far, in the evening, as to *make a beginning*. ... I sat for a long time before a *blank sheet of paper* ... . Finally I went out.

(ch. 17, p. 62)

We will later learn that this letter from the governess to the Master will never be, in fact, more than just an envelope containing that same blank sheet of paper: the beginning as such is only written as *unwritten*, destined to remain anterior and exterior to what can be learned from a letter:

'I've just begun a letter to your uncle', I said.
'Well then, finish it!'
I waited a minute. 'What happened *before*?'
He gazed up at me again. '*Before* what?'
'*Before* you came back. And *before* you went away.' ... he was silent.

(ch. 17, pp. 64–5)

In so far as the narrative itself is an effect of writing and as such is dependent on the letter of its text, its very *telling* involves the non-possession of its beginning. If the story is a letter and if a letter is the materialisation of the absence of the beginning of a story, then the very act of telling, of narrating, must begin as the transgressive breaking of a seal – the seal of the silence from which the story springs. The story then is nothing but the circulation of a violated letter which materially travels from place to place through the successive changes of its addressees, and through a series of 'address-corrections'. While the letter is never really begun, it is nonetheless ceaselessly *forwarded*.

The letters *in* the story, then, strikingly resemble the letter of the manuscript of the story. And although these letters either remain unwritten or are intercepted and destroyed, although their content is either missing or undecipherable, their *function* nonetheless, like that precisely of the manuscript-letter which contains them, is to *constitute a narrative*, to *tell the story* of the goings-on which they partake of, the story which has necessitated their being written.

> 'Do you mean you'll write?' Remembering she couldn't, I caught myself up. 'How do you communicate?'
> 'I tell the bailiff. *He* writes.'
> 'And should you like him to *write our story*?'
> My question had a sarcastic force that I had not fully intended, and it made her ... inconsequently break down... .
> 'Ah, Miss, *you write*!'
>
> (ch. 16, pp. 61–2)

Clearly, what the letter is about is nothing other than the very story which contains it. What the letters are to tell is the telling of the story: how the narrative, precisely, tells itself *as an effect of writing*. The letters in the story are thus not simply *metonymical* to the manuscript which contains them; they are also *metaphorical* to it: they are the reflection *en abyme* of the narrative itself. To read the story is thus to undertake *a reading of the letters*, to follow the circuitous paths of their changes of address.

The first thing such a 'letter-reading' must encounter is the fact that, paradoxically enough, it is not what the letters *say* which gets the story started, but what they *don't say*: the letters are as such *unreadable*, illegible as much for the reader as for the characters in the story, who are *all the more* affected by them for not being able to decipher them. The letters are thus unreadable in precisely the same way the unconscious is unreadable: like the letters, the unconscious also governs an entire (hi)story, determines the course of a whole life and destiny, without ever letting itself be penetrated or understood.

If the letters' very resistance to daylight, to transparency and to meaning, is indicative of their participation in an unconscious economy; if, as signifiers *par excellence* of that unconscious economy, they can only be meaningful *through their own censorship*, signify through their own *blacking-out*; if the very story of the unconscious is a story of the circulation of undecipherable letters, – then the crucial theoretical question for both literature and psychoanalysis, for the reader of textual letters as well as for the interpreter of the text of the unconscious, would be the following one:

how can *unreadable* letters be *read*, even as they demand to be *read as unreadable*? This question, which is indeed raised by *The Turn of the Screw* on all levels, is crucial as much for the reader as for the characters of the story, whose fortunes are wholly determined by the mystery that the letters at once point to and withhold.

How can we read the unreadable? This question, however, is far from simple: grounded in contradiction, it in fact subverts its own terms: to actually *read* the unreadable, to impose a *meaning* on it, is precisely *not* to read the unreadable *as unreadable*, but to *reduce* it to the readable, to interpret it as if it were of the same order as the readable. But perhaps the unreadable and the readable *cannot* be located on the same level, perhaps they are *not* of the same order: if they could indeed correspond to the unconscious and to the conscious levels, then their functionings would be radically different, and their modes of being utterly heterogeneous to each other. It is entirely possible that the unreadable as such could by no means, in no way, be made *equivalent* to the readable, through a simple effort at better reading, through a simple *conscious* endeavour. The readable and the unreadable are by no means simply *comparable*, but neither are they simply *opposed*, since above all they are not *symmetrical*, they are not mirror-images of each other. Our task would perhaps then become not so much to read the unreadable *as a variant of the readable*, but, to the very contrary, to *rethink the readable itself*, and hence, to attempt to read it as a *variant of the unreadable*. The paradoxical necessity of 'reading the unreadable' could thus be accomplished only through a radical modification of the meaning of 'reading' itself. To read on the basis of the unreadable would be, here again, to ask not *what* does the unreadable mean, but *how* does the unreadable mean? Not what is the meaning of the letters, but in what way do the letters *escape* meaning? In what way do the letters *signify via*, precisely, their own *in*significance?

We have seen how the letters become a crucial dramatic element in the narrative plot precisely because of their unreadability: their function of 'giving the alarm' (ch. 21, p. 78), of setting the story in motion and keeping it in suspense through the creation of a situation of tension and of contradiction in which ambiguity reigns, is correlative to the persistent opacity of their informative function and to the repeated failure of their attempts at narration, of their endeavour to tell the story of a beginning, to 'write a story' which would itself know its own origin and its own cause. But it is precisely *because* the letters *fail* to narrate, to construct a coherent, transparent story, that there is a story at all: there is a story *because* there is an unreadable, an unconscious. Narrative, paradoxically, becomes possible to the precise extent that a story becomes *impossible* – that a story, precisely, *'won't tell'*. Narrative is thus engendered by the displacement of a 'won't tell' which, being transmitted through letters, forwards itself as a *writing-effect.*

It is indeed the unreadable which determines, in James's text, the narrative structure of the story. The narrative events themselves arise out of the 'alarm' the letters invariably produce. And each of the letters will end up, indeed, giving rise to another letter. There is therefore a *chain* of letters, in much the same way as there is a *chain* of narrative voices, of narrators. The letters, however, relay each other or give rise to each other by means of the very *silences,* of the very *ellipses,* which constitute them: the letters are only linked to each other through the very 'holes' in their contents. From the enigmatic letter of the Director of Miles's school, to the unfinished letter of the governess to the Master which Miles intercepts and destroys, the story of *The Turn of the Screw* is structured around a sort of necessity short-circuited by an impossibility, or an impossibility contradicted by a necessity, of *recounting an ellipsis,* of writing, to the Master, a letter about the head-master's letter, and about what was missing, precisely, in the head-master's letter: the reasons for Miles's dismissal from school. The whole story springs from the impossibility, as well as from the necessity, of writing *a letter about what was missing in the initial, original letter.*

Thus it is that the whole course of the story is governed by the hole in a letter. The signifying *chain* of letters, constituted less by what the letters *have* in common than by what they *lack* in common, is thus characterised by three negative features which can be seen as its common attributes: (1) the message or content of the letters is elided or suppressed; (2) in place of the missing message, what is recounted is the story of the material movement and fate of the letters themselves: the letters' circuit, however, becomes, paradoxically enough, a short-circuit of the direct contact between receiver and sender; (3) the addressee, who determines the letters' displacements and circuit, becomes the privileged element in each one of the letters: the *address* is the only thing that is readable, sometimes the only thing even *written.* And, curiously enough, *all* the letters in *The Turn of the Screw* – including the one from the school director, forwarded to the governess – are originally addressed to one and the same person: the Master. What is the structural significance of this convergence of the unreadable upon one crucial address?

The need to write to the Master to inform him of the uncanny happenings for which Bly has become the arena, stems from the fact that the Master is the *lawful proprietor* of Bly: for the governess and for the children as well, the Master embodies at once the supreme instance of Law as such and the supreme figure of Power. But the Master, before the story's beginning, in its unwritten part for which the prologue accounts, had precisely exerted his power and dictated his law to the governess through the express *prohibition* that any letters be addressed to him.

> 'He told her frankly all his difficulty – that for several applicants the *conditions* had been *prohibitive*. ... It sounded strange; and all the more so because of his main condition.'
>   'Which was–?'
>   'That she should never trouble him – but never, never; neither appeal nor complain nor write about anything; only meet all questions herself; receive all moneys from his solicitor, take the whole thing over and let him alone. She promised to do this, and she mentioned to me that when, for a moment, disburdened, delighted, he held her hand, thanking her for the sacrifice, she already felt rewarded.'
>   'But was that all her reward?' one of the ladies asked.
>   'She never saw him again.'
>
>   (Prologue, p. 6)

The paradoxical contract between the governess and the Master is thus from the outset a contract of *disconnection*, of *non-correspondence*. Constitutive of an aporia, of a relation of non-relation, the Master's discourse is very like the condition of the unconscious as such: Law itself is but a form of Censorship. But it is precisely this censoring law and this prohibitive contract which constitute, paradoxically, the story's condition of possibility: the condition of possibility of the story of the impossibility of writing the Master a letter about what was initially missing, *not said*, in yet another letter (equally addressed to, but refused by, the Master). Through the Master's inaugural act of forwarding *unopened* to the governess a letter addressed to him from the Director of Miles's school, mastery determines itself as at once a *refusal of information* and a *desire for ignorance*. Through its repressive function of blocking out, of suppressing, the instance of Law is established as the *bar* which will radically separate signifier from signified (S/s),[2] placing the letters, by the same token, under the odd imperative of the *non-knowledge* of their own content, since, written *for* the Master, the letters are, from the outset, *written for their own Censor*. The situation, however, is even more complex than this, since the governess also, quite clearly, falls in love – right away – with the Master. The Master therefore becomes, at the same time, not only an authority figure as well as an instance of prohibition, but also an object of love, a natural focus of transference. Written not only *for* the very personified image of power, but also *for* their own censorship and their own prohibition, the letters addressed to the Master are in fact, at the same time, *requests for love* and demands for attention. What, then, is the nature of a demand addressed both to the instance of power and to the instance of active non-knowledge? What is the status of *love for the Censor* – of *love for what censures love*? And how can one write *to the Censor*? How can one write *for* the very figure who signifies the suppression of what one has to say to him? These are the crucial questions underlying the text of *The Turn of the Screw*. It is out of this double bind that the story is both recounted and written.

The letters to the Master can convey, indeed, nothing but silence. Their message is not only erased; it consists of its own erasure. This is precisely what Miles discovers when he steals the letter the governess has intended to send to the Master:

'Tell me ... if, yesterday afternoon, from the table in the hall, you took, you know, my letter.'

...

'Yes – I took it.'

...

'What did you take it for?'
'To see what you said about me.'
'You opened the letter?'
'I opened it.'

...

'And you found *nothing*!' – I let my elation out.
He gave me the most mournful, thoughtful little headshake. '*Nothing.*'
'*Nothing, nothing*!' I almost shouted in my joy.
'*Nothing, nothing*', he sadly repeated.
I kissed his forehead; it was drenched. 'So what have you done with it?'
'I've burnt it.'

(chs 23–4, pp. 84–6)[3]

It is no coincidence, doubtless, that the letters to the Censor end up being intercepted and materially destroyed. Just as the governess intercepts the children's letters to the Master, Miles intercepts the governess's letter to the Master and ends up throwing it into the *fire*. The reader may recall, however, that the fire, as of the very opening line of the prologue, appeared as the centre of the narrative space of desire out of which the story springs: 'The story had held us, *round the fire*, sufficiently breathless ...' Symbolically narrative frame: in the centre of the circle, in the centre of the prologue, the same central place, with respect to the circle of readers-listeners, as that of the story's content with respect to the narrative frame: in the centre of the circle, in the centre of the frame, fire and story's content seemed indeed to act as foci – as *foyers* – upon which the space both of narration and of reading seemed to converge. But through Miles's gesture of throwing the governess's letter into the fire, the *fire inside the story* turns out to be, precisely, *what annihilates the inside of the letter;* what materially destroys the very 'nothing' which constitutes its *content*. And since the letters in the story are metaphorical to the manuscript of the story as a whole, i.e., to the narrative itself as an effect of writing, we can see that what the fire indeed consumes, in burning up the content of the letter, is nothing other than the very *content* of the story. If the story here is one of letters, it is because, in every sense of the expression, *letters burn*. As that which burns in the letter and which burns up the letter, the fire is the story's centre only in so far as it *eliminates the centre:* it is analogous to the story's *content* only in so far as it consumes, incinerates at once the content of the story and the inside of the letter, making both indeed impossible to read, *unreadable*, but unreadable in such a way as to hold all the more 'breathless' the readers' circle round it. 'We do not see what is burning', says Lacan in another context, referring to another fire which, however, is not without resemblance in its fantastic, funereal presence to the one which, here, is burning up the letter – 'we do not see what is burning, for the flame blinds us to the fact that the fire catches ... on the real.'[4]

From *Literature and Psychoanalysis: The Question of Reading: Otherwise*, ed. Shoshana Felman (Baltimore and London, 1982), pp. 119–20; 138–48.

NOTES

[Shoshana Felman's influential essay, 'Turning the Screw of Interpretation', was first published in *Yale French Studies* in 1977 (94–207); it was reprinted in the above volume (with the same pagination) and again in Shoshana Felman, *Writing and Madness: Literature, Philosophy, Psychoanalysis* (Ithaca, NY, 1985), pp. 141–247. The essay as a whole, which may be said to mark the beginning of modern *Turn of the Screw* criticism, takes an approach, combining psychoanalysis with communication theory, that is ultimately deconstructive, to interrogate reading, writing and madness. The short excerpt published here discussing letters (picked up by Schleifer – see essay 1 – and many subsequent commentators) and using the writings of Lacan, equates letters with the unconscious in the governance of 'story'. Unreadability is signified via insignificance in an elliptical process of epistolary mistransmittance, transferal and incineration. Ed.]

1.   All quotations from *The Turn of the Screw* are taken from the Norton Critical Edition, ed. Robert Kimbrough (New York, 1966), by section and page number in the text. All italics within the quoted texts are mine, unless otherwise indicated.

2.   Cf. J. Lacan, 'L'Instance de la lettre dans l'inconscient', in *Ecrits* (Paris, 1966), especially pp. 497–8 and 502.

3.   The fact that the letter of *Nothing* can in fact signify a *love letter* is reminiscent of Cordelia's uncanny reply to King Lear: by virtue of his imposing paternal and royal authority, King Lear, although soliciting his daughter's expression of love, can symbolically be seen as its censor. In saying precisely 'nothing', Cordelia addresses her father with the only 'authentic' love letter:

> Lear   Now, our joy,
>   Although the last, not least, to whose young love
>   The vines of France and milk of Burgundy
>   Strive to be interested, what can you say to draw
>   A third more opulent than your sisters? Speak.
> Cordelia Nothing, my lord.
> Lear   Nothing!
> Cordelia Nothing.
> Lear   Nothing will come of nothing. Speak again.
>
> (*King Lear*, I. i)

4.   J. Lacan, *Le Séminaire – Livre XI: Les Quatre concepts fondamenteaux de la psychanalyse* (Paris, 1973), p. 58. It is perhaps not

indispensable, but neither would it be here out of place to recall the crucial importance of fire in Henry James's life, and its recurrent role, both real and symbolic, as a *castrating agent*: just as James's father lost a leg in attempting to put a fire out, James himself injured his back in the course of a fire, as a result of which he was afflicted for the rest of his life with a mysterious, perhaps psychosomatic back ailment. Cf. Dr Saul Rosenzweig, 'The Ghost of Henry James: A Study in Thematic Apperception', in *Character and Personality* (Dec. 1943).

3

The Use and Abuse of Uncertainty in *The Turn of the Screw*

JOHN CARLOS ROWE

The transference of authority from ruler to ruled in James's writings is especially interesting because it seems regularly to result in the displacement of political and economic issues into psychological concerns of individual characters. Both *The Turn of the Screw* and the history of its interpretations are excellent illustrations of this sort of transference; both the narrative structure and diverse critical views of this work seem to concentrate on the psychology of the Governess to the significant exclusion of the work's wider social implications. Edmund Wilson's analysis of the Governess, of course, represents best this tendency among the early Freudian analyses. Wilson, to be sure, does not disregard the few sociological details and hints provided by James, but he equates the Governess's psychology with the central and controlling values of the culture:

> Her sombre and guilty visions and the way she behaves about them seem to present, from the moment we examine them from the obverse side of her narrative, an accurate and distressing picture of the poor country parson's daughter, with her English middle-class class-consciousness, her inability to admit to herself her natural sexual impulses and the relentless English 'authority' which enables her to put over on inferiors even purposes which are totally deluded and not at all in the other people's best interests. Remember, also, in this connection, the peculiar psychology of governesses, who, by

reason of their isolated position between the family and the servants, are likely to become ingrown and morbid.[1]

For Wilson, the anomalous character of the Governess's position in society all the more emphatically makes her representative of its gravest prejudices and ills. The critical argument that pits good against evil, governess against ghosts, has not won much support recently, and this argument also tends to trivialise the social issues in the work. Because the Governess's social standing is so ambivalent in Victorian society, whatever moral good she may be made to represent must be all the more archetypal and distinct from the particular values of a culture that may well have lost the controlling moral righteousness that she represents.[2] The narrative itself certainly seems to encourage this concentration on the 'psychology' or 'morality' of the Governess in the closed circle of romance that is Bly. The frame tales that introduce the Governess's manuscript (which focuses exclusively on the events at the country house) provide the reader with abundant ambiguities but precious few facts and details about anything or anyone outside the magic circle of Bly. Yet if the principal purpose of these diverse narratives is to effect the sort of transference of concerns of social and political authority that we have discussed above onto the psychological concerns of characters like the Governess and Mrs Grose, both of whom have no real social power, then the ambiguities involving all that lies beyond the estate of Bly would appear to be perfectly designed, to be 'facts' in their own right.

Before attempting to read this relation of transference between the 'inside' of the narrative (Bly, country, psychology of Governess, family of orphans) and its 'outside' (frame tales, Harley Street Uncle, London, society, power), I must return to the complicity of literature itself in what thus far has been considered a *theme* in a particular literary work. James's own literary authority often seems to function in the manner of those 'absent authorities' in his works or those subversive social powers I have described above. James's mastery of his form is accomplished by characters and by readers (always implicit 'characters' in his work) who appear all the more true to their forms as they seem to escape the control of other 'authors'. Read thematically in James's writings, this issue of authority seems to be worked out rather unproblematically in the protagonist's educational progress toward self-consciousness and independence. Interpreted in terms of the reader's response to the work, this issue seems to argue for the reader's following the dictates of the text to achieve his/her own interpretation of the ambiguous human problems presented. The implicit relation between the epistemological themes of a literary narrative and the hermeneutic processes prompted in the reader is maintained by many modern theories of literature (notably the New Criticism, Russian Formalism, the Geneva School, and those *Rezeptionstheorien* based on phenomenological models) that have followed the principal aims of idealist philosophy from Hegel to Sartre. On the other hand, such a literary intention might be read as the strategic effort of the author to employ the apparent 'freedom' and 'self-realisation' of character and reader alike to disguise and defend that author's own will to power. The usual response to this charge that the literary author shares the political ruler's subversive strategies is that a work of fiction always announces its author and never ceases to declare its fictionality, whereas social authorities use all their power to disguise their art as law, their styles as truth.[3] Literature is nevertheless as much a mode of psychic defence as one of exposure, revelation, and confession. Literature's appeal to its fictionality may be read as the subtlest of all ruses, because it so often transforms its fictionality – its ephemerality – into a claim for unique insight into and understanding of reality.

James considered Shakespeare's genius in terms that recall Coleridge's conception of Shakespeare as a protean, metamorphic figure, who is recognised only in his various disguises. In his introduction to *The Tempest*, James writes: 'The figured tapestry, the long arras that hides him, is always there, with its immensity of surface and its proportionate underside.'[4] James's image is strangely ambivalent, recalling as it does Polonius hiding behind the curtain in the Queen's bedroom and Hamlet's mistaken murder of the veiled figure he considers to be a hidden king. Indeed, James figures the critic as just such a Hamlet: 'May it not then be but a question, for the fullness of time, of the finer weapon, the sharper point, the stronger arm, the more extended lunge?'[5] The artist is also a Polonius – hypocrite, voyeur, speaker of others' wisdom – who hides himself precisely to be mistaken for the king. Our most violent critical lunges, prompted by our suspicion of a king, will undo both us and the hidden Polonius. Such 'undoing', however, such 'uncanniness', belongs neither to reader nor to 'author', both of whom seek to master the text: the first by uncovering its hidden depths, the second by hiding himself *within* the distracting folds, the wayward patterns of his woven style.

Secrecy is one of the principal devices of such social and literary artistry. Secrets in James appear at first to be lures for the reader and devices of suspense and drama, but the revelation of a secret in James almost always ends in radical ambiguity. Even in an early novel like *The American*, the central secret of the old marquis's murder at the hands of his wife, Madame de Bellegarde, is 'revealed' in Newman's conversation with Mrs Bread in the most profoundly ambiguous manner. Tina's possible illegitimacy in *The Aspern Papers* is as paradoxical in its 'revelation' as the discovery of Aspern's private letters to Juliana: a 'discovery' confirmed only by Tina's announcement to the narrator that she has burnt all evidence. The incriminating letter that Graham Fielder locks up in the ivory tower in the beginning of *The Ivory Tower* is deliberately unread by him or Rosanna Gaw, and their knowledge of its contents seems a function of their preservation of it as secret. James's literary strategy is often to demonstrate how a character's very desire to know the truth of such enabling secrets reveals the secret of that character's personality rather than the truth of the ostensible secret in the plot. In this use, the secret is merely a device James borrows from the popular romance and ironises for the sake of his psychological themes. On the other hand, the radically ambiguous secret is also a means of *disguising by displacing* an original arbitrariness in the power structure; its ambiguity prompts those who 'read' its truth to assume responsibility for it. The very ambiguity of the secret may be considered a strategy that initiates the sort of interpretive activities that will transfer its authorship to others, especially those whom it would rule. Thus Newman's ambiguous knowledge of the Bellegardes' family secret implicates him in that secret, so that he ends by perpetuating it. Mrs Tristram understands this 'aristocratic' manipulation of honour and respectability quite well: 'My impression would be that since, as you say they defied you, it was because they believed that, after all, you would never really come to the point. Their confidence, after counsel taken of each other, was not in their innocence, nor in their talent for bluffing things off; it was in your remarkably good nature! You see they were right.'[6] Mrs Tristram's ironic characterisation of Newman's 'good nature' equates social honour and respectability with an essential morality, which has now been made to serve the perpetuation of those aristocratic pretensions that mark the authority of the Bellegardes. Indeed, the 'services' performed by Newman's 'good nature' are precisely what exclude him from the secret power of the Bellegardes. Even so, Newman is left with the knowledge of his own complicity, his own ambivalent sense of what he has done, and confusion concerning his own psychic motives. On the one hand, James's characters do become implicated in the secrets of their cultures, in so far as they refuse initially to discover in themselves the sin, illegitimacy, and weakness represented by such secrets. Such a theme is a common concern in many critical studies of Henry James. On the other hand, these characters are also forced to perform in response to such secrets in ways that will preserve them, but displaced into uncanny and ultimately undecidable hieroglyphs of human psychology and 'nature'. One of the consequences of this narrative secrecy is the interesting drama of James's psychological experiments; another equally important effect is the preservation of the secret as an aristocratic 'privacy' that governs the public events of the narrative.

In *The Turn of the Screw*, the children's uncle represents this sort of aristocratic *and* literary 'secrecy' in the most explicit and complicated way. The critics' concentration on the psychology of the Governess (or her 'morality') may be read in terms of the Uncle's originating transference of his authority to her, itself a complicated strategy for maintaining his power while keeping it from exposure. Critics have by no means ignored the Uncle, but their attention has been governed principally by his ostensible irresponsibility and extravagance. Even those critics who insist that the Uncle's employment of the Governess involves a subtle seduction, whose sexual implications are manifest in her subsequent behaviour, maintain that his primary motive is to escape the unpleasant family obligations posed by the little orphans, Miles and Flora. Introduced in Douglas's prologue to the Governess's manuscript as 'a gentleman, a bachelor in the prime of life, such a figure as had never risen, save in a dream or an old novel, before a fluttered anxious girl out of a Hampshire vicarage', the Uncle appears as little more than a literary convention of the well-mannered, aristocratic rake, who is always 'rich' and 'extravagant' and exudes 'a glow of high fashion, of good looks, of expensive habits, of charming ways with women' (*TS*, p. 4).[7] Although his money, property, and position would seem to entitle him to a certain mastery in this culture, the Uncle's refusal to assume any direct responsibility for the care and education of his younger brother's children makes it easy for critics to trivialise his power as that of some *deus absconditus* who leaves the field to the Governess. His power in the subsequent narrative is almost exclusively a function of his taboo against communication from the Governess. 'He' figures in the text only to the extent that the Governess fears breaking silence, a fear confirmed by his only communication with her: 'The postbag that evening – it came late – contained a letter for me which, however, in the hand of my employer, I found to be composed but of a few words enclosing another, addressed to himself, with a seal still unbroken. "This, I recognise, is from the headmaster, and the head-master's an awful bore. Read him please; deal with him; but mind you don't report. Not a word. I'm off!"' (*TS*, p. 10). By virtue of his irresponsibility, the Uncle confirms all the more his secret power – itself a power of secrecy and censorship – over the actors at Bly and their audience. Invisible and silent in the course of the dramatic action, with the exception of his one appeal *for* silence, the Uncle prompts a psychodramatic struggle between masters and servants at Bly that he has already inscribed and continues to control in and by his absence.

James's own will to power in *Hawthorne*, 'Greville Fane', and, more generally, his career as an international modern may be addressed adequately by means of Bloom's anxiety of influence. The dispossessed identities of such characters as Olive Chancellor, Mrs Gereth, Fleda Vetch, and Tina Aspern are understandable in relation to the particular men (Basil Ransom, Owen Gereth, the narrator and Jeffrey Aspern) who control them by various legal means. Nevertheless, these issues remain 'psychological themes', which are little more than the chief stocks of many traditional approaches to Henry James. The Uncle in *Turn of the Screw*, however brief his appearance, provides us with an occasion to carry such themes beyond their interpersonal horizons and still maintain the larger social relevance of the particular issues they represent. The Uncle is never characterised in the manner of James's customary realism; instead, he is merely allegorised, so that we understand him only as a sign of larger social forces. In ultimate and practical service to the Uncle, the Governess gathers in her character the feminist issues of the preceding chapter.[8] In her competition with others for authority at Bly, the Governess thematises any 'author's' struggle for a voice and especially Henry James, Jr's, own anguished bid for novelty. Viewed in this way, then, the Uncle in *The Turn of the Screw* provides us with the means of continuing the narrative of our study of James by carrying both poetic influence and the social role of woman over to a more direct confrontation with the rhetoric of those ideological forces that subordinate poet and woman alike.

In order to read the Uncle, I must allow myself to be duped by
the text's ambiguities and commit myself to a reductive allegory, in
which 'overlooked' and 'surprising' details about him are offered
as determinate facts. Shoshana Felman's brilliant reading of *The
Turn of the Screw* depends upon her assumption that critics (like
Wilson, like me) will refuse the uncanniness of the text and insist
upon substituting their own conclusive meanings at the very
moment that they would argue for the most radical literary ambiguity.[9] Felman's deconstruction of Edmund Wilson's psychological
interpretation of the tale concludes that the reader lacks James's
mastery just in proportion as the reader asserts mastery over the
text: 'James's very mastery consists in the denial and in the deconstruction of his own mastery.' In this same context, Felman makes
a significant association between James and the Uncle: 'Like the
Master in his story with respect to the children and to Bly, James
assumes the role of Master only through the act of claiming, with
respect to his literary "property", the "licence", as he puts it, "of
disconnexion and disavowal". ... Here as elsewhere, "mastery"
turns out to be self-dispossession.'[10] Elsewhere Felman reads the
Uncle as the Lacanian other, the signifier of the unconscious, and
thus the source of the indeterminacy of the text: 'Constitutive of an
aporia, of a relation of non-relation, the Master's discourse is very
like the condition of the unconscious as such: Law itself is but a
form of Censorship. But it is precisely this censoring law and this
prohibitive contract which constitute, paradoxically, the story's
condition of possibility.'[11] And still elsewhere, the Uncle is associated with the reductive impulse of psychoanalysis to control and
master literature: 'In its efforts to master literature, psychoanalysis
– like Oedipus and like the Master – can thus but blind itself: blind
itself in order to deny its own castration, in order not to see, and
not to read, literature's subversion of the very possibility of psychoanalytical mastery.'[12] In her own effort to demonstrate the
ways in which literary undecidability deconstructs the mastery of
such determinate forms of discourse as psychoanalysis, literary
criticism, and social authority, Felman personifies in the Uncle
both the paradoxical genius of James and the mystified drives for
completed meaning characteristic of the criticism and psychoanalysis that would 'master' James and literature. Thus *any* reading of
the Uncle must end in its own allegorical displacement of his
protean power, if we accept the diverse functions he serves in
Felman's analysis.

As the differential other of the Governess's own efforts to read, the Uncle is metaphorised by Felman as that which remains 'unreadable', the 'hole' constituted in all the letters (including James's) that circulate in quest of their 'proper' meanings. Felman argues, however, that the relation between 'readable' and 'unreadable' is not to be understood in terms of opposition, in the same sense that the relation of the Freudian unconscious to consciousness is not to be construed as bipolar. Felman reformulates the relationship between literature and psychoanalysis – the larger issue of her work – in terms of the readable as *a variant of the unreadable*: 'To read on the basis of the unreadable would be, here again, to ask not *what* does the unreadable mean, but *how* does the unreadable mean?'[13] Just how the 'unreadable' Uncle's mastery means in the course of this narrative is precisely a study in the ways in which the 'unreadable' maintains its sway. The Uncle's social power (of the aristocracy, law, censorship) is to be understood only in its *deviance*, in its *perversion by* transference to the 'individual psychology' of the Governess and even the children, who represent notably marginal classes within the social hierarchy: the daughter of a country parson, the orphaned children of a younger brother in a culture governed principally by primogeniture.

These details concerning class, inheritance, and legal guardianship are given in Douglas's prologue to his reading of the Governess's manuscript. This fine technical discrimination between prologue and manuscript allows James to offer the Governess's 'own' handwritten account in such a way as to represent the Uncle only in his absence. The information that Douglas provides is offered as essential to an understanding of the story, but it is nonetheless information that must be left out of the Governess's manuscript. Yet it is information that Douglas could have received from none other than his sister's tutor, the Governess herself, following the events of the narration. I would contend that the prologue is the delayed effect of narration itself, the *Nachträglichkeit* that the displacements of the narrative constitute as an 'unreadable' background that may be read as such only in terms of its exclusion from the narrative 'proper'. This prologue becomes a necessary introduction once it has been determined as that which the Governess's written narrative seeks to exclude. And what her narrative principally excludes is the *fact* of the Uncle's potent and active authority that governs her own bid for mastery as the guarantee of the Uncle's secret power.

Because Douglas's prologue is oral and based on his reconstruction of what the Governess has 'told' him, it excludes itself from the narrator's (the 'I') suspect claim that the narrative he gives the reader is 'from an exact transcript of my own made much later' based on the Governess's manuscript which 'poor Douglas, before his death – when it was in sight – committed to me' (*TS*, p. 4). Based as it must be on a chain of oral transmissions (Governess, Douglas, 'I'), this prologue either distinguishes itself from the 'exact transcript' of the manuscript or questions the narrator's claim to have made an 'exact transcript' of a manuscript 'in old faded ink and in the most beautiful hand' (*TS*, p. 2). If the prologue is a necessary introduction to the narrative, then no transcript would be 'exact' without it. Yet because the narrative cannot be transcribed 'exactly', its imperfect telling by its various narrators already argues for the substitution of the term 'translation' in the place of 'transcription'. Unless, of course, we are supposed to read 'from an exact transcript of my own' as the narrator's ironic suggestion that the *only* 'exact transcript' of any story is the narrator's 'own' story, its exactness assured by his appeal to however feeble a memory. Indeed, Douglas answers the narrator's question 'And is the record yours? You took the thing down?' by claiming: '"Nothing but the impression. I took that *here*" – he tapped his heart. "I've never lost it"' (*TS*, p. 2). We should recall here Socrates' objections to writing in the *Phaedrus*, in which he rejects Thoth's invention on the grounds that writing 'will implant forgetfulness in their souls' and supplant the living truth 'veritably written' in the soul of philosophical man.[14] The Governess's manuscript is, in fact, transmitted by her own bequest to Douglas and then by Douglas to the narrator as something each in turn 'possesses'. Yet the possession of writing occurs only in the appropriations one makes of its signs, which is to say that there can be no 'exact transcript' of writing except in those wilful interpretations that would offer themselves as the 'living truth', the 'speech' of an author.

For these reasons, it is all the more important that what little we learn of the Uncle should be given in this oral prologue, itself an explicit instance of a speaker's will to become author, to substitute his/her own 'impression' for the texts that have commanded him/her to exist. In the midst of these narrative problems, we are introduced to the Uncle's story and circumstances:

> He had been left, by the death of his parents in India, guardian to a
> small nephew and small niece, children of a younger, a military

brother whom he had lost two years before. These children were, by the strangest of chances for a man in his position – a lone man without the right sort of experience or a grain of patience – very heavy on his hands.

(*TS*, p. 5)

The interpolation of the prepositional phrase 'by the death of his parents in India' immediately after the verb 'left' causes the reader momentarily to understand 'left' as referring to his own orphan status. The complete predication of the verb, however, explains that he has been 'left ... by death ... guardian', which suggests a legal title conferred by default. In legal terms, such lineal descent of guardianship in a landed family is quite appropriate in nineteenth-century England: the grandparents would have first obligation to care for the children, followed on their deaths by the oldest surviving son, heir to the family estate. Because the children's father was the Uncle's 'younger, ... military' brother, the reader should assume that this military vocation indicates that the usual primogeniture governs inheritance in this family and that the Uncle is the principal heir to the land. As William Blackstone states the custom of English inheritance laws: 'And, among persons of any rank or fortune, a competence is generally provided for younger children, and the bulk of the estate settled upon the eldest, by the marriage-articles.'[15] Despite the general application of primogeniture to the majority of the estate, most nineteenth-century English gentry devised some means (generally during the father's lifetime) of settling a 'suitable' inheritance on younger sons, especially those who had married and had children. In any event, it is most likely that Miles is heir to some competence or other inheritance descending from his father, the Uncle's younger brother.

More important than the possible estate Miles stands to inherit from his father is Miles's status as the next in line to inherit from his Uncle the family estate, unless the Uncle marries and has children of his own. This circumstance complicates the Uncle's legal claim to Bly, 'his country home, an old family place in Essex' (*TS*, p. 4). English law distinguishes between two basic claims to property: *possession* of property and the *right* to property. According to Blackstone, a 'title completely legal' depends upon the joining of the right of possession and the right of property.[16] The most basic right of possession is 'the mere *naked possession*, or actual occupation of the estate'.[17] The younger, military brother, by virtue of his military service, would have had no occasion to establish any claim even to mere 'naked possession' of Bly. His son, Miles, however, might begin to establish such a claim on the basis of his residency in the ancestral home. The Uncle, faced with the choice of keeping the children in his London residence or at his country estate, risks his reputation as 'a gentleman, a bachelor' on the one hand and (however remotely) his full title to Bly on the other hand. Given the legal significance of the term 'possession' as well as its diverse connotations in the rest of the narrative (ghostly visitation, knowledge, mastery, intuition), the description of the Uncle's choice to send the children to Bly is curious: 'He had put them in possession of Bly, which was healthy and secure' (*TS*, p. 5). Even in the non-legal idiom 'to be put in possession of', there is in the word 'possession' a strong suggestion of what one owns but still only at the grace of a donor. Further, the Uncle chooses Bly as the 'proper' place, both 'healthy and secure', because it is in the 'country'. By implication, the city where he resides is improper, unhealthy, and insecure, at least as far as children are concerned. In legal terms, the Uncle's employment of a governess to represent his guardianship at Bly enables him to maintain his 'right of possession' without requiring his physical presence. The legal propriety of the Uncle's strategy masks his improper motives, just as the health and security of the country estate disguise the source of their maintenance in the urban world of the Uncle.

Still other improprieties may be masked by the establishment at Bly that the Uncle contrives so carefully, so seductively. John Clair has already uttered one of the 'horrors' that Douglas's spare prologue tempts us to read in its silences: that the children are the illegitimate offspring of the Uncle and Miss Jessel.[18] In a similar vein, we might be tempted by the description of the Uncle's brother as one 'whom he had *lost* two years before' (*TS*, p. 5). Given the prologue's care with respect to the legalities involved in the Uncle's position and the children's relations, it is curious that no mention is made of the brother's wife, who would be the natural guardian. Such a significant omission encourages us to read the brother's 'loss' as a 'fall' resulting from some prodigality, rather than as a literal death. Indeed, the word 'loss' is used only one other time in the prologue: 'There had been for the two children at first a young lady whom they had had the misfortune to lose' (*TS*, p. 5). Although the next sentence refers explicitly to the former governess's 'death', the children's 'loss' and Uncle's 'loss' bring the former governess and the younger brother into some stylistic association prompted by our own quest for 'general uncanny ugliness and horror and pain' (*TS*, p. 2). This perversely reductive reading of the children as the illegitimate offspring of the younger brother and Miss Jessel certainly would be reinforced by the Victorian literary conventions concerning the romantic exploits of soldiers. Confronted with such circumstances, the Uncle might well be inclined to maintain the respectability of his family name by hiding these bastards and their 'natural' mother away at Bly, in the care of servants well trusted or at least seduced into silence.

These imagined illegitimate dealings of the younger brother with Miss Jessel would find a curious association in the Uncle's identity as 'a gentleman, a bachelor', whose extravagance involves both 'expensive habits' and 'charming ways with women'. Even the modifiers describing the identities of the brother are parallel in construction: 'a gentleman, a bachelor'; 'a younger, a military brother'. The Uncle, too, is associated with martial exploits that confuse the military, the sexual, and the natural: 'He had for his town residence a big house filled with the spoils of travel and the trophies of the chase' (*TS*, p. 4). Even the parents, who have died in India, are associated with militancy, since British colonial rule in India at the time of their deaths (roughly 1845) was being consolidated and strengthened by social and economic reforms increasingly dependent on the force of the army.[19] Indeed, were the style of the prologue the 'proper' evidence for arguing the secret and tragic affair of the younger brother and the former governess, then we would be forced to conclude that the signs of such illegitimacy contaminate the entire family: parents as well as the two sons.

Let me now abandon this allegory of reading, which has stretched the barest hints of the prologue to suggest the more particular sorts of legal, sexual, and political illegitimacies disguised by the artistry of the aristocracy. Allowing myself to have been duped by the text in my quest for a reductive meaning, a governing secret, that would transform the prologue into the formal boundary enclosing the subsequent narrative's meaning and truth, I may now swerve from this inevitable compulsion of interpretation and insist that precisely what the prologue maintains is the *essential ambiguity of illegitimacy*. Displaced from uncle to brother to Miss Jessel to children, the hints of illegitimacy seduce the reader into repeating that transference which is the actual 'illegitimacy' of this ruling class. By particularising the arbitrariness of authority as the 'extravagance' of an individual character, the 'excess' or 'imbalance' of a neurotic psychology, the interpreter re-enacts and thereby *serves* the power of the master. For convenience and for certain strategic reasons, I shall continue to refer to this authority and mastery as 'the Uncle', recognising that this name – like that other name, 'the Master' – is employed only in the *written* narrative by characters explicitly involved in the process of transference. In Douglas's prologue the Uncle is only a pronominal function, a 'he' or 'him', the grammatical character of whose identity reminds us of the presence of a speaker, a narrator, an author: Douglas, governess, 'I'.

In fact, the name 'Uncle' is appropriate for 'him' only in relation to these children – and then only on the condition that they are in fact the legitimate offspring of his brother. And yet this name 'Uncle' functions only in relation to those with whom 'he' will have nothing to do, except by way of assigning his authority, transferring his 'name'. All of this might encourage the interpreter to understand what I have termed the 'essential ambiguity of illegitimacy' as the absolute arbitrariness of all claims to social authority. As I have suggested above, this is a common conclusion in many deconstructive approaches to literature and culture. Just as the transference of social authority's illegitimacy into the madness of an individual character preserves and disguises such illegitimacy, so the abstraction of a particular kind of arbitrary social rule as the essential arbitrariness at the origin of all rules hides its illegitimacy. The Uncle's ambiguous identity and ambivalent claim to authority are themselves the truths of a very particular and thus historical social power. This power is the power of extravagance and 'freedom': from labour, service, other masters.

As 'a gentleman, a bachelor', the Uncle is 'figured' by the Governess 'as fearfully extravagant', and as living in a 'big house' 'filled with ... spoils ... and ... trophies' (*TS*, p. 4). Everything she 'sees' in him seems to suggest that his only 'affairs' involve the design and maintenance of his own 'image': 'Saw him all in a glow of high fashion, of good looks, of expensive habits, of charming ways with women' (*TS*, p. 4). Indeed, his 'extravagance' seems defined by its intransitivity: that is, the product of this expense of vision is nothing other than an expensive vision. The Uncle's fashionable appearance seems in direct contrast with the 'respectability' of his servants at Bly. Indeed, any argument concerning the former governess's hidden identity as the natural mother of Miles and Flora would have to contend with her characterisation in the pro-

logue: 'She had done for them quite beautifully – she was a most respectable person' (*TS*, p. 5). The word 'respectable', however, is
rendered ambivalent in the very next sentence: 'Mrs Grose, since
then, in the way of manners and things, had done as she could for
Flora; and there were, further, a cook, a housemaid, a dairywoman,
an old pony, an old groom and an old gardener, all likewise thoroughly respectable.' As if to emphasise that Douglas's tone has
further qualified the meaning of 'respectability', someone in the audience asks: 'And what did the former governess die of? Of so much
respectability?' In the superlative form and modifying 'person',
'most respectable' signifies moral quality and social propriety.
When applied to 'an old pony', however, 'respectable' describes the
functional rather than the moral value of the noun. 'Respectable',
used to mean something 'serviceable' but not necessarily of the best
or newest (as in the idioms 'a respectable suit of clothes' and 'he
does a respectable job'), seems to apply to the other nouns in the
series, all of which denote people in terms of their jobs rather than
their personalities or moral natures. The former governess, whose
'respectability' the subsequent narrative will question, is identified
as respectable in close association with others whose respectability
seems more dependent on their modestly adequate performance of
contractual tasks than on their social standing or moral distinction.
Such an interpretation is strengthened by the use of the adverb
'likewise' to suggest an equivalence of respectability among the
items in the series *and* with the previous use of 'most respectable
person' to describe the former governess: '... all likewise thoroughly
respectable'.

The prologue's irony regarding the term 'respectability' depends
upon an ambivalence that emphasises the division between labour
and title, service and property, servant and master. In a culture in
which labour has some relation to both economic and moral value,
the 'respectable' services of 'an old gardener' would be the measure
of his social 'respectability'. Indeed, the highest aim of such labour
might be generalised as the production and maintenance of the
common social well-being or good. The division within the term
'respectability' in Douglas's prologue marks the essential divisions
in a class society. Every reader of James's novels knows that the
rare character who works for a living is viewed by the others as eccentric to that hermetic aristocratic world where position and social
standing are measured principally by one's freedom from labour.
James was fascinated by this aristocratic extravagance, because it

justified itself in terms of its sheer style and artistry, whose apparent ephemerality was capable of exercising profound social power. The 'art of life' that seems the ultimate labour of James's aristocrats is, in fact, an artistry akin to the rhetoric involved in the production of capital, the 'style' of what Marx termed the 'theory of surplus value'. In a capitalist system of economics, the very identity of the capitalist depends upon his ability to generate a 'surplus' product in excess of the cost of the labourer's maintenance. In one sense, the capitalist's own labour is precisely the artistry required to exploit his workers to produce such a surplus. One of the reasons James developed the character of the art-collecting businessman (Newman, Mr Touchett, Adam Verver) may have been his sense that the apparent 'leisure' of the dilettante disguises a subtler kind of economic and social manipulation, which produces an extravagance or surplus. Even though these businessmen are most often represented as mere collectors rather than artists, their business is precisely the production of 'art'. Just as James renders ambivalent the apparent oppositions in his fiction between the worlds of business and society, America and Europe, male and female, reason and imagination, so he subverts the opposition between economics and art.[20]

The rhetorical strategies of the ruling class in a hierarchical society follow generally the process of psychic transference I have described above as governing the narrative of *The Turn of the Screw*. Such transference serves to produce the indeterminacy of both its origin and end, and it is precisely this indeterminacy that is the surplus (an *I*) by which the ruler stakes his claim. The contractual relation between the Uncle and Governess depends upon his singular, determinate prohibition: 'That she should never trouble him – but never, never; neither appeal nor complain nor write about anything; only meet all questions herself, receive all moneys from his solicitor, take the whole thing over and let him alone' (*TS*, p. 6). On the one hand, this censorship of any intercourse between master and servant is the absolute necessity of a system in which ownership and labour are divided. On the other hand, the effect of this prohibition, this dispossession of the servant, is the assignment to the Governess of 'supreme authority' and full possession. The Uncle's prohibition may be quite specific, but its governing principle is its ambiguity: the ambivalence of 'possession'/ 'dispossession'. The seductive power of the Uncle resides in just such duplicity: 'She promised to do this, and she mentioned to me that when, for a moment, disburdened, delighted, he held her hand, thanking her for her sacrifice, she already felt rewarded' (*TS*, p. 6). The periodic sentence reinforces the reader's sense of equivocation between 'sacrifice' and 'reward'. We have seen already how such sacrificial gains are common to James's female characters, whose very identities in a patriarchal society compel them to interpret sacrifice as reward and fetishise surrender or self-denial as their own property.[21] Such surrender becomes 'will to power' in its most extreme formulations, as in May Bartram's manipulation of her surrender to John Marcher and his beast in order to preserve a secret control of another who ostensibly 'rules'. At its furthest extreme, then, this characteristically feminine 'surrender' in James's writings repeats the secret authority of the Uncle, which is expressed best in his extravagance, uselessness, irresponsibility, wilful castration, and general ambiguity. Yet in the Uncle's seductive contract, he has already transferred such 'qualities' to the Governess, whose only token of reward should be that fleeting contact – 'he held her hand' – whereby sexual flirtation and the 'honourable' conclusion of a business contract are so beautifully confused.

Thus the 'seduction' accomplished by the Uncle cannot be reductively explained as sexual or economic or legal or political. These separate discourses constitute a chain of metonymies, whose links are forged by the transferences and displacements occasioned by the extravagance, the surplus, the undecidability that constitute the Uncle's property and propriety. Felman characterises the shared will to mastery of Edmund Wilson and the Governess as their mutual denial of the essential undecidability of sexuality: 'In their attempt to elaborate a speech of mastery, a discourse of *totalitarian* power, what Wilson and the governess both *exclude* is nothing other than the threatening power of rhetoric itself – of sexuality as *division* and as meaning's *flight*, as contradiction and ambivalence; the very threat, in other words, of unmastery, of the impotence, and of the unavoidable castration which inhere in *language*.'[22] Felman's analysis transforms the impotence and castration of the Uncle ('a gentleman, a bachelor') as well as his duplicitous and threatening power into the essential undecidability of the rhetoric of sexuality, of sexuality as rhetoric. And yet the 'totalitarian power' Felman attributes to Wilson and the Governess is merely a cruder and more explicit version of the totalitarianism of the Uncle, who appropriates the essential undecidability of language and transforms it into his own proper 'name'. Because he identifies himself with all that exceeds the determinate meanings of culture (represented in the narrative by written 'letters') and thus all that escapes consciousness, he does indeed become identified with the 'unconscious', with the other that is the ultimate and elusive object of all significations. As the one who refuses to read and writes only to refuse to read, he excludes himself from the central and inevitable labour of the culture to 'produce' meanings. In his extravagance, he becomes the figure of what cannot be read, in such a manner that every image of mastery in the remainder of the narrative is merely a simulacrum or fetish representing him. Interpreting the episode in which Flora fits a mast into a toy boat, Felman notes the phonic and sexual associations between 'mast' and 'master': 'While the governess thus believes herself to be in a position of command and mastery, her *grasp* of the ship's helm (or of "the little master" or of the screw she tightens) is in reality the grasp but of a *fetish*, but of a simulacrum of a signified, like the simulacrum of the mast in Flora's toy boat, erected only as a filler, as a stopgap, designed to fill a hole, to close a gap.'[23]

Seducing the Governess by prohibiting her any further intercourse with him, assigning her *duty* as 'supreme authority', communicating with her only by means of unread letters, the Uncle preserves his paradoxical identity: the authority of castration, the power of impotence, the presence of absence. He is the subtlest of all Scheherazades, who avoids seduction by virtue of his seductive narrative, which is 'itself' only when it is told by another. The relation between the Uncle's extravagant authority and the characters' and critics' respectable labours is thus one of exclusion and negation, whereby the dialectic of master and servant is effectively barred and the threat of usurpation forestalled indefinitely.

It is not necessary to interpret in detail the Governess's obedience to the Uncle's authority in the subsequent narrative. Felman's analysis of the Governess's will to meaning in sexual, familial, social, and finally linguistic terms serves as a remarkably complete commentary on this idea. I would note here only how uncanny doublings control the narrative structure of the Governess's manuscript and thus serve as ghostly simulacra of the basic contract between the Uncle and the Governess. The critical argument that insists upon the Governess's insane projection of her own repressed fears in the form of the ghosts of Peter Quint and Miss Jessel often cites as evidence the Governess's systematic re-enactment of each ghostly visitation. Peering through the window where Quint had appeared, sitting at her own table where Miss Jessel had appeared to be writing, the Governess dramatises these ghostly visitations as if to give them body, to reify them. Her repetition represents her competitive struggle to substitute her own body for their ghostly presences, but this is merely a conflict among the master's servants and thus merely another instance of the uncle's transference, which by now has assumed the power of law. The war that is waged between governess and ghosts, children, Mrs Grose is itself 'ghostly', the simulated conflict between master and servant that has been disguised in the initial contract, in which the Uncle figures himself as undecidable, indeterminate, 'extra-vagant', even 'improper'.

I shall offer only one exemplary instance of this displaced and displacing aggression, which effectively transfers the conflict between master and servant to one between servant and servant. In a discussion with Mrs Grose in which the Governess considers the appropriateness of informing the Uncle that Miles has been dismissed from school, the Governess actually blames the Uncle:

> 'I'll put it before him', I went on inexorably, 'that I can't undertake to work the question on behalf of a child who has been expelled –'
> 'For we've never in the least known what!' Mrs Grose declared.
> 'For wickedness. For what else – when he's so clever and beautiful and perfect? Is he stupid? Is he untidy? Is he infirm? Is he ill-natured? He's exquisite – so it can be only *that*; and that would open up the whole thing. After all,' I said, 'it's their uncle's fault. If he left here such people –!'
> 'He didn't really in the least know them. The fault's mine.' She had turned quite pale.
>
> (*TS*, p. 61)

I interrupt the passage at this point only to note that the Governess charges the Uncle with the responsibility for having *left* such servants at Bly: that is, for his inaction. Even so, Mrs Grose immediately defends him precisely on the grounds of his ignorance, assuming full responsibility herself. The effect is to turn her quite ghostly: 'She had turned quite pale.'

> 'Then what am I to tell him?'
> 'You needn't tell him anything. *I'll* tell him.'
> I measured this. 'Do you mean you'll write –?' Remembering that she couldn't, I caught myself up. 'How do you communicate?'
> 'I tell the bailiff. *He* writes.'
> 'And should you like him to write our story?'

> My question had a sarcastic force that I had not fully intended, and it made her after a moment inconsequently break down. The tears were again in her eyes. 'Ah Miss, *you* write!'
>
> (*TS*, pp. 61–2)

Mrs Grose's defence of the uncle in terms of his ignorance and absence does not quite accord with what is said in the prologue: 'He ... had done all he could ... parting even with his own servants to wait on them and going down himself, whenever he might' (*TS*, p. 5). Mrs Grose forgets the Uncle's former relations with his servants and his earlier visits to the children at the very moment that she assumes responsibility for the children – a 'forgetfulness' that itself repeats the Uncle's prol ibition. Yet, her assumption of responsibility also involves her commitment to 'tell him', which would involve a violation of that taboo (properly the *Governess's* contract). Mrs Grose's bold move to assume responsibility and authority can be realised only by writing to the Uncle – indeed, the transformation of 'telling' into 'writing' is a function of his absence. And writing is that task of which she is incapable, and it is an incapability often cited by critics as a sign of her lowly station in the class structure. Mrs Grose's bid for authority immediately invokes yet another master: 'I tell the bailiff. *He* writes.' Whether this bailiff is the administrative official of the district in which the estate of Bly is located or, more likely, overseer or steward of the estate itself (the English term 'bailiff' was commonly used in both senses in the nineteenth century), he represents a legal mediation between public and private, social and family law. The Governess's sarcastic response is thus all the more significant: 'And should you like him to write our story?' In this crucial moment in the narrative, the Uncle's responsibility for the children is uttered in a form that threatens to violate his law, but it is precisely this threat that produces a series of defensive gestures that effect a movement from Mrs Grose to the bailiff back to the Governess: 'Ah Miss, *you* write.' Mrs Grose's sentence is itself ambivalent, suggesting the imperative mood (and thus Mrs Grose's subtler authority) as well as a mere assertion, 'you are capable of writing', that would mark Mrs Grose's surrender of authority and confession of subservience to the Governess. Thus the threatened rebellion against the Uncle is defused by a displacing movement from Governess to Mrs Grose to bailiff and back to Governess. Felman comments on this passage: 'Clearly, what the letter is about is nothing other than the very story which contains it.

What the letters are to tell is the telling of the story: how the narrative, precisely, tells itself *as an effect of writing*. The letters in the story are thus not simply *metonymical* to the manuscript which contains them; they are also *metaphorical* to it: they are the reflection *en abyme* of the narrative itself. To read the story is thus to undertake *a reading of the letters*, to follow the circuitous paths of their changes of address.'[24] What those changes of address constitute is, as Felman makes clear, the genesis of the story itself, which she would have us believe is the 'unconscious' of language. Yet that genesis must be said to be traceable to the Uncle as master, who has made himself over according to this idea of language, so that the *mise en abyme* of the manuscript is an effect of the Uncle and his disguised power. The narrative thus speaks his name endlessly, even though that name is nothing other than the chain composed of its surrogate, fetishised, 'assigned' authorities: Peter Quint and Miss Jessel, Mrs Grose, the bailiff, Governess, Douglas, 'I', audience around the fire, reader, formal critic.

The interpretive effort to master *The Turn of the Screw* is the deployment of the Uncle's power, producing merely displaced images of his repressive authority, his authority as repression and censorship. Any allegorical reading of the hidden sexual or moral drama that governs the narrative serves to hide his mastery from view, to ascribe responsibility to another agent, who is always in the Uncle's secret service. What does this say, then, about reading *The Turn of the Screw* as fundamentally concerned with uncertainty, with the *aporia* that is language: the rhetoric of sexuality and the psyche? I am in complete agreement with Felman's assertion of language's essential undecidability, of its originary indeterminacy and arbitrariness, just as much as I am in agreement with her Lacanian extension of 'language' to the functioning of the psyche. My own argument regarding the 'abuse' of uncertainty in *The Turn of the Screw* does not derive from some formalist desire to discover a determinate or reductive meaning for the text, even though I have 'played' with such an intention as a means of demonstrating my own complicity in such an ineluctable will of interpretation. My own interpretation of the Uncle's 'secret power' may be applied quite democratically to any agent of such undecidability, whose goal would remain the maintenance of a certain 'extravagance' that would exempt his work from the determinations of more wilful readings. Such a 'position' would provide textuality (of society, of the psyche) with an 'outside' free from the possession and aggression governing the power struggles of language, history, and culture. Felman ultimately equates the Uncle and Henry James as the true ghosts haunting the space of literature: 'It is because James's mastery consists in knowing that mastery as such is but a *fiction*, that James's law as master, like that of the Master of *The Turn of the Screw*, is a law of flight and of *escape*. It is, however, through his escape, through his *disappearance* from the scene, that the Master in *The Turn of the Screw*, in effect, *becomes a ghost*. And indeed it could be said that James himself becomes a phantom master, a Master-Ghost *par excellence*.'[25]

The transformation of mastery into ghostliness does not subvert or undo mastery, because the text itself tells us quite explicitly that *ghosts haunt*, even as they appear to be no more than the fictive projections of disturbed dreamers. Ghosts haunt precisely because we recognise them as impossible fictions, whose power we assume must derive uncannily from ourselves. The 'supreme fictionist' argument, so prevalent in the modernism of Wallace Stevens, T. S. Eliot, William Faulkner, and other ostensible heirs of the Jamesian tradition, transforms the world into a fiction of language only to disperse the authority for such fiction making to 'everyman'. Such a strategy, however, merely disguises the sources of social and political power that would have us believe that their nightmares are our dreams. Our invention of their fictions has already been motivated by those who discover their immortality as a function of their displaced circulation through the psyches of their characters, readers, dreamers. The law of the Uncle remains powerful in so far as the Governess remains true to herself; the law of Henry James persists in the reassertion of his mastery, his genius, in the most triumphant interpretations of his readers. Felman's textuality 'proves' that we cannot know, that we are forever 'dupes' of the language that employs us: 'It is with "supreme authority" indeed that James, in deconstructing his own mastery, vests his reader. But isn't this gift of supreme authority bestowed upon the reader as upon the governess the very thing that will precisely *drive them mad*?'[26] Literary authority as much as social authority has the power to drive us mad, precisely because such authority is capable of compassing those differences and duplicities that constitute madness as external, as the other of cultural normality. Yet such a concept of madness depends upon our ability to *isolate* it analytically from the wilful intentions of language and communication. It would not differ substantially from Kant's conception of aesthetic intransitivity, since it would maintain itself precisely as the remainder or surplus of what cannot be made to perform 'useful' work or 'respectable' service of our needs and appetites. Such intransitivity would escape the determinations of society, politics, law, history, and psychology, by means of its own law of self-preservation and repetition. The law of the Uncle is the repetition of his absence as a presence, the repetition of his prohibition against transgressing the boundary separating master and servant. In the struggles for authority prompted by this censorship in the course of the narrative, each of the characters serves to preserve the Uncle from action, sustaining him as an image of intransitivity, extravagance, and surplus.

Similarly, uncertainty, indeterminacy, ambiguity, and irony cannot as 'concepts' escape their destinies as laws or 'centres' in the purely classical sense that Derrida has defined: 'Thus it has always been thought that the centre, which is by definition unique, constituted the very thing within a structure which, while governing the structure, escapes structurality.'[27] As such, these concepts reinstate the metaphysics and politics they would escape: self and other, master and servant, legislator and citizen, unconscious and conscious, 'literature' and ordinary language. Linguistic undecidability is not itself a concept or a content, in fact ceases to be 'itself' the moment that it is made to serve as a concept, a centre, a principle. Undecidability is merely what echoes in every act of communication, every will to determine meaning and form, the echo of the will to utterance and at the same time the supplement of interpretation. In this sense, undecidability is always implicated in the labour that is performed, always itself a product of the repression and forgetting that are the motives for additional work. In so far as it is working to be worked, linguistic undecidability, the necessity of the supplement, is never the same and has no 'name' outside those differences constituting history and society. In so far as it is excluded, *abstracted*, from the labour of culture and history, outside of and remote from every mystified will to meaning and truth, undecidability preserves itself as sheer denial, pure negation: the *death* of Hegel's *Verneinung*. As the agent of such denial, as the abstraction or extravagance that refuses complicity in the lies of human language, undecidability merely reasserts that Nietzschean ressentiment against time and becoming that is the stammer of the nihilist, the arbitrary power of the aristocrat and mystic, the 'genius' or 'madness' of art.

There is no 'proper' undecidability; it is always the effect or product of a certain forgetting of motives and drives that have awakened interest. The particular, determinate, and eminently *historical* circumstances governing the production of literary, social, and political uncertainties are what we wish to study. On the one hand, we might consider the 'history' of interpretations prompted by *The Turn of the Screw* to argue in favour of this work's strategic and finally irreducible indeterminacy, itself the measure of its 'literariness' and thus its endurance as an immortal classic. On the other hand, I would argue that the history of this work's interpretations is the history of the production of ambiguities – of conflicting readings – that point clearly to their specific social and historical determinants. The endurance of *The Turn of the Screw* is precisely this historicality, which is a timeliness forever displacing its author, forever remaking the name of 'Henry James'.

From John Carlos Rowe, *The Theoretical Dimensions of Henry James* (Madison, WI, 1984), pp. 123–46; 271–3.

NOTES

[John Carlos Rowe's purpose in probing beyond the time-honoured psychological preoccupations of *Turn of the Screw* criticism is to reveal its wider social implications. His materialist examination of class relations (with an admixture of psychoanalysis and deconstruction, using Felman and Derrida) analyses concepts of secrecy and power, in this text concentrated in what is seen as 'the law of the Uncle'. 'Mastery' at various levels (from Uncle to James himself) is exercised by transference, seduction and surrogation over the more, or less, marginal social classes to perpetuate property rights, division of labour and consequent class influence. The ambiguity of illegitimacy and ambivalent authority, with absence effectively signifying presence in a ghostly form of mastery, enables James to subvert the usual opposition between the economic and art. Ed.]

1. Edmund Wilson, 'The Ambiguity of Henry James', in *A Casebook on Henry James's 'The Turn of the Screw'*, ed. Gerald Willen (New York, 1960), p. 121.

2. See Glenn Reed's objections to the psychological thesis in 'Another Turn on James's "The Turn of the Screw"', *American Literature*, 20 (1949), 413–23.

3. An argument generally supported by the evidence of literature's manifest strangeness or uncanniness, as J. Hillis Miller suggests in the opening chapter of *Fiction and Repetition: Seven English Novels* (Cambridge, MA, 1982), p. 18: 'One of the most obvious characteris-

tics of works of literature is their manifest strangeness as integuments of words. Poets, novelists, and playwrights say things which are exceedingly odd by most everyday standards of normality. Any way of interpreting literature would need to account for that oddness.'

4. Henry James, 'The Tempest' (1907), in Selected Literary Criticism, ed. Morris Shapira (Harmondsworth, 1968), p. 357.

5. Ibid.

6. Henry James, The American (New York, 1960), p. 382. I am using the 1877 text of The American for this interpretation. The New York Edition of The American incorporates James's infamous revisions of this ending – revisions that render Mrs Tristram's final judgements of Newman far less problematic than her ambivalent judgement of his 'good nature' in the first edition.

7. Henry James, The Turn of the Screw, ed. Robert Kimbrough (Norton Critical Edition, New York, 1966); page references are given in the text as TS.

8. See the preceding chapter [of Rowe, The Theoretical Dimensions of Henry James: 'Feminist Issues: Women, Power and Rebellion'. Ed.].

9. Shoshana Felman, 'Turning the Screw of Interpretation', in Literature and Psychoanalysis: The Question of Reading: Otherwise, ed. Shoshana Felman (Baltimore, MD, 1982), p. 155.

10. Ibid., p. 205.

11. Ibid., p. 145 [see p. 49 above. Ed.].

12. Ibid., p. 199.

13. Ibid., p. 143 [see p. 47 above. Ed.].

14. Plato, Phaedrus, trans. R. Hackford (Indianapolis, 1952), p. 161 (277 D-E). I am alluding in this instance to Derrida's deconstruction of the Platonic ranking of philosophic speech above the mere 'notation' of writing: 'La pharmacie de Platon', in La dissémination (Paris, 1972), pp. 95–108.

15. William Blackstone, Commentaries on the Laws of England, a facsimile of the first edition of 1765–69, 4 vols (Chicago, 1979), 1: 438.

16. Ibid., 2: 199.

17. Ibid., 2: 195.

18. See John Clair's arguments for the illegitimate relations between the uncle and Miss Jessel in The Ironic Dimension in the Fiction of Henry James (Pittsburgh, 1965), pp. 37–58.

19. The events of the narrative seem to be 'dated' by the suggestive hints of chronology in the frame tales somewhere around 1845–55, a

period roughly equivalent with the marquess of Dalhousie's service as governor-general of India (1848–56). Dalhousie's rule served effectively to shift control in India from the economic influence of the East India Company to the direct authority of the British crown. Social and economic 'reforms' made under Dalhousie are generally considered the causes of the Indian Mutiny of 1857, during which thousands of British subjects were massacred by Indian sepoys who composed the majority of the British army in India. The consolidation of India's dominion by the British crown was symbolised by the coronation of Queen Victoria in 1876 as 'empress of India'. See Thomas George Percival Spear, *India: A Modern History* (Ann Arbor, MI, 1972), pp. 264–76, for a convenient account of this consolidation of British imperialism in nineteenth-century India.

20. James tended to idealise such societies as the Venetian republic, on the grounds that the culture's art, economics, and politics were so integrally related. In 'Venice' (1882), James romanticises the modern Venetians, whose poverty finds compensation in 'their lives in the most beautiful towns' and whose 'good and ... evil fortune [is] to be conscious of few wants': *Italian Hours*, intro. Herbert Mitgang (New York, 1968), pp. 5–6. As mystified a view as this may be, it calls attention all the more forcefully to what James considers the decadence of modern Anglo-American societies, which he considers based on personal ownership.

21. Nicola Bradbury, *Henry James: The Later Novels* (Oxford, 1979), p. 120, characterises the ultimate achievement of Jamesian renunciation to be a sort of knowledge: an acceptance of human mystery. Philip Sicker, *Love and Quest for Identity in the Fiction of Henry James* (Princeton, NJ, 1980), p. 129, stresses the relation between renunciation and the extreme idealisation of the loved one that results in fetishism.

22. Felman, 'Turning the Screw', p. 192.

23. Ibid., p. 173.

24. Ibid., p. 141 [see p. 46 above. Ed.].

25. Ibid., p. 206.

26. Ibid.

27. Jacques Derrida, 'Structure, Sign and Play in the Discourse of the Human Sciences', *Writing and Difference*, trans. Alan Bass (Chicago, 1978), p. 279.

4

Repetition and Subversion in Henry James's *The Turn of the Screw*

JOHN H. PEARSON

> He who would only hope is cowardly, he who would only recollect is a voluptuary, but he who wills repetition is a man, and the more expressly he knows how to make his purpose clear, the deeper he is as a man. But he who does not comprehend that life is a repetition, and that this is the beauty of life, has condemned himself and deserves nothing better than what is sure to befall him, namely, to perish.
>
> (Søren Kierkegaard)

The purpose of Kierkegaard's defence of repetition is the maintenance of thoroughly engendered power. He contends that responsible contribution to patriarchal succession requires recognition of one's manly role in it; irresponsibility and ignorance in this regard lead to political and biological damnation, which is nothing less than absence in the next generation's structures of power and authority. Unmanly men, in other words, will suffer the political fate of women. Manliness, however, promises assurance of posthumous representation (and, implicitly, posthumous participation) within the structures of power. Although for his part Kierkegaard is sufficiently responsible to reveal that repetition and articulation are the means of entailing power, this logic did not originate with him. As Emily Brontë shows in *Wuthering Heights*, the laws of primogeniture, which assure the maintenance and containment of family fortune under male auspices, complicated the lives of women for generations. Even in the absence of immediate male heirs, power remained engendered, as Jane Austen describes in *Pride and Prejudice*. The repetition of Mr Bennet's patriarchal neglect of his wife and daughters is assured because his estate is entailed in perpetuity by the written wills of previous patriarchs. All rights and privileges associated with the estate are devised to the nearest male relative rather than bequeathed to any female kin. It should not be surprising that women like Brontë and Austen have written of engendered structures of power, exposing the excesses of, and sometimes subverting, male hegemony; it is surprising, however, that so canonical a writer as Henry James, from such a privileged family as that of Henry James, Sr, would contribute *The Turn of the Screw*, his most enigmatic tale, to this body of subversive literature. Within the frame of the governess's narrative, James enacts the logic of repetition that maintains patriarchy, yet he does so with a difference – in the voice and guise of a woman. The governess seems to understand and finally to use the logic of repetition as a means to power as she struggles with the ghostly authority of her absent employer, the Harley Street uncle of her charges, Miles and Flora. Outside the frame of the governess's narrative, James re-enacts the logic of repetition and uses it subversively in the startlingly similar preface and prologue. These repeated 'pre-readings' embed the governess's tale in an engendered struggle for authority, attempting to bring full circle the subversive repetitions by recalling authority in a male voice.

Kierkegaard's logic of repetition and the subversion of the governess's narrative authority by the prologue exemplify the two distinct modes of repetition, Platonic and Nietzschean, identified by J. Hillis Miller in *Fiction and Repetition*.[1] Platonic repetition asserts that identity and delegated authority devolve from similarity between the original and the repetition. This is repetition that Kierkegaard would recognise and validate. In *The Turn of the Screw*, Platonic repetition is represented as patriarchy and the governess's reiteration of its logic. As John Carlos Rowe has noted, Miles will one day accede to his uncle's economic power and authority not because of individual virtue, but because he carries his uncle's name and genetic material and, most importantly, because he carries these things as his uncle does – that is, as a male happily governed by the laws of primogeniture.[2] The logic of Platonic repetition also accounts for the authority delegated to Peter Quint.

Although the governess's predecessor, Miss Jessel, was intellectually – as the housekeeper, Mrs Grose, was morally – the most capable governor of Bly in the owner's absence, Peter Quint, the owner's 'own man' in the owner's 'own clothes', was granted the rights and responsibilities of authority at Bly in his employer's stead. The one characteristic that qualified Quint for leadership is his gender; his Platonic repetition of the employer's gender guaranteed his participation in the patriarchal structure that ultimately empowered Quint only as a repetition (a likeness, a delegate) of the Harley Street uncle.[3]

Through Nietzschean repetition, in contrast, identity and potential authority devolve from difference. This mode of repetition ultimately leads to subversion of established authority, as evidenced by the governess, who first repeats the master's power by exercising the authority that he has granted and that is entirely dependent upon his will to empower her as his ambassador at Bly, and who then distinguishes herself from him and his method of governance by establishing authority beyond his control, and in ways that he does not – through knowledge (gained by reading) and the power to act appropriately that she gains from the knowledge. The governess's fervent desire to read the signs and letters that permeate her world is a continual reminder of the master's equally fervent desire to remain ignorant and irresponsible. She asserts herself by insisting on reading even what is not, or is hardly, written, whereas her employer refuses to read even that which is most clear. Although the Harley Street employer has ultimate authority, he has effectively abdicated it by refusing to participate in the lives of the children. He will write – that is, he will signify himself by exercising his will – but he will not read – he will not acknowledge the will of another. He thereby shuns his responsibility for the children and, eventually, neglects his duties to the patriarchal structure that enables him to act in such a reckless manner. Unidirectional action of the sort that the uncle commits when he refuses to read anything is irresponsible.[4] It delegates governance to substitutes whose interests do not always coincide with his own. His irresponsibility forces him outside the governess's text, in which he is everywhere represented as absence.

Both preface and prologue argue that writing/acting and reading/responding must be balanced responsibly, or else the succession of Platonic repetitions comes to an end, and with its demise comes the loss of authority. In the preface James says that the uncontrolled imagination, the will to act, must not break its bounds and get 'into flood'; it must not violate 'by the same stroke our sense of the course and the channel, which is our sense of the uses of the stream and the virtue of the story' (*TS*, p. xvii).[5] The challenge is to navigate between the tyranny of excessive writing and the chaos of excessive reading. One must repeat established forms, in other words, but one must not be enslaved by them. The uncle personifies unbridled freedom, aflood without determinants. He forfeits all his rights and privileges in the governess's narrative because he refuses to acknowledge the restrictions of the channel that valorises his authority. Furthermore, by undermining the patriarchal succession, through which he inherited authority, he has nothing to bequeath to his heir and successor, Miles.[6] This is assured by the governess, who withholds the greatest sign of her employer's patriarchal succession – his surname. Yet it is not an individual that she seeks to subvert but an institution, particularly her employer's familial and authoritarian roles in it. The uncle is corrupted by his desire for ultimate power – the power freely and irresponsibly to treat others as personal possessions. By tyrannically fulfilling that desire even against the codes of responsibility that ultimately support his patriarchal claim to power, he abdicates his place in the succession. Such irresponsibility, as Kierkegaard implies, invites supplementation and displacement, causing the structure that empowers the Harley Street uncle to collapse if some way is not found to shore it against his absence. The uncle's initial solution is a succession of ambassadors – a series of Platonic repetitions that are identified and authorised by similarity to the original, whose purpose is the containment of power. The first is the ill-chosen Quint; the second is the ill-prepared and unhappy boy, Miles.

The uncle is absent from the structure that evolved from, and that constantly gestures toward, his authority. The governess, in the role of governess – a woman employed to care for another's (in this case, a man's) wards – is granted 'supreme authority', but it is contingent on her employer's original authority as the legal guardian of Miles and Flora (*TS*, p. 154). The governess's 'supreme authority' always recalls the uncle, for it exists only by his imposing absence. The governess strives to fill with her forceful presence the channel that generations of patriarchal succession had hollowed out and that her employer has abandoned. She must read, interpret, and write. But first she must subjugate herself to the system in order to appropriate its form. Only then can she make her mark on it and assert her authority. Luce Irigaray explains that in the initial phase of the subversion of patriarchy, woman has 'only one "path", the one historically assigned to the feminine: that of mimicry. One must assume the feminine role deliberately': for the governess, this means she must allow herself to be seduced into her assigned position of subservience and dependence upon the absent uncle's authority. This 'play with mimesis', Irigaray continues, leads to subversion, for it converts 'a form of subordination into an affirmation [of patriarchy] thus to begin to thwart it'.[7]

The uncle's absent authority is strangely mimicked by the apparition of Peter Quint. (Whether Quint and Jessel are ghosts or delusions is ultimately irrelevant in this reading. What they signify, and that they do signify, both to the governess and in her text, are important here.) When alive, Quint was the uncle's representative and therefore the ruling figure at Bly, the vessel for the uncle's abdicated authority. When alive, Quint was overly present while the uncle was, and remained during the governess's eventful tenure, conspicuously absent. Both men corrupt, but their corruptions are known by different names and have very different social values. In their extremes of absence and presence, the two men form a unity of male hegemony that refuses to surrender its power even as it throws it all away.

The governess's encounters with Quint show her as a Nietzschean reader: a reader whose reading differs from the writing, for she seeks to assert her own 'absolute freedom of hand' rather than mirror either the uncle's absent authority or Mrs Grose's loss of authority – a loss occasioned by the governess's arrival as the absent uncle's delegate. She struggles in her rewriting to uncover what the 'text' – the situation – that she reads suppresses. She channels her freedom carefully. The governess's first encounter with Quint reflects her ties to patriarchy; however, as narrator (with the temporal distance of retrospection), she takes control of the meeting by antedating it with her desire:

> It was plump, one afternoon, in the middle of my very hour: the children were tucked away and I had come out for my stroll. One of the thoughts that, as I don't in the least shrink now from noting, used to be with me in these wanderings was that it would be as charming as a charming story suddenly to meet some one. Some one would appear there at the turn of a path and would stand before me and smile and approve. I didn't ask more than that – I only asked that he

should know; and the only way to be sure he knew would be to see it, and the kind light of it, in his handsome face.

(*TS*, p. 175)

The governess desires precisely what the uncle will not do: she wants him to 'read' her, to evaluatively interpret her, and thus to (re)write her. Her desire for his approval valorises his power over her. He retains authority in his absence because patriarchy is sufficiently powerful to induce the governess to replicate its figures when they are otherwise not available. Her desire repeats the uncle's authority, but acknowledges its own role in the repetition.

The model that the governess relies on is revealing: 'it would be as charming as a charming story' to encounter her employer. Narrative, she tells us, is the means of acquiring what life will not offer. Her desire to be another's text is subverted by her desire to textualise that other, to write him reading her. Therefore, when the governess first sees Quint, she is 'arrested ... on the spot' not by his presence, but by 'the sense that [her] imagination had, in a flash, turned real' (*TS*, p. 175). She sees him in a tower above her (perhaps a metaphor for the distinction of social class and gender, perhaps a reliance on received narrative form – romance), and she is shocked at the appearance of one who she supposes is her employer, and then shocked again, she says, that 'the man who met my eyes was not the person I had precipitately supposed' (*TS*, p. 176). Quint meets her eyes just as she meets his: each is reading the other in this scene. The governess offers two clues to her will-to-power. First, she does not think that her employer or fate preternaturally reads her desire and fulfils it; she momentarily believes that her imagination has such projective power as to turn real. Second, thinking she sees her employer, she does not show submission or embarrassment by diverting her glance; she stares wilfully and directly into his eyes. This sign of territorial struggle with the patriarch she thinks the man to be suggests that the governess is staking a claim to authority at Bly.

She claims that what she first thought was a repetition of her previous encounter on Harley Street is not repetition at all: 'I had not seen [this face] anywhere. The place moreover, in the strangest way in the world, had on the instant and by the very fact of its appearance become a solitude. ... It was as if, while I took in, what I did take in, all the rest of the scene had been stricken with death' (*TS*, p. 176). At this moment the governess begins her active subversion of patriarchy. She is no longer being channelled through the powerful banks of its authority; her channel is its ghost. Originality always speaks of death, for it must do away with the order that it replaces. Everything changes at this instant; everything familiar becomes strange. A new author is born: 'I can hear again, as I write', the governess says. She is reading her own writing: the apparently hermetic duality suppresses the patriarchy it seeks to replace.

The governess's second encounter with Quint follows another, fainter set of signs of the uncle's abdication of authority and her own position in the hierarchy. She returns to 'that cold clean temple of mahogany and brass, the "grown up" dining-room' where the children have their tea on Sundays (*TS*, p. 183). The governess presides in the dining room only as an employee, never as mistress or guest. No proper head of house ever dines there; thus, she shares the cold temple with an absence. She returns specifically to retrieve her gloves, which she had been sewing earlier. The need to repair gloves ('with a publicity perhaps not edifying', she concedes) indicates that the governess does not receive the rewards sometimes accorded to women in patriarchy: she is not 'cared for' nearly so well as she cares for the children. She is not used as the signpost of a man's economic prowess. In fact, as the youngest daughter of a parson, she was never sufficiently cared for. The very need to seek employment, and to accept it under such strange circumstances, clearly indicates that she was forced to earn her own way. Second class by virtue of her gender and her socioeconomic status, the governess, as Rowe suggests, is a marginal member of society at best.[8] She seems destined either to be swallowed up by a society that must seem oppressive to her, or to seek power through revolutionary means.

Into this vacant temple of male authority and personal privilege the governess steps, and instantly she becomes 'aware of a person on the other side of the window and looking straight in'. Her vision, she says, 'was instantaneous; it was all there' (*TS*, p. 184). She recognises the figure as the same face – identity by similarity – that she saw on the tower. As she reads him, however, she acknowledges a threatening difference: 'He appeared thus again with I won't say greater distinctness, for that was impossible, but with a nearness that represented a forward stride in our intercourse and made me, as I met him, catch my breath and turn cold. He was the same – he was the same' (*TS*, p. 184). Once again the two read each other, but the effect is for the governess to reconceive their first meeting as meaningful (not some chance encounter with a forward tourist) and dramatically intense. Both the governess and Quint, inside and outside, take in a vision framed by the window. Their reciprocity recalls the double frame of preface and prologue that begins the tale and, like that double frame, their reciprocity questions the location of 'true' authority. The governess recognises the figure as someone she 'had been looking at ... for years and had known ... always' (TS, p. 184). Though yet unnamed, the figure is the ghost of corrupted patriarchal succession, of its abuses of power and its pervasiveness, that rises to meet the threat that the governess poses as an interloper in its temple. The 'knowledge in the midst of dread' that the figure 'had come for someone else', whom she later believes to be Miles, is the governess's interpretation of the intruder's stare that left her and fixed 'successively several other things' (TS, p. 184). The intruder is looking into the temple of his domestic authority, from which he is being excluded by the governess's growing power. The forward stride that this encounter takes signifies the dual threat of the governess to patriarchy and of patriarchy's response to her. In addition, the circumstances under which Quint reappears suggest the governess's paradoxical desire for the master to be more forward in their intercourse.

What marks this second encounter, however, is that the governess meets the intrusion more aggressively than before: she runs outside to meet and displace the male figure in the window. She assumes his vision of the temple and is herself replaced therein by Mrs Grose. She situates herself outside the frame that separates inside from outside, thus placing herself in the position that the preface, as we shall see, defines as the location of authority. 'With this I had the full image of a repetition of what had already occurred', she says. Inside-outside, more importantly, self-other, are now dualities of two women. The governess recognises her likeness in Mrs Grose: 'She saw me as I had seen my own visitant; she pulled up short as I had done; I gave her something of the shock that I had received. She turned white, and this made me ask myself if I had blanched as much. She stared, in short, and retreated just on my lines' (TS, p. 186). The governess, with supreme authority, is establishing channels of behaviour into which Mrs Grose is being directed. Ironically, as she displaces the figure of male authority, she disguises it by revealing to Mrs Grose's vision only herself. Nevertheless, the instinct to (re)write that is so redolent in the governess surfaces as she aggressively questions Mrs Grose until she has material for a narrative that understands the encounters.

Thus, in the absence of authority that Quint represents, the governess situates herself. She takes his place and the place of that which he signifies, and in so doing she reinscribes patriarchal lines of domination, authority, and class division through Platonic repetition because those are the only channels of aggressive enactment of authority with which she is familiar. Through these channels of domination, she actively reads and writes the story of patriarchal succession that will lead to her final struggle with Miles. Quint's arrival is eventually read by the governess as an attempt to extend patriarchal succession to Miles by granting him Quint's version of his patrimony: corruption. But the governess is still asking critical questions about Quint; she has not assumed authority over him.

Absence characterises the third and final encounter with Quint. At daybreak, on the stairway, the governess discovers that she is fixed in Quint's stare just as she was twice before. His reading momentarily stuns her, and Quint's presence is more forceful than ever: 'the thing was as human and hideous as a real interview' (*TS*, p. 223) – as the interview of Harley Street that began her adventure. However, the governess is remarkably fearless: 'dread had unmistakably quitted me', she says; 'I had no terror' (*TS*, p. 222). What the governess discovers is that silence, a figure of both ultimate absence and infinite meaning, is her most powerful weapon against Quint:

> It was the dead silence of our long gaze at such close quarters that gave the whole horror, huge as it was, its only note of the unnatural. If I had met a murderer in such a place and at such an hour we still at least would have spoken. ... I can't express what followed it save by saying that the silence itself – which was indeed in a manner an attestation of my strength – became the element into which I saw the figure disappear; in which I definitely saw it turn, as I might have seen the low wretch to which it had once belonged turn on receipt of an order, and pass ... straight down the staircase and into the darkness in which the next bend was lost.
>
> (*TS*, p. 223)

Making Quint a text that she refuses to read, the governess imitates the employer's mode of exercising authority, subverting it to her own ends. Quint responds just as he had been accustomed to respond to such authority; he succumbs to her exercise of will that negates him by effacing himself.

Quint cannot enter the governess's silence; he can neither incite speech nor speak. He is a figure of absence, of authority that has been abdicated, and she has met him with the truthful reflection. Furthermore, by remaining silent, by neither speaking his name nor responding to his presence, she emits no sign of his existence. Thus Quint ostensibly does not exist because he has no effect; the governess wills him not to be. Into the abyss of her silence Quint disappears. Perhaps without realising the implications, the governess has gained total narrative control over Quint. Her silence, a gap in her narrative, opens up a great hole to the flood of imagination that, James says in the preface, violates 'our sense of the uses of the stream and the virtue of a story' (*TS*, p. xvii): Quint falls through a hole in the text and is swept away by the flood of abdicated responsibility. When he is recalled at the very end, the governess summons and banishes him at will, demonstrating her ability to channel the flood. She exercises her supreme authority by enslaving the name of her opposition.

Having repeated the encounters with the figure of degenerate male authority until she could dominate it, the governess turns more fixedly to the last remnant of patriarchal succession. Miles, whom the governess repeatedly refers to as 'the little Master', is (we assume) the uncle's legal heir. He seems to be the epitome of aristocratic breeding. He also seems to be the secret vessel of male degeneracy. Abandoned by his uncle and expelled from his all-male school, Miles enters a world of typically disempowered women. As the only male with pretence to authority, Miles seems assured of a place of considerable authority and respect at Bly. His salvation from the certain destinies of irresponsible male absence and from corrupt male presence obsesses the governess, for she must sever him from the patriarchal form he would repeat in order to ensure her own authority, her own individual presence.

But Miles is already fully patriarchal. He has learned at least the outward means of dominating women: his relations with the governess are increasingly clouded by sexual innuendo. Both the master at Harley Street and Quint subjugated the women invested with at least a modicum of authority by seducing them (literally or figuratively). In fact, Quint, who would view Miss Jessel not so much as an ambassador of his authority (which is the way the employer would see her) but as a potential rival for power at Bly, attempted to subjugate her by making her the unwilling agent of the transference of his own power. Impregnating Miss Jessel with his offspring, Quint transformed her into the vessel of his progeny and a sign of his prowess. But Miles's sexuality is superficial charm; he repeats those educated, upper-class characteristics of his uncle that Quint distinctly does not. For example, when the governess seeks out Miles in his bedroom, she asks him if he has been asleep. Miles answers,

> 'Not much! I lie awake and think.'
> 'What is it ... that you think of?'
> 'What in the world, my dear, but you?'
>
> (*TS*, p. 263)

His flawless charm is seductive, but it does not have the force of sexual intent that clearly identifies Quint. In this sense, Quint and Miles are Platonic repetitions of the uncle. Yet as repetitions of different aspects of the master's seductive powers, neither is complete. Division is less forcefully patriarchal, but it demonstrates patriarchy's willingness to compromise some attributes of original authority (class distinctions, for example) in order to secure another, apparently more fundamental attribute of power – namely, its maleness. And together Miles and Quint form a synthesis of absence and presence, force and a channel, that might prove a very powerful opponent to the governess.

Miles is preceded by narratives of absence: the letter from his uncle and the unopened letter from Miles's school that the uncle's letter frames. These twin writings abdicate responsibility for the boy while they make the governess doubly responsible for him. The uncle's letter reminds her of her supreme authority within the frame of forced silence. The headmaster's letter arouses her desire to fill the empty channel of Miles's history with the force of her imagination. She yearns to write what the headmaster has not; she will fill the silence with self-empowering discourse.

Miles himself threatens her authority by representing the future of the order that she seeks to subvert and by refusing to submit to her authority. Confronted by her often subtle requests for information, Miles remains obstinately unyielding, suggesting his suspicion that the governess is seeking narrative authority over him. His charm is meant to disconcert the governess; however, as she presses him for the information she needs to write her narrative, Miles responds with more sexually forceful speech. When asked why he wants to leave Bly, Miles responds by asserting, 'Oh you know what a boy wants' (TS, p. 265). He devolves the subject of conversation now, as before, to the governess and reminds her of her female role as caretaker of male desire. He is evasive because he is a hollow repetition of patriarchy, an empty shell with no force of imagination. In fact, he relies on the governess for the details of his own history. The scene of impotent seduction is framed by references to a letter to the uncle about Miles, a letter that would tell Miles's story and establish the governess's narrative authority over the boy. Before she leaves her room to confront Miles, she stares at the blank piece of stationery. Soon thereafter, when the governess informs Miles that she has begun writing the letter, he angrily orders her to finish it: to tell his history and to summon the source of authority to which he aspires. Miles needs his uncle to 'settle things' with the governess (TS, p. 265), for he fears that his identity (as his uncle's repetition) is being eroded and that his education is being blocked by the governess. Therefore, Miles must steal the governess's letter to his uncle, the letter that represents (as Shoshana Felman forcefully argues) Miles's existence: he must appropriate what his own hollow state cannot create – his history and, really, his place in the succession of patriarchal power. The letter that the governess writes but that the uncle never reads would force the abdicated male authority to assume its responsibilities and reinforce patriarchy. Of course, as a result the governess would write herself out of power and back under the ideology that entitles male identity. However, as Miles finds out, the letter contains nothing (TS, p. 305). It is a figure of absence – of silence.

Like the governess's narrative itself, the letter is a trap or bait to patriarchy to reveal its theft of the subjugated imagination. The letter proves an effective weapon against Miles, almost as powerful as silence is against Quint. Miles not only suppresses his history, but he also talks constantly, as if he is afraid that silence will reveal what he cannot face. And in fact, his discovery of 'nothing' in the letter to his uncle leads ultimately to his destruction. Miles never reveals, for he has no content. He has been cut off from history and will inherit no future. The uncle will not read; Quint cannot speak; Miles does not tell. Unlike his uncle, however, Miles reads what the governess has written; the 'coward horror' that is there for Miles to face is his destiny in her narrative world: Nothing.

The narrative ends with Miles's death for this reason. He is the last living presence with any pretensions to authority over the governess. His survival to adulthood would defeat the governess's subversion of patriarchy. She could not allow him to repeat the degenerate presence of Quint, nor the irresponsible absence of his uncle. He dies into silence and absence: forced to confront the governess's narrative authority over Peter Quint (and so over that which Quint signifies), Miles 'jerked straight round, stared, glared again, and [saw] but the quiet day' (*TS*, p. 309). Like Quint, he is 'hurled over an abyss', and like Quint, he falls out of the text.

To maintain authority independent of her employer's desire to remain absent, the governess must not only disempower the succession of his transferred authority, but must also appropriate its essential logic of manifesting authority through exercise of will, control over property (including its inhabitants), and mastery of meaning, which, as Kierkegaard claims, must eventually be articulated. She does not introduce a new order into her world; ultimately she replaces the old regime with her own, for the forms of patriarchy are the only forms of authority she has known. However, as Rowe explains, such displacement merely disguises the 'original arbitrariness of the power structure; its ambiguity prompts those who "read" its truth to assume responsibility for it': the governess's assumption of the powers of patriarchy are doomed to initiate 'the sort of interpretive activities that will transfer its authorship to others, especially those whom it would rule'.[9] Her means of gaining and maintaining power, in other words, doom the governess's industry to failure, for her narrative not only attempts to reveal the truth of the suppression of female identity, but also betrays itself by revealing the means of its own subverson.

The text of *The Turn of the Screw* is a history of the suppression of female identity, a history of forced female absence. The women in the narrative and its prologue are repeatedly cast away: women leave the country house before the manuscript arrives and therefore are not among the select few who hear it; Miss Jessel leaves Bly, dying in childbirth; the governess leaves her home because she is a financial burden, and she is exiled to Bly after succumbing to her employer's seductions; Flora is sent away from Bly when she becomes disturbed, and Mrs Grose attends her in her flight. Yet female absence in this text refuses to become silence: the unexplained absence of Miss Jessel opens the space for a text that the governess takes it upon herself to write. Whereas male presence continually signifies male absence, female absence continually signifies female presence: Flora and Mrs Grose leave because of the presence of Miss Jessel (and/or the governess), and they head for the centre of absence – the uncle's home. The governess takes over the reins at Bly because Miss Jessel has left. Even the very temporary void created in the study when the governess pursues the apparition of Quint outside the window is filled almost immediately by Mrs Grose. There seems to be a tacit understanding among the women that absence must continually be filled. This, it seems, is the way to power. Such, however, is the lesson that Douglas and the prologue narrator learn from the text.

The narrative of her tenure at Bly that the governess confides to Douglas verbally and later in manuscript form repeats her struggle with male authority. The manuscript is a palpable sign of patriarchy's deviance and announces the break in patriarchal succession, yet it compromises the governess's authority. With no defence against textual corruption, it offers itself for a Nietzschean reading and (re)writing. Douglas and the prologue narrator, in fact, collaborate to gain authority over the governess's text: Douglas keeps it under lock and key as if it were both a valuable and a dangerous item; eventually, he reads it 'with a fine clearness that [is] like a rendering to the ear of the beauty of his author's hand', thus producing an echo of the original text that seems to be a nearly exact translation of it into another medium and yet that provides an opportunity for the final subversion of the text. The narrator stops asking critical questions of the text and begins making substantive claims of content and, ultimately, of the power of entitlement (as Shoshana Felman has shown).[10] Even as they signify the original power of the text by repeating it, Douglas and the narrator recover what they believe the governess's text suppresses in order to recover the authority of patriarchal succession that her text usurps. The narrator hears, then receives, and then transcribes the text, takes the considerable liberty of prefixing the prologue, seeking, as Douglas does not, to repeat the text he reads by a text he writes, one that signifies him by its differences from the 'original'. In effect, he unleashes the repressive powers of discourse that historically, Irigaray contends, have subjugated if not obliterated women.[11] He repeats the means of hearing and writing that James admits in the preface led to his own text.

James himself is neither outside the repetitious structures nor free of the desire for power that informs them: he adds the preface as another (which the reader experiences as the first) reading and writing of the tale. The preface to volume 12 of the New York Edition, which contains 'The Aspern Papers', *The Turn of the Screw*, 'The Liar', and 'The Pupil', frames the prologue with a nearly identical, contextualising tale of origin, one that features Henry James as the appropriating reader-turned-narrator: the 'starting-point itself', James says in the preface, is 'the sense, ... of the circle, one winter afternoon, round the hall-fire of a grave old country-house. ... Our distinguished host expressed the wish that he might but have recovered for us one of the scantest of fragments of [the ghost story]. ... He himself could give us but this shadow of a shadow. ... On the surface there wasn't much, but another grain, none the less, would have spoiled the precious pinch addressed to its end as neatly as some modicum extracted from an old silver snuff-box' (*TS*, p. xv). When later asked for 'something seasonable by the promoters of a periodical dealing in the time-honoured Christmas-tide joy', James took possession of the tale and contributed, he says, 'the vividest little note for sinister romance that I had ever jotted down' (*TS*, p. xv). The prologue offers a ghostly reflection of this tale of origin: 'the story had held us, round the fire, sufficiently breathless, but except the obvious remark that it was gruesome, as on Christmas Eve in an old house a strange tale should essentially be, I remember no comment uttered till somebody happened to note it as the only case he had met in which such a visitation had fallen on a child' (*TS*, p. 147). Authority might be ascertained by tracing the succession of repetitions to an origin: the uncle might trace his power and position to an early male relative who first established himself, and so his heirs, in some position of authority within cultural structures of power. This same tracing of origins – or the narrative's genealogy – seems to be the work of both preface and prologue. Yet no origin is ever located, nor does an origin exist. The two frames are in collusion: they mask the absence of their original power simply by repeating their claim to it.[12]

Yet repeating a claim to originality, and therefore relying on Platonic repetition to entail power, is not the only work or logic of the preface and prologue. As each repetition adds itself to the succession of voices that recall and mythologise the first articulation of the story, the authority of the original is subverted. The double frame actually seeks to corrupt any delegation of power because it seeks to remove power from the predecessor and contain it within its own structure. James seeks to be empowered as author, not delegated to the role of transcriber of another's tale. To this end he claims to have taken only the scantest of seeds and nurtured the growth of what he would have readers believe is essentially an original tale. Douglas and the prologue narrator seek to exercise similar powers by authoring the prologue and substantially supplementing the governess's tale. Therefore, both framing texts undo the business of writing and then author it anew. Following the logic of Nietzschean repetition, each adds its own signifying mark: the preface reveals that James took the thread of a tale and wove it into his own cloth. The prologue offers a history of the manuscript, its transcriptions and performances, that also subverts the authority of an original: the governess inscribes her story with remarkable handwriting; Douglas verbally prefaces the manuscript and translates the author's handwriting into a noteworthy vocal performance; the prologue narrator embeds the governess's tale in a narrative that describes the scene of the telling, the tale of the text, and his claim to the title of his rewritten, revised version. Each writing/telling, rewriting/retelling of the text, in other words, produces a repetition of it that differs in some significant degree from the original. Through these differences, power describes itself, for each degree of difference is a veritable sign of the relocation of power, until finally 'the frame, far from situating, as it first appeared, the story's origin, actually situates its loss, constitutes its infinite deferral'.[13]

Both Felman and Rowe suggest that the repeated acts of suppression and recovery of knowledge and authority that accompany the prologue's successive writings and readings of the governess's text are attempts to gain mastery over the tale by establishing mastery of its meaning. In effect, they both argue toward different ends that the prologue insinuates that its introduction is essential to proper interpretation. Felman and Rowe imply that the prologue is supplemental: it is ancillary to the governess's tale yet necessary, and its presence implies that the governess's tale is lacking some essential portion of its full embodiment. Felman attributes the presence of the prologue to the gross ambiguities of the framed tale. By continually reading and amplifying the governess's tale with information that the tale does not contain, the prologue narrator attempts to transfer the authority of the presumably original manuscript to his own text.[14] In other words, the prologue repeatedly articulates the governess's text to gain both physical and interpretive authority over it.

Similarly, Rowe argues that the prologue recovers what the governess has suppressed. While Rowe agrees with Felman that authority is signified in the prologue by interpretive power and possession of the manuscript, in his own palimpsestual reading of Felman's argument Rowe concludes that the significance of such authority extends into political and ideological realms rather than into the psychological and theoretical. Rowe argues that *The Turn of the Screw* is the story of 'transference of authority from ruler to ruled', which results in 'the displacement of political and economic issues into psychological concerns'.[15] Rowe explains that the desire for authority within these political and economic contexts ultimately compels the governess to exclude 'the fact of the Uncle's potent and active authority that governs her own bid for mastery as the guarantee of the Uncle's secret power'.[16] The secret power that the governess attempts to undermine, Rowe says, is signified by the details that she omits: 'details concerning class, inheritance, and legal guardianship' – the characteristics of patriarchy that the prologue recovers from the governess's autobiographic narrative and that Rowe recovers from the margins of Felman's argument.[17] He suggests that the prologue repeatedly articulates its differences from the governess's text. It repeats the governess's strategy, speaking over and over what the framed text does not, as if it would drown out the governess's voice while naming her as a dangerous subversive.

In the double frame of *The Turn of the Screw*, Henry James participates in the engendered maintenance of power and in its relocation. James frames the governess's tale, in other words, with a volatile border that both asserts and subverts its own authority as well as the authority of the governess's narrative. As 'a prologue to the prologue, an introduction to the introduction', the preface is the beginning of the beginning of James's text.[18] By raising its voice at the outermost step of the textual threshold, the preface undermines the prologue by doubling yet distinguishing itself from the prologue as the 'true' model of which the prologue is implicitly revealed as the supplemented imitation. The reality of the world inhabited by Douglas and the narrator, in which the governess's manuscript palpably exists and is transcribed, is unmasked by the preface as a fiction, but as a fiction based largely on fact. As a result, the relationships between fact and fiction, between the real and the created, between originality and repetition, between authority and the delegate of authority, are made unstable. This instability virtually becomes the substance of the narrative that is doubly framed.

The double frame does not support Kierkegaard's belief that wilful repetition results in maintenance of power. On the one hand, repetition of the border attempts to make the border stronger, as if by doubling the frame James doubles the frame's power and presence. Yet repetition of the border also questions the very concept of the border: the preface-frame and the prologue-frame suppress mutual recognition, each claiming to be the line between the inside and outside of the narrative and to contain the origin of the story. Each frame silently discredits the other's implicit claim to originality. Thus the double frame of preface and prologue initiates the twin logics of Platonic and Nietzschean repetition that characterise the patriarchal structure and the governess's attempts to subvert it. What the double frame repeats are the modes of entailing power: articulating the self and silencing the other.

James engenders these actions by engendering his narrative. The preface and prologue are unquestionably male voices that do not recognise each other, though both seek authority over the female voice of the governess's narrative by subsuming it into its own structure. This female voice, in turn, refuses to recognise or enter into any sort of dialogue with either male voice. In a sense, then, James has at least described two models of engendered transference of authority. One is the struggle between male and female, between frame and framed narratives. This model makes power a dynamic of the relation between male and female rather than an attribute of static, engendered hegemony. This relation is fuelled by the insatiate desire of one to subsume the other into its own structure, into its own logic, and yet it is an implicit recognition that authority is a function of the Self-Other duality, a relation in which the self requires the other that it seeks to consume.

The other model is also engendered, but it is a dialogue of two male voices – the preface and the prologue. The governess's text becomes the location of the dialogue, though it is simply a pretext for the interaction of the two frames. This model is what Eve Kosofsky Sedgwick refers to as 'homosocial': it employs the female other as a means for interaction between males. Because preface and prologue repeat without either acknowledging repetition or consuming the other, neither usurps the other's power; each maintains its own authority and is empowered by its silent relationship with the other, and by the joint subversion of the governess's narrative. This silent homosocial cohabitation of the feminine text both begins (physically) and ends (temporally) the governess's narrative.

The double frame therefore claims the authority of origin and the rights of consumption. The masculine frame cannot, however, make invisible what has been exposed. As Irigaray explains, this masculine 'cover-up of a possible operation of the feminine in language' is fruitless. Through Nietzschean repetition of masculine logic, the feminine, though partially 'resorbed' in masculine discourse, will always 'also remain elsewhere':[19] outside or beside masculine discourse the feminine will leave its mark, the very existence of which subverts the exclusivity of patriarchal authority.

From *The Henry James Review*, 13 (1992), 276–91.

NOTES

[John H. Pearson's essay builds on Kierkegaard's defence of repetition, using J. Hillis Miller's identification of Platonic and Nietzschean forms of repetition. This framework is employed to explore the delegation in *The Turn of the Screw* of a 'ghostly' hegemony, through the agency of 'ambassadors', purporting to conserve patriarchal succession in circumstances of abdicated authority. Such authority, both patriarchal and narrative, is seen to be subverted: by the feminine discourse of the governess, as well as by James's dual framing devices – of preface (to the New York Edition) and prologue. Developing arguments taken from Felman and in particular Rowe, Pearson posits a relocation of power, through a series of repetitions of 'text', that serves in consequence to undermine both patriarchal and textual stability. Ed.]

1. J. Hillis Miller, *Fiction and Repetition: Seven English Novels* (Cambridge, MA, 1982).

2. John Carlos Rowe, *The Theoretical Dimensions of Henry James* (Madison, WI, 1984), p. 133 [see p. 63 above. Ed.]

3. On delegation in James's work, see Julie Rivkin, 'The Logic of Delegation in *The Ambassadors*', *PMLA*, 101 (1986), 819–31.

4. The moral significance of the uncle's refusal to read is made apparent by the contrast with Mrs Grose, who is another non-reader. Unlike the uncle, she is not an anti-reader: she finds reading and writing doubles (the bailiff and the governess) who perform the tasks she cannot. By implication, she shames her employer, for she overcomes obstacles in order to perform her duties, obstacles that he forcefully maintains in order to escape his own.

5.   'The Turn of the Screw', in *The Selected Novels and Tales of Henry James*, vol. 12 (New York, 1906–8); all page numbers are given in the text under the abbreviation *TS*.

6.   Rowe sees Miles as a potential usurper of the uncle's authority. Although Miles's father was a younger brother, and therefore probably heir to only a small portion of the family estate, Miles's tenancy at Bly establishes a basis for his claim to that estate based on physical possession; thus one might argue that the uncle intentionally jeopardises the line of succession in order to prevent Miles from both intruding upon his London life as a bachelor and entangling his estate and fortune in legal proceedings: see Rowe, *Theoretical Dimensions*, p. 133 [p. 63 above. Ed.].

7.   Luce Irigaray, *This Sex Which Is Not One*, trans. Catherine Porter (Ithaca, NY, 1985), p. 76.

8.   Rowe, *Theoretical Dimensions*, p. 130 [see p. 61 above. Ed.].

9.   Ibid., p. 126 [see p. 57 above. Ed.].

10.   The prologue reveals its obsessive call for what Felman calls 'entitlement' to the governess's manuscript, a right contingent on a succession of knowledge and physical possession of the tale, by tracing the succession of owners (*TS*, p. 127): see Shoshana Felman, 'Turning the Screw of Interpretation', *Yale French Studies*, 55/56 (1977), 94–207. The governess confides a tale of her experiences to Douglas. Before her death, she sends him a manuscript version of her confessions. A few days after he furtively alludes to the tale, Douglas possessively reveals the manuscript that he has been hoarding for years and, after prefacing the narrative with a few words of introduction that supplement the tale, he reads it aloud to a fireside circle of entranced listeners, one of whom, the nameless narrator of the prologue (the ineluctable I that Rowe says is the accumulation of the narrative's indeterminacy – Rowe, *Theoretical Dimensions*, p. 138 [see p. 68 above. Ed.]), eventually inherits the manuscript as a legacy when Douglas dies. The narrator in turn exercises the rights of ownership by supposedly transcribing the manuscript; however, as Rowe reminds us, he actually translates it and revises it by adding his own considerable mark, the framing prologue that contains and further supplements Douglas's introduction. The history of the manuscript is a history of the desire for and succession of power; it relates a tale of repetitions, of repeated readings and writings, each of which leaves a trace of new ownership on the text.

11.   Irigaray, *This Sex Which Is Not One*, p. 76.

12.   Loss of discernible origins does not necessarily result in loss of authority, however. Barbara Parker argues in her essay on R. W. Emerson that eighteenth-century and early nineteenth-century high criticism of

the first three gospels, for example, resulted in acknowledgement that the irreconcilable differences among these texts could only be accommodated by forsaking the search for their origin (or the desire to identify one of the three as the original). Once the 'very notion of origin is exploded', authority might be derived from Nietzschean repetition: Barbara Parker, 'Origin and Authority: Emerson and the Higher Criticism', *Reconstructing American History*, ed. Sacvan Bercovitch (Cambridge, MA, 1986), pp. 67–92 (91). Emerson claims of the bard who speaks with authority that 'All the debts which such a man could contract to other wit would never disturb his consciousness of originality; for the ministrations of books and of other minds are a whiff of smoke to that most private reality with which he has conversed': *The Complete Works of Ralph Waldo Emerson*, ed. Edward Waldo Emerson, 12 vols (Boston, 1903–4): 4, 199 (quoted in Parker, 'Origin and Authority', p. 91). Authority is derived through Nietzschean repetition – that is, from the individuating mark one leaves on that which one appropriates.

13. Felman, 'Turning the Screw', p. 122.

14. See ibid., p. 121.

15. Rowe, *Theoretical Dimensions*, p. 123 [see p. 54 above. Ed.].

16. Ibid., p. 131 [see p. 61 above. Ed.].

17. Ibid., p. 130 [see p. 61 above. Ed.].

18. Felman, 'Turning the Screw', p. 125.

19. Irigaray, *This Sex Which Is Not One*, p. 76.

5

Blanks in *The Turn of the Screw*

T. J. LUSTIG

If *The Turn of the Screw* is concerned with slippages and turns of meaning, it is also deeply preoccupied with gaps and voids: James wrote in his Preface that the 'values' of the story were 'positively all blanks'.[1] Shlomith Rimmon has argued that *The Turn of the Screw* constructs its ambiguity around 'a central informational gap'.[2] But this notion of an absent core, a single and central enigma, seems to secure its lucidity by avoiding any explication of the teeming voids which haunt *The Turn of the Screw*. Few fictions deploy such extensive and disparate lacunae, and *The Turn of the Screw* uses its blanks to undermine all attempts to establish relations and to join references into a coherent pattern. One could even argue that the tale blanks its overt blanks. 'Blankley' is the name of a country house in 'The Wheel of Time'. In *The Turn of the Screw*, by contrast, the revealing blank is elided and contracted into 'Bl...y', a placename as suggestive as 'Paramore', though a more reticently monosyllabic one.[3]

The Turn of the Screw is repeatedly concerned with the act of telling. More often than not, however, its predicament is that of not being able to tell. Fragmented and vestigial, the existing text looks like the ruined remains of a fuller story. The introductory chapter of *The Turn of the Screw* begins just after a story has been told and ends just before a story is about to begin. It occupies a space between two acts of telling, framing and mediating a narrative which, as Douglas points out, takes up the tale 'at a point after it had, in a manner, begun', and which ends in the air, with a death whose consequences are not registered in the narrative of the governess, except in the sense that her narrative is the effect of that death.[4] The formal beginning and ending of the introductory chapter and of the main narrative do not conclude with actual, absolute, chronological beginnings and endings: they are, as Christine Brooke-Rose puts it, 'truncated, at both ends'.[5]

The frame chapter serves to mediate a further mediation, since it seems that the events at Bly do not constitute a complete and discrete story so much as a border between a past defined in terms of social relations and a future made up of literary or textual relations. Miles and Flora are passed from their dead parents to their disappearing uncle and on to Quint and Jessel, who die to make way for an evanescent nursemaid, a temporary school, Mrs Grose and the governess herself.[6] Some time after the events of the main narrative the governess tells her story directly to Douglas. The story is subsequently written down by the governess and sent to Douglas before her death. Douglas reads the governess's narrative to the circle gathered in the old house and in turn transmits it, before his own death, to the narrator of the introductory chapter, who finally makes an 'exact transcript' of the manuscript (*Complete Tales*, x, 19). The events at Bly thus form the mid-point in a sequence of transmissions, each of which begins and ends in death or absence, all of which lead away from genetic sources and reproductive pairs to single parental substitutes and from primary spoken narratives to written, read and copied ones.[7]

The spaces which intervene between the separate events of this skeletal history are complete blanks – mere spaces of time – but the events themselves are almost equally shadowy, permeated and punctured by the voids which they supposedly separate. At first sight the attempt to date the sequence of events following those at Bly seems to meet with some success, although Douglas simply informs his listeners that the governess was ten years older than him, that she has been dead for twenty years (p. 17) and that she answered the uncle's advertisement 'at the age of twenty' (p. 19). Only by relying on Griffin's assertion that it is forty years since the governess told Douglas her story (p. 18) and assuming that Douglas, at Trinity, was about twenty 'on … coming down the second summer' can one relate the succession of events to an independent chronological scale (p. 17). The governess, it appears, told Douglas her story at the age of about thirty, approximately ten years after the events at Bly and twenty years before her death at the age of fifty. The events occurred about half a century before the Christmas house party, at which Douglas is approximately sixty years old. Importantly, however, no information is provided as to how much time elapses between the reading and the narrator's reception of the manuscript shortly before Douglas's death, or between these events and the production of the transcript 'much later' (p. 19). Positioned at the end of the sequence of events, the frame narrator's silence produces a retroactive ripple of uncertainty which, as Edwin Fussell points out, prohibits all attempts to tie the beginning of the narrative to a fixed date.[8]

A similar reticence affects the frame narrator's account of the series of events in the old house. Only three evenings are dramatised in the introductory chapter and with reference to the first of these (Christmas Eve) the narrator initially states that Douglas's reading occurred 'two nights later', that is to say on 26 December (p. 15). Speaking of events on the second day (25 December), however, the narrator now affirms that Douglas received the manuscript 'on the third of these days' and began to read it 'on the night of the fourth' (p. 19). This implies that the reading took place on 27 December, or even (if the narrator is counting from the second day, of which he is speaking at the time) on 28 December.[9] Such a discrepancy is particularly odd because the narrator subsequently repeats his first assertion that Douglas's reading occurred 'the next night' after the second dramatised evening (p. 22). If the reading did in fact take place on 26 December, then one is left with an apparently superfluous reference to a gap which does not exist. If the reading took place on 27 or 28 December, however, the gap now consists of a mysteriously undramatised period. No hypothesis which adheres to one date for the reading can close these mutually exclusive references, and yet these contradictions are not directly related to the field occupied by 'ambiguity' in *The Turn of the Screw*, at least as it is usually formulated.

Naturally no fiction is required to take out a stop-watch and calendar to account for its chronological lapses and transitions. Nor is a novel bound to represent time as a smooth linear succession of events: in *The Ambassadors*, as both Ian Watt and Charles Thomas Samuels have shown, James repeatedly employs proleptic and analeptic shifts.[10] One would be tempted to dismiss the temporal discrepancies in the frame chapter as oversights on James's part were it not for the fact that he rarely made such errors and for the far more important fact that the frame chapter seems to act as a small-scale model of the temporal uncertainties of the governess's own narrative, which contains, or rather skirts, a chronological haemorrhage consisting not of days but weeks. The governess arrives at Bly in June and the final scene of the tale occurs in November (see pp. 23, 129). All the dramatised scenes in the main narrative (which thus covers a minimum four-month period) occur on one of a mere thirteen days.[11] The first six dramatised days must all take place in June since on the day of Quint's second appearance the governess tells Mrs Grose that she saw Quint for the first time 'about the middle of the month' and she has already made it clear that this first apparition was encountered 'at the end of a long June day' (pp. 46, 35). The last six dramatised days take up a longer period – one of some seven weeks – but are as unequivocally accounted for as the first six days. The governess's discovery of Miles on the lawn at night (Day 9) takes place on the 'eleventh night' following Quint's third appearance on Day 8 (p. 74). Days 9 and 10 succeed each other, 'a month' separates Days 10 and 11, and the last three days are also successive (p. 84). The first six and the last six dramatised days therefore occupy some eight weeks of at least sixteen spent by the governess at Bly. On either side of the seventh dramatised day (that of Miss Jessel's first appearance), therefore, and lying at the dead centre of the sequence of represented days if not of the chapter plan, two transitional passages (one between Days 6 and 7, the other between Days 7 and 8) must bear the burden of accounting for a blank period of at least two months which lasts throughout July and August and occupies up to a half of the narrative's predicated timespan.

Mrs Grose's tears on the evening of the sixth dramatised day are followed by frequent conversations with the governess 'for a week' and the imposition of a 'rigid control' (p. 52). Since this period of 'disguised excitement' lasts only until it is 'superseded by horrible proofs', one might plausibly conclude that only a week separates Day 6 from Miss Jessel's first appearance on Day 7 and that seven of the missing eight weeks remain to be accounted for (p. 53). But the transitional passage between Days 7 and 8 sheds little light on this blind spot. The last word of the governess on the seventh dramatised day and at the end of chapter 8 is that she 'must just wait' (p. 66). Chapter 9 almost immediately begins with the news that 'a very few' days in the company of Miles and Flora were sufficient temporarily to allay the governess's anxieties (p. 66).

Because the governess continues to describe the effects of the children's companionship, it seems that her allusions to 'this period' and 'these days' relate to the same few days (pp. 67, 68). If this is true then it would appear that the remaining seven weeks flash past with a reference to a further 'lull' separating Days 7 and 8 (p. 69).

The governess seems to compensate for the hole at the heart of the time-scheme by multiplying her references to specific periods of time. These references either have an ungrounded precision or refer simply to intervals between events, to gaps in which nothing happens. The governess tells Mrs Grose that Miss Jessel appeared 'two hours ago, in the garden', but there is a strange disparity between this scrupulous chronological precision and her admission that she 'can give no intelligible account' of how she has 'fought out the interval' (p. 56). Occasionally the governess's temporal references are simply inaccurate: on the twelfth dramatised day she refers to Miss Jessel's first appearance on Day 7 as 'the other day', although by her own account this event occurred at least six and possibly up to thirteen weeks previously (p. 110).

I have tried to show that the history of the children before Bly, like the history of the governess's narrative after Bly, is a telescoped series of circles within circles. Given the chronological lacunae in *The Turn of the Screw*, this concentric patterning might provide a succession of reassuring enclosures. Examined more closely, however, the line of circles begins to seem more like a run of blanks within blanks. There is a social 'circle' at Bly and Douglas's audience make up a 'hushed little circle' (pp. 89, 19). Unnervingly, however, it is impossible to determine the contents of these circles. Besides the narrator, Douglas and the Griffins, the frame section introduces an unspecified number of 'ladies whose departure had been fixed' (p. 18). On the first evening in the old house they voice their intention to stay on for Douglas's reading. Referring a little later to the events of the second day, the narrator mentions the fact that the ladies departed before the reading 'in a rage of curiosity' produced by the 'touches' with which Douglas had 'already worked us up' (p. 19). Almost immediately, however, and apparently referring exclusively to the second evening, the narrator goes on to relate 'the first of these touches' (p. 19). Evidently the 'departing ladies' are still present and leave at some point before the night of the reading (p. 19). One might assume that it is one of these departing ladies who remains (after her own disappearance has been narrated) to issue the two remarks attributed to 'one of the ladies' on this second evening (p. 22). This cannot be the case, however, because 'the same lady' puts a further question to Douglas on the very night of the reading (p. 22). To acquire even the shadowy identity of the departing ladies is nevertheless something of an achievement in the old house. Six remarks are made by voices identified simply as 'somebody' (pp. 15 [twice], 17, 18) or 'someone' (pp. 15, 21). It is not possible to establish whether these speeches belong to guests already mentioned, to six separate voices or to a single otherwise unidentified speaker.

Does this vagueness matter? Narratives indicate but do not have to catalogue their worlds. Yet the fact that a similar tenuity affects the edges of the circle at Bly reinforces one's sense of a strategy in the blanks. According to Douglas, the master informs the governess that, besides the housekeeper Mrs Grose, Bly is staffed by a cook, a housemaid, a dairywoman, a pony, a groom and a gardener (see p. 21). Aproned and with a room which smells of lately-baked bread (see pp. 33, 98), Mrs Grose seems to take over the role of the cook, who does not appear in the narrative of the governess, although presumably somebody must have provided the roast mutton consumed by Miles and the governess after the housekeeper's departure in chapter 21 (see p. 127). The solitary housemaid mentioned by the master is almost immediately replaced by a 'pair of maids' in the governess's narrative and a reference is subsequently made to 'a couple of the maids' as if there are even more than two (pp. 22, 126). The governess does mention a pony (see p. 86) but it belongs to the Hampshire vicarage where she was brought up and not to Bly. The dairywoman, groom and gardener do not appear in the main narrative. Instead one encounters a bailiff (see p. 100) who may or may not be 'Luke' (p. 109) and a nursemaid who temporarily replaced Miss Jessel but seems no longer to be present (see p. 32).

These are not the only disparities and blanks amongst the peripheral members of the cast in *The Turn of the Screw*. The governess makes two allusions to her brothers (see pp. 69, 85) although according to the frame narrator, Douglas speaks of her only as 'the youngest of several daughters' (p. 19). Both Douglas and the governess mention the latter's father (see pp. 19, 85) but neither speaks of her mother. The uncle mentions his mother (see p. 20) but not (at least in *The Two Magics* text of 1898, which is used in Edel's edition of James's *Complete Tales*)[12] his father, and refers to the children's father (see p. 20) without mentioning their mother. 'Mrs'

Grose has no conspicuous husband. The relationships between the frame narrative and the main narrative, therefore, and the relationships which each of these narratives in turn postulate give rise to a perturbing, subliminal sense of mutual discontinuity if not of open conflict.

Considered in its entirety, *The Turn of the Screw* systematically blanks out beginnings and endings. This overall strategy is replicated on a reduced scale in many of its parts. Hardly a chapter of the tale possesses a beginning or ending which coincides with the initiation or completion of a distinct structural unit, whether this is a time, a place, a scene, an action or a dialogue. The interstices which separate the chapters are an active part of the text and occasionally its most charged moments. Like the final chapter, chapters 3, 6 and 10 break off suddenly at points of crisis. Events following these crises, like the narrative as a whole, are reported subsequently and indirectly. This sometimes creates the curious impression that the governess is not simply recalling the events at Bly but remembering *remembering* those events. In contrast to the chapters which lack endings, chapters 5, 10, 15, 19, 20, 23 and 24 seem, rather like the first chapter of the governess's narrative, to take up the tale after it has already begun. The formal breaks which separate these chapters from their immediate predecessors occur within a single piece of consecutive action.

Whenever texts and writings crop up as objects within the narrative, they too are almost always characterised by emptiness and incompletion.[13] Letters in *The Turn of the Screw* tend not to be written or, when written, not to be sent or, when sent, to be unmentioned or unmentionable. 'Not a word. I'm off!' writes the master to the governess, dropping her a line only to sever their correspondence and speaking only to preserve and enforce silence (p. 28). His note encloses a letter from Miles's headmaster which apparently makes no charges to back up the boy's dismissal from school and of which the governess decides to say 'nothing' – 'nothing' to the uncle and 'nothing' to Miles himself (p. 33). The governess receives 'disturbing letters from home' but goes into no details about their contents (p. 41). She allows the children to write to their uncle but keeps their letters. When she does eventually write to the master she simply describes herself as sitting before 'a blank sheet of paper' and later claims that her letter contained only 'the bare demand for an interview' (pp. 101, 124). Miles confirms the bareness and blankness of this letter when he admits that he has found 'nothing' in it (p. 134):

> 'Nothing, nothing!' I almost shouted in my joy.
> 'Nothing, nothing,' he sadly repeated.
>
> (p. 135)

There are so many 'nothings' in *The Turn of the Screw* that the negative begins to define the positive rather than vice versa. The governess's story can only be spoken of in terms of its blanks. It has 'not been out for years'; 'nobody' but Douglas has ever heard of it and 'nothing' that he knows touches it (p. 16). But it is not even that nothing touches it for 'sheer terror': it is 'not so simple as that' and Douglas seems 'at a loss how to qualify it' (p. 16). The experience is not his own and nor is the record of it, since he took down 'nothing but the impression' (p. 16). The governess did not tell Douglas that she had 'never told anyone' her story (p. 17). 'Neither' he nor the governess mentioned the reasons for her silence and nor does the manuscript, which, as Douglas points out, *'won't* tell' (pp. 17, 18).

Whatever it was that Miles said at school, the negative manner in which he alludes to it resembles nothing so much as Douglas's way of speaking about the governess's manuscript. Miles admits that he 'said things' but cannot remember to whom he said them (p. 135). It was not to everyone, nor to many, but he cannot recall their names. He 'didn't know' that they would tell and the governess confirms that his masters at least 'never told' (p. 137). When the governess comes upon Quint, she can only define him in the same negative way that Douglas defines her manuscript and Miles speaks of what he said at school.[14] The figure on the tower is 'not the person I had precipitately supposed' and the governess has 'not seen it anywhere' (p. 36). She can arrive at 'no living view' of the bewilderment produced by the apparition, at 'no account whatever' of it (pp. 36, 39). She does not mention the incident to Mrs Grose and cannot explain her reasons for this reticence (see p. 39). The figure is nobody from Bly and nobody from the village: 'nobody – nobody' (p. 45). Indeed, Quint looks 'like nobody' (p. 46). He has 'no hat', wears clothes that are 'not his own' and is connected with 'missed' waistcoats (pp. 46–7). He is 'never – no, never! – a gentleman' and resembles an actor, although the governess has 'never seen one' (p. 47).

For a narrative which is so concerned with remembering (the verb is used in the first lines of the frame chapter and the first words of the governess are 'I remember'), *The Turn of the Screw* records a great deal of forgetting (p. 23). The governess is 'unable ... to remember' what plans she made for the resumption of Miles's studies (p. 34). She forgets what 'remarkable person' she was playing in Flora's Sea of Azof game (p. 54). She has 'no subsequent memory' of 'what first happened' after Miss Jessel's final appearance (p. 117). The governess repeatedly draws attention to the difficulty of narrating her experiences, resorting to certain phrases because she 'can express no otherwise' what she means, 'can call them nothing else', 'can use no other phrase', 'can describe only as' (pp. 40, 88, 117, 133). She asks herself with perplexity how she can 'express' and 'describe' events (p. 40). She wonders how to 'retrace' her experiences (p. 87). She searches for 'terms' which will adequately convey the action but feels that her language 'represents but grossly' what actually occurs (pp. 88, 133). She becomes aware that she can 'scarce articulate' and later finds 'no sound on my lips' (pp. 56, 80). She is faced with the 'unspeakable' (p. 86), the 'unutterable' (p. 56) and the 'indescribable' (pp. 58, 75), with things that 'no words can translate' (p. 106). At various points she is unable to 'name' (p. 137), 'say' (pp. 37, 38, 70, 102), phrase (see p. 39), 'speak' (p. 43), 'tell' (p. 65), 'express' (pp. 67, 71, 131), explain (see p. 68), present (see p. 81), represent (see p. 78) and 'convey' (p. 79).

Blanks occur even at the phonemic level of *The Turn of the Screw*. On the first night in the old house Douglas exclaims that the garden in which he had once heard the governess's story 'wasn't a scene for a shudder; but oh – !' (p. 17). This 'oh' syllables the inexpressible, offers a vestigial emblem of the absent. On the second evening in the Griffins' house another 'oh' is said to be 'the only other word of importance contributed to the subject' until, on a subsequent night, Douglas opens the governess's album and admits that he has no title for the narrative (p. 22). 'Oh, *I* have!' exclaims the narrator in the final utterance of the introductory chapter (p. 22). The narrator's 'oh', echoing back through the other oh's, returns in a full circle to the first utterance of the frame chapter. 'If the child gives the effect another turn of the screw', Douglas then asked, 'what do you say to *two* children – ?' (p. 15). The narrator's final 'oh' therefore seems to act as a suspended reference to the title of the text and by implication to the narrative itself – one long 'oh' of hung meaning.

The play of circles within circles and of blanks within blanks does not, however, end with the 'oh'. Flora's first lesson from her new governess consists in being given 'a sheet of white paper, a pencil and a copy of nice "round O's"' (p. 29). This first act of writing in the main narrative acts as a token of the blankness and circularity which affects the other writings recorded by the text, repeats a bordered void in the same way as the frame narrator's copy of the governess's manuscript. Simultaneously present and absent, Flora's O's are, however, by no means the final stage in the run of lacunae. Below even the letter as message and the letter as character or cipher stands the typographic mark ' – '.[15] One could say that the long dash bears a metonymic relation to the text as a whole; it certainly operates as an effective index of the extent to which the narrative becomes pitted and vesicular at times of crisis. The ghostly in particular tends to be accompanied by an almost telegraphic scattering of dashes, and it is especially appropriate that Quint first emerges from between the lines by means of the dash. 'I mean that's *his* way – the master's', says Mrs Grose, leaving the governess with the 'impression of her having accidentally said more than she meant' (p. 31). In a sense, Quint is a ghost created by the predicative power of language, which, as Darrel Mansell points out, 'can never quite get rid of the thing it says does not exist'.[16] Yet it is not only the language but the silence or pause implied by the typography ('*his* way – the master's') which directs attention to a space occupied by a 'he' other than the master.

There are some sixty uses of the word 'oh' in *The Turn of the Screw*, but there are over 600 long dashes. The average of twenty-five dashes per chapter is considerably exceeded in chapter 21 (forty-five) and the frame chapter (forty-three). But it is particularly apt that the void in the time-scheme, located either before or after Miss Jessel's first appearance, is associated with the highest density of dashes in chapter 6 (fifty-four) and chapter 7 (fifty). Passages of dialogue account for approximately 280 dashes but the average of eleven per chapter is significantly exceeded in chapters 7 and 21, with forty dashes apiece. Douglas's reference to the 'turn of the screw' occurs in the first of seventy-five speeches in the text which peter out in the long dash, emphasising the ' – ' as well as the 'oh' connotation of the phrase (p. 15). The remaining 360 or so dashes occur in passages of narrative, the average of approximately fourteen per chapter being notably exceeded in chapter 6 (forty-one), chapter 3, that of Quint's first appearance (thirty-four) and in chapter 4, that of his second appearance (twenty-seven).

From T. J. Lustig, *Henry James and the Ghostly* (Cambridge, 1994), pp. 115–25; 271–2.

NOTES

[T. J. Lustig's book examines the theme of the ghostly throughout James's *oeuvre* and includes as its centrepiece a substantial chapter on *The Turn of the Screw* (pp. 105–89). The excerpt presented here makes a close examination of gaps in narrative and in dating, in respect of the prologue and the tale proper. Circles within circles and blanks within blanks relate to absent or missing people, letters, amnesia and other negative qualities, evidenced in the text by the use of negative statements, 'nothings', 'oh's' and dashes. While there is no obvious label to put on Lustig's eclectic approach, he combines a sophisticated close reading with a plentiful use of historical and intertextual data. Ed.]

1. *Henry James: Literary Criticism; French Writers, other European Writers, the Prefaces to the New York Edition*, ed. Leon Edel and Mark Wilson (New York, 1984), p. 1188.

2. Shlomith Rimmon, *The Concept of Ambiguity: The Example of James* (Chicago, 1977), p. 51. Tzvetan Todorov, *The Poetics of Prose*, trans. Richard Howard (Oxford, 1977), p.145, has also argued that 'the Jamesian narrative is always based on *the quest for an absolute and absent cause*'.

3. For possible expansions of the syllable 'bly', see Lustig, *Henry James and the Ghostly*, pp. 170, 176. The name 'Bly' may well have occurred to James during August or September 1897 when, shortly before beginning work on *The Turn of the Screw*, he spent some time at Dunwich in Suffolk, four miles from Blythburgh and six from Blyford. Also suggestive is the following sequence of names in James's notebooks for 1892: 'Gaye (name of house) – Taunt – Tant (Miss Tant, name of governess)', *The Complete Notebooks of Henry James*, ed. Leon Edel and Lyall H. Powers (New York, 1987), p. 67.

4. *The Complete Tales of Henry James*, ed. Leon Edel, 12 vols (London, 1962–4), vol. 10, p. 19; page numbers hereafter given in the text, are for *The Turn of the Screw* in this edition.

5. Christine Brooke-Rose, *A Rhetoric of the Unreal: Studies in Narrative and Structure, especially of the Fantastic* (Cambridge, 1981), p. 184; see also note 14 below.

6. In the revised version of the tale James further multiplied the intervening stages in the children's history by inserting a reference to some grandparents, who take care of Miles and Flora after the death of their parents and before their uncle: see *The Novels and Tales of*

Henry James, New York Edition, 26 vols (vols 1–24, London, 1907–9; 25–6, London, 1917), vol. 12, p. 153.

7. On the problem of origins and the relation between narrative and death in *The Turn of the Screw*, see Shoshana Felman, 'Turning the Screw of Interpretation', *Yale French Studies*, 55/56 (1977), 94–207 (122, 128).

8. See Edwin Fussell, 'The Ontology of "The Turn of the Screw"', *Journal of Modern Literature*, 8 (1980–1), 118–28.

9. On the temporal discrepancy in the introductory chapter of *The Turn of the Screw*, see Donal O'Gorman, 'Henry James's Reading of *The Turn of the Screw*', *The Henry James Review*, 1 (1980), 125–38, 228–56 (133–5).

10. See Ian Watt, 'The First Paragraph of *The Ambassadors*: An Explication', *Essays in Criticism*, 10 (1960), 250–74 (257–8); Charles Thomas Samuels, *The Ambiguity of Henry James* (Urbana, IL, 1971), p. 199.

11. Day 1 (pp. 23–6), Day 2 (pp. 26–8), Day 3 (pp. 28–32), Day 4 (pp. 32–3). Quint first appears on Day 5 (pp. 35–9). His second appearance occurs on Day 6 (pp. 41–52). Miss Jessel first appears on Day 7 (pp. 53–66). Quint appears for a third time on Day 8 (pp. 69–74). Day 9 (pp. 74–6), Day 10 (pp. 77–84). Miss Jessel's third appearance occurs on Day 11 (pp. 90–105) and her fourth appearance on Day 12 (pp. 106–18). The final encounter with Quint appears on Day 13 (pp. 118–38). Days 1–4 are successive, as are Days 9–10 and 11–13. Gaps of time occur between Days 4 and 5, Days 5 and 6, Days 6 and 7, Days 7 and 8, Days 8 and 9, and Days 10 and 11. It is coincidental that Donald P. Costello detects a sequence of thirteen *non-chronological* units in the text: 'The Structure of *The Turn of the Screw*', *Modern Language Notes*, 75 (1960), 312–21.

12. See note 6 above.

13. See Felman, Turning the Screw', p. 144 [p. 48 above. Ed.].

14. Brooke-Rose, *Rhetoric of the Unreal* (p. 162), points out that Quint is never completely described in physical terms and, like the narrative, seems to be 'truncated'.

15. On James's use of the dash to create ambiguity, see Ralf Norrman, *Techniques of Ambiguity in the Fiction of Henry James, with Special Reference to 'In the Cage' and 'The Turn of the Screw'* (Åbo, 1977), pp. 29–32, 63–7 and, regarding *The Turn of the Screw*, pp. 153, 174.

16. Darrel Mansell, 'The Ghost of Language in *The Turn of the Screw*', *Modern Language Quarterly*, 46 (1985), 48–63 (52).

6

Getting Fixed: Feminine Identity and Scopic Crisis in *The Turn of the Screw*

BETH NEWMAN

> Is there no satisfaction in being under that gaze that circumscribes us, and ... which in the first instance makes us beings who are looked at, but without showing this?
>
> (Jacques Lacan)[1]

> ... looking was food enough to last. But to be looked at in turn was beyond appetite. ...
>
> (Toni Morrison)[2]

Like narrative, the 'gaze' has become an object of suspicion, especially within feminist discourse. One source of this suspicion has been Laura Mulvey's ground-breaking article 'Visual Pleasure and Narrative Cinema', which argued that narrative in classic Hollywood cinema works together with cultural and cinematic codes of looking to sustain a phallocentric cultural unconscious.[3] Foucault's discussions of surveillance, 'panopticism' and the 'clinical gaze' have from another direction contributed to more general suspicions of what is being called the 'gaze'.[4] In a critical climate that frequently represents the gaze as something sinister, as a sign of power and a means of control, it is easy to forget that being the object of someone's look can in some circumstances be pleasurable – even sustaining and necessary.

What makes this easy to forget, at least for those of us concerned with the position of women in society, is that women (according to Mulvey's influential argument) have been tethered to the passive side of looking. As Mulvey observes, '[i]n a world ordered by sexual imbalance, pleasure in looking has been split between active/male and passive/female' a 'division of labour' that defines woman as spectacle, man as bearer of the look. Others have argued that in various forms of representation (novels, film) and in the discourse of psychoanalysis, women's active participation in looking is represented as castrating or otherwise threatening to male subjectivity and is therefore punished.[5] Breaking out of the gendered positions of looking might therefore seem more important than claiming that what a woman wants might be, in certain circumstances, precisely to be seen. Yet I intend here to make such a claim.

The words *look* and *gaze* that will recur in my argument require some preliminary unpacking, especially since the meaning of *gaze*, in anything like a technical sense, is far from settled. Partly through the influence of Sheridan's translations of *le regard* in both Lacan and Foucault, the word *gaze* is now often used casually in contemporary literary criticism to refer to almost any kind of looking. But in some feminist film theory of the 'seventies and 'eighties (which has provided much of the impetus for the term's adoption by literary critics) one is more likely to meet with the word *look*: Mulvey's 'Visual Pleasure' article, for example, uses this word almost exclusively. More recently, Kaja Silverman has argued for a distinction between *look* and *gaze*, the former referring to an embodied seeing and the latter to an 'unapprehensible' seeing that is 'by no means coterminous with any individual viewer, or group of viewers'. *Look* is thus to *gaze* as *penis* in psychoanalytic theory is to *phallus*; therefore 'the look ... may masquerade as the gaze'. She concludes that '[t]he gaze ... remains outside desire, the look stubbornly within'.[6] Silverman derives her distinction from Lacan's insistence on the difference between eye and gaze in *Four Fundamental Concepts*. In an effort to honour what seems to me a theoretically useful distinction (one difficult to sustain, however, in practice), I use *look* whenever an embodied mutual seeing is in question. I reserve *gaze* for three other aspects of visual relations: to refer to a phantasmatic psychical structure – an internalised or introjected seeing of oneself as if by some other; to denote a visual relation in which the mutual, intersubjective aspect is obscured or mediated by a function of supervision (since in Foucault's account of the Panopticon and panopticism more generally, the goal is the introjection of the observer's gaze by the objects of surveillance); and finally, to invoke the abstract structure of visual relations as an object of fantasy or (as in this essay) of discourse, i.e., the relations of looking abstracted from its embodied local specificity.

I focus here on a single text: James's *The Turn of the Screw*, a text whose explorations of the visual dimensions of power, pleasure, and self-definition have already been remarked.[7] The governess's crisis, as I read it, arises in her struggle to define herself (as we all must) in terms of the gaze – the interplay of her own look with that of others, both real and imagined. Part of this struggle involves a certain ambiguity about which side of the gaze the proper middle-class woman is supposed to be on. I shall argue here that nineteenth-century social codes produced two competing and mutually exclusive definitions of femininity, each placing the woman on the opposite side of the gaze. The situations of many nineteenth-century heroines – the rivalries that structure their stories, the tensions that divide them from themselves – may be understood as attempts to work out the contradictory relations of looking in which nineteenth-century middle-class women found themselves. *The Turn of the Screw* suggests, moreover, that the gaze is not necessarily the controlling, pernicious enactment of (patriarchal) power it is sometimes understood to be (though it may be that, too). It is better understood as one aspect of the visual dynamics in which we are all produced as subjects, and through which we achieve, however problematically, the sense of identity. Though another's look can be experienced as threatening – as a bid for mastery or an assertion of power – that other's look is also necessary to one's sense of self. It can therefore be desired as much as dreaded or resented. In a culture where relations of looking and being looked at are inevitably burdened with gendered meanings, however, the stakes of that desire will be different for women than for men.

I

Because James so assiduously withheld any decisive signs about the gender of the nameless narrator in the story's frame, it is striking that professional readers of *The Turn of the Screw* have until recently assumed this narrator to be male.[8] The paucity of female narrators in James's *oeuvre*, together with the convention of presuming masculinity in the absence of feminine markers, are no doubt behind this assumption, but perhaps another more subtle reason is the narrator's behaviour, when he is 'fixed' by Douglas's penetrating look:

> He continued to fix me. 'You'll easily judge', he repeated: 'you will.' I fixed him too. 'I see. She was in love.'[9]

The narrator does not assume a demure 'feminine' passivity but 'fixed' him in return, suggesting that he (she?) regards him (her?) self as Douglas's equal in status and power. Yet when Douglas looks at the narrator it is 'as if, instead of me, he saw what he spoke of' – that is, 'general uncanny ugliness and horror and pain' (p. 2). What Douglas sees as he looks at the narrator who assertively looks back – horror, pain, and an ugliness described as 'uncanny' – recalls the male spectator's responses to the sight of Medusa's head in Freud's reading of it as a signifier of castration. It is tempting therefore to 'read into' this flirtation between Douglas and the narrator the gendered dynamics of looking whereby a woman's returning look paralyses ('fixes' in a sense) the male subject with horror. (And if such a look threatens castration, the second 'fixed' begins to resonate for the modern reader as it probably would not for James, with the sense of 'neutered', 'castrated'.)

But since the text steadfastly refuses to specify the narrator's gender, such a reading would surely be an over-reading. And since criticism has had no trouble seeing both parties to the flirtation as male though it has had no textual reason to do so, this subtle flirtation should instead discourage us from involving any simple formulae about gender and the 'gaze'. Though it is possible to argue that Douglas's penetrating look 'feminises' the narrator – that is, places a putatively male figure in a feminine 'subject position' – the persistence with which this figure has nevertheless been presumed male reveals that serving as the object of the look is not reserved for women alone. What the flirtation in the frame of *The Turn of the Screw* suggests is that a man can indeed be the object of a libidinal and even mastering look – that the association of that position with the woman is conventional, but neither essential nor exclusive.[10] Thus *The Turn of the Screw* begins by unsettling any easy equation of bearing the look with masculinity, or of being the object of the look with femininity.

I have already called attention to the word *fix* in this scene, which recurs later in the text to refer to the act of staring intently at another person. The syntax in which this word appears here and elsewhere, while not absolutely unidiomatic, stretches slightly the more usual English usage, and reveals some of the issues at stake for both sexes in the relations of looking. According to the *OED*, the word was first used in English in expressions like 'to fix (one's eyes) upon an object', a usage reflected in two of the relevant modern definitions of the word: '[t]o direct steadily and unwaveringly, fasten, set (one's eyes) attention, affections, etc.) *on*, *upon*, and *to* (an object)', and 'to direct upon [someone] a steady gaze from which he cannot escape'. But most of the examples that illustrate this meaning include a word like 'eyes' as the object of the verb, which in English is almost always used reflexively.[11] (Thus a more idiomatic phrasing would be 'He fixed his eyes upon me ... I fixed mine upon him too.') Nevertheless, the narrator is not alone in the story in using the word this way. The governess uses the same word and syntax in her own narrative to describe Peter Quint's stare:

> '[T]his visitant, at all events ... seemed to fix me.'
> (p. 17)

The governess's habit of dropping the reflexive reference to eyes and using the verb transitively – a usage more typical of French, and thus perhaps too learned or genteel to make immediate sense to the unlettered Mrs Grose – is unusual enough to puzzle the housekeeper when the governess describes her sighting of Miss Jessel:

> 'She only fixed the child.'
> Mrs Grose tried hard to see it. 'Fixed her?'
> (p. 32)

When the narrator in the tale's frame silently adopts the governess's idiom, he or she signals some kind of identification with the woman whose story he or she retells, and offers a testimony to Douglas's powers as a storyteller. The narrator signals this identification, moreover, while recounting a moment of special insight into the governess's actions ('I see. She was in love'). The process of identification, in which the narrator implicitly claims 'I am like that' (i.e. like the governess or some aspect of her), leads to a subtle self-alteration; the narrator adjusts his or her self-presentation so that in some small way (here, through diction) it more nearly approximates that of the governess. Through this seeping of the governess's language into the narrator's the text suggests that identity is always being constituted and reconstituted, continually bolstered – but also altered, remade, hence potentially undermined – by forces that lie 'outside' the self. These forces include not only other people's stories, as in this example, but also images – particularly those of other people, or even oneself, seeing oneself.

My claim is, then, that identity and its stability (or its tenuousness) are precisely at stake in the intense looks that Douglas and the narrator exchange, and more specifically in the word *fix* as it occurs in *The Turn of the Screw*. Indeed, the meaning of *fix* that the OED lists first is 'to make firm or stable' – a meaning invoked, just a few lines after the exchange of glances between Douglas and the narrator, with reference to 'the ladies whose departure had been *fixed*' (p. 3, my emphasis). This use of the word *fix* so soon after Douglas and the narrator have 'fixed' one another in searching, insistent looks, together with the syntactical anomaly that confuses Mrs Grose, might permit us to collapse the two meanings into one. The resulting pun would suggest that 'to direct ... one's eyes, attention, affections, etc.' upon another is in some way to 'fix' that other in the sense (more usual in the transitive use of the verb) of making him or her in some way firm or stable. When the narrator remarks of the governess's employer a few paragraphs later that '[o]ne could easily *fix* his type' (p. 4, my emphasis), he or she means that the employer is easily recognisable as a particular kind of character; but the turn of phrase again invokes identity as something which, whatever shifts it may undergo, can seem susceptible of being pinned down, held fast, 'fixed'.

The word 'fix' then, captures the potential dangers that the other's look poses for one's sense of self. Potentially erotic (as in a flirtation), that look may nevertheless threaten a paralysis that goes beyond mere firmness or stability. Yet other moments in the text suggest that certain kinds of looks can reassuringly if problematically 'fix' an identity that seems dangerously fleeting and uncertain. The prototype of such scenes occurs soon after the governess's arrival at Bly when, alone in her room, she surveys herself in the mirror – 'the long glasses in which, for the first time, I could see myself from head to foot' (p. 7). Some contemplation of self and image seems the logical response to a young governess's situation. Her sense of her identity has just sustained some shocks: uprooted and displaced, she has been removed from the confirming and familiar images of herself reflected back to her at home. Moreover, she is required to assume an unaccustomed authority, and yet the lavish surroundings where she is to exercise it make this poor clergyman's daughter keenly feel her own social insignificance. As such, the governess's confrontation with her image in the mirror might be understood as reassuring at a moment when she needs reassurance, especially because it shows her an unfragmented image of herself – an image of self as whole and complete – 'for the first time'.

Such reassurance, though, is surely ambivalent. In returning to the governess an unfragmented image, the full-length mirror invokes not simply a confrontation with the self, but more specifically a return to the Lacanian 'mirror stage', a time when a small baby (aged six to eighteen months) whose previous experience of the body is one of fragmentation, recognises its image in the mirror and so gains a sense of wholeness and identity.[12] But in Lacan's analysis of the mirror stage, this experience of wholeness is undermined by an alien and alienating quality of the mirror image, which always remains irreducibly outside of, and different from, the self: the child, after all, does not yet experience the wholeness and completeness it sees in its mirror reflection. James's rendering of this confrontation too makes the governess's experience of wholeness and self-possession before the mirror potentially as threatening as it is reassuring. First of all, the image of a whole, coherent self that the governess sees in the mirror would be undermined by its own multiplication in the 'long glasses' (*plural*), which would produce multiple images and possibly, though the governess does not say so specifically, even the dizzying *mise-en-abyme* effect of mirrors reflecting mirrors – the effect of the frame structure of the text as a whole with its multiple embeddings. The experience of wholeness, control, and authority might be undermined, moreover, by the daunting size and grandeur of the 'long glasses', which, along with the other furniture in the 'large impressive room' – 'the great state bed, ... the figured full draperies' – would dwarf the image they give back to her. Her image in the mirror might thus return her not only to an early anticipation of future wholeness but also to an experience of vulnerability, and so reinforce the anxieties produced by her new surroundings and in her new role: feelings of being lost, adrift, in charge of what she cannot manoeuvre.[13]

There is a related ambivalence in Lacan's account of the mirror stage – an ambivalence associated with being 'fixed'. The (French) word *fixer* occurs in Lacan's essay 'Le Stade du Miroir' in precisely the sense that James uses its English equivalent – to mean 'to gaze at intently'; moreover, the vagaries of translation point to a convergence of this meaning with one of making stable. Lacan describes the infant jubilantly overcoming the constraint represented by his caretakers' arms or the '*trotte-bébé*' that supports him 'pour suspendre son attitude en position plus au moins penchée, et ramèner, pour le *fixer*, un aspect instantané de l'image' (i.e., 'in order to suspend his attitude in a more or less forward-leaning position, and to bring back, in order to *fix* it, an instantaneous aspect of the image' – my translation of 'Stade du Miroir', p. 94, and my emphasis). Translator Alan Sheridan is surely correct in rendering this *fixer* in English not as 'to fix' but rather as 'to hold ... in his gaze'.[14] But the word 'fix' does not disappear entirely from the English sentence; it has merely migrated to an earlier phrase where it translates 'suspendre' and provides the sense of holding still or stabilising. (Sheridan's translation reads: '[the baby], *fixing* his attitude in a slightly leaning-forward position, in order to hold it in his gaze, brings back an instantaneous aspect of the image' [my emphasis].[15]) Thus the translation registers both meanings of the word *fix* exploited by James – and implicit in the French as well.

The two meanings of 'fix' underscore the ambivalence of the 'mirror stage' for the subject who has passed through it. On one hand, the subject gains a sense of a stable self, an identity; the image it sees and recognises is stable, partly because of the 'fixed' attitude with which the baby contemplates it: yet this same stability contrasts sharply with the subject's experience of itself as it looks at its image. For what it has been experiencing is not only fragmentation, a sense of the body in bits and pieces, but also turmoil: the 'flutter of jubilant activity' that accompanies his approach to the mirror, and the 'turbulent movements that [he] feels are animating him' as he looks.[16] Being 'fixed', then, offers the promise of a future stability and wholeness. On the other hand, such fixing also exacts its price, marking the beginning of the constitutive self-alienation of the subject. Lacan writes (and Sheridan translates): the image of 'the total form of the body ... appears to [the subject] above all in a contrasting size (*un relief de stature*) that fixes it [*le fige*] and in a symmetry that inverts it'.[17] Thus the whole image 'by these two aspects of its appearance, symbolises the mental permanence of the *I*, at the same time as it prefigures its alienating destination'.[18] The 'fixed' image, that is, is a misrepresentation, showing stability where there is turbulence, and simultaneously shrinking and inverting the body it gives back to the subject as a picture of itself. (Hence one's recognition of oneself in it is always a misrecognition.) The price we pay for a sense of a coherent self is that we must accept what is always a misconstruction; yet such a misconstruction is nevertheless what enables identity and serves as its foundation. More ominously, it ultimately serves also as a kind of prison – 'the armour of an alienating identity, which will mark with its rigid structure the subject's entire mental development'.[19] This reference to identity as a rigid armour emphasises the negative side of what it means to be 'fixed' – whether by one's own look at oneself, or by that of others. It suggests forced conformity to an image or structure supplied by something *outside* the self, something to which the self is then moulded.

I am not arguing that all of this 'fixing' happens to the governess as she beholds her image in Bly's 'long glasses'. I want to suggest rather that *The Turn of the Screw*, through its peculiar use of the word 'fix' and its emphasis on specular relations, accords with some of the claims that psychoanalysis makes about the relationship between subjectivity, identity, and vision. In Lacan's text, an image of oneself 'fixed' or objectified, and then internalised from outside oneself, is both a necessary condition of identity and a trap in which one becomes caught. *The Turn of the Screw* suggests that the other's look is another source 'outside' the subject of an image of the self necessary for identity – for a sense of who or what one is when one says *I* – and a threat.[20] Moreover, this need for the other's look, I shall argue, is complicated by the way gender relations in the nineteenth century were structured around the gaze, and by a contradiction that inhabited the definition of (middle-class) femininity in the nineteenth century. For the narrator of James's tale, an already complicated need to see herself seen is further exacerbated by her social position.

II

Studies of the governess in mid-nineteenth-century England – the period in which James carefully places *his* governess – point to a confusion about how to categorise the woman forced by economic necessity to pursue the only calling open to 'respectable' women. The social position of the Victorian governess was inherently unstable, marked by what M. Jeanne Peterson has termed 'status incongruence'.[21] Governesses occupied an ambiguous divide between middle-class women, whom they usually resembled in manners and origins, and working-class women who – like the governess but unlike the middle-class wife – had to support themselves by working outside the home. Worse still, in caring for children they did for pay what the middle-class wife and mother did for free, a fact that brought the governess perilously close to the figure of the prostitute. In the middle-class Victorian imagination, then, such women belonged to no clear category or social class; we might say that it was difficult to 'fix' them, though one solution was to place them alongside the working-class woman, the 'fallen woman', and the madwoman or lunatic as another of the 'deviant' female figures against which the middle-class wife and mother was defined as the female norm.[22] *The Turn of the Screw* invokes this perceived proximity of the fallen woman and the madwoman to the governess by suggesting that Miss Jessel, the previous governess, left Bly to have Peter Quint's child, and by raising the possibility of the governess-narrator's madness. It emphasises the problem of 'status incongruence' by relating Miss Jessel's 'fall' to violations of class boundaries as well as to sexual impropriety – whereas '*She* [Miss Jessel] was a lady', according to Mrs Grose, Quint was 'so dreadfully below' (p. 33). The governess-narrator's unspecified difficulties at home, whence she receives 'disturbing letters' (p. 20), hint at the downward mobility of her own family, headed by a poor parson burdened with several daughters.

The problem of social identity compounds the more personal onslaughts to the governess's sense of self – her youth and inexperience, her isolation at Bly, her unrequited love for her absent employer, the problems with the family from whom she is separated, and so on. Her self-contemplation in the mirror, along with the sometimes frenzied scopic activity in which she sees things not seen by other people or alternatively, imagines herself being seen, may be partially understood as responses to this crisis of identity. While there is nothing inherently gender-specific in these responses, gender enters the picture – and complicates it – in the governess's ambivalence about being the object of a male gaze. Furthermore, gender relations produce another, more profound ambivalence about which side of the gaze she wants to be on.

This ambivalence emerges in the contrast between her pleasure in indulging in a certain fantasy, and her horrified response when she

finds that 'my imagination had, in a flash, turned real' (p. 16).
Describing what she calls her 'own hour', a quiet time when, Miles
and Flora having been put to bed, she is alone, she recalls:

> One of the thoughts that, as I don't in the least shrink now from
> noting, used to be with me in these wanderings was that it would
> be as charming as a charming story suddenly to meet some one.
> Some one would appear there at the turn of a path and would stand
> before me and smile and approve.
>
> (p. 15)

Thoroughly versed as she is with romance novels, the governess
constructs here a romance of her own – one perhaps conditioned by
Jane Eyre's encounter with Rochester as she walks the grounds of
Thornfield.[23] Though she denies 'shrinking' from what she here
confesses, her elliptical pronouns betray some reluctance to confess
it just as her wording suggests that she had once found the confession harder to make. She makes it no real secret, however, that the
'some one' in question is her employer, the absent master; she has
already recalled the pleasure she felt at such moments in imagining
'that by my discretion, my quiet good sense and general high propriety, I was giving pleasure – if he ever thought of it – to the
person to whose pressure I had yielded. What I was doing was what
he had earnestly hoped and directly asked of me, and that I *could*,
after all, do it proved even a greater joy than I had expected'
(p. 15). As a daydream, the governess's 'charming story' of meeting
the master on the path is subject to all the mechanisms of secondary
elaboration, to the ego's demands for coherence and a limited credibility, demands that the governess meets by making her daydream a
modest one: 'I didn't ask for more than that [his smile and ap-
proval] – I only asked that he should *know*' (p. 15). But the very
modesty of the scenario she depicts expresses another fantasy embedded in, or supporting, the conscious one: that she is the object of
the master's look, a look imagined (masquerading, Silverman might
say) as an all-seeing gaze that regards her as discreet, quietly sens-
ible, highly proper, competent, and in control.

Significantly, the governess *wants* to be seen: she wants to receive
the recognition of an important other as a confirmation of her identity. Her isolation in a place that offers 'little company [and] really
great loneliness' (p. 6) sharpens her desire for such recognition.
Sequestered in the provinces and confined there to the domestic
sphere, she has only two young children and the servants, especially

Mrs Grose, from whom she can receive confirming images of herself, those necessary supports from the other of one's internalised sense of self.[24] But the children and the servants can only confirm her in her socially unstable and insignificant identity as governess. Moreover, even though Mrs Grose does remark to the governess that she is 'young and pretty' (p. 12), her inmates at Bly necessarily deprive her of images of herself as a sexual being. Such images would be especially important to her now, when she has just fallen in love, presumably for the first time.

Seeing herself seen and approved at least in fantasy, she gains some tenuous support for her uncertain authority, her shaky identity. So long as she sustains the illusion she gains a sense of the mastery over her situation that she otherwise feels lacking: 'I could take a turn into the grounds and enjoy, almost with a sense of property that amused and flattered me, the beauty and dignity of the place. It was a pleasure at these moments to feel myself tranquil and justified ...' (p. 15). The fantasy of the approving look of the other, and specifically of a masculine other (a 'master', someone endowed with power and authority), converges with the consciously elaborated fantasy of a romance with the master to bestow a sense of 'property' upon the governess. That is, being seen and approved by the master is tantamount in her fantasy to becoming the lady of the manor, almost the owner of the estate upon which she knows herself to be merely a dependent employee.

Such moments of illusory wholeness and mastery, of course, are prone to deflation. Predicated on the misplaced certainty of self-contemplation, the experience of 'seeing oneself seeing oneself' denies or conceals, at least in the Lacanian account of subjectivity, one's lack of complete self-knowledge – given that parts of the self will always remain unconscious, precisely outside of one's knowledge. It conceals as well (or rather, at the same stroke) the desires by which one feels oneself incomplete, lacking. Predictably, what disturbs the governess's moment of satisfied self-observation is her sudden sense of someone else on the scene watching her, whom she later identifies with Mrs Grose's help as the dead Peter Quint. His presence indicates a blind spot in her own seeing – she thought she was alone and unobserved – and so arrests her 'with a shock much greater than any vision had allowed for' (p. 16). It opens a chink in the closed and complete self-image she has been constructing by imagining her employer's approval, and moreover, brings the desire motivating this fantasy closer to consciousness – catches her in the act of desiring, so to speak. The shame of a desire she cannot consciously acknowledge expresses itself in her shock and lingers in her equivocation, as she writes her story years later, between the claim that she does not 'in the least shrink *now* from noting' her fantasy of meeting someone, and her coyness, even as she divulges that conscious fantasy, about its object.

If we understand the governess's desire to be seen precisely as repressed, then Quint's 'bold hard stare' (p. 18) falls into place as the return of the repressed, with all the uncanniness – that combination of strangeness and familiarity – such a return implies. '[I]t was as if I had been looking at him for years and had known him always', she writes as she records his second appearance (p. 20). The uncanniness of Quint's look is emphasised by her eventual discovery that Quint is dead, that she has seen and been seen by a ghost.

Moreover, when she perceives that she is being looked at by someone she immediately recognises is not a 'gentleman', the governess confronts the sexual component of the imagined look she has been investing with such benign omniscience. The loss of social status that the gaze undergoes when it appears in a 'base menial' rather than in the fantasised master at once demystifies and remystifies it. That is, in Quint the master's gaze is turned back to an embodied look, but one that (to recall Silverman's account of these issues) nevertheless masquerades as the gaze – more precisely, as the voyeuristic, appropriating 'male gaze' that has been the object of feminist critique. Associated with a 'base menial', the gaze transferred from the master is thus subject to a kind of debasement: a reduction to the sexual of what seemed, in the governess's fantasy of being seen, to have the more heroic, less directly erotic associations of being 'a remarkable young woman' (p. 15). As a prop for this appropriating 'male gaze', Quint's look evokes all of the unpleasure bound up with the governess's ambivalence towards being the object of a scopic relation. Here we can perhaps detect a hint of the harassing, aggressive attitude familiar in any society where men regard looking women over as their prerogative. What strikes the governess is Quint's 'strange freedom' and undue 'familiarity' (p. 17) as he stands 'very erect' on the tower (p. 17). His look seems not only phallic and sexually aggressive but even somewhat sadistic in the control over its object implied by his moving deliberately 'from one of the crenellations to the next' while never taking his eyes from the governess, who remains 'fixed' on the grounds below. Quint's look thus not only returns to the governess the repressed fantasy of herself as the object of the gaze and the libidinal aspect of that fantasy, but also causes her to revise the fantasy, when it enters consciousness, as an unpleasurable one. Put differently, Quint's look represents the risks to self for women of heterosexual relations in a world ordered by a sexual hierarchy. The consciousness of being the object of a male look can entail the feeling of being claimed as property as surely as the governess's fantasy of being under the master's approving look provides her with a 'sense of property' experienced more positively as being in charge.

Given the importance of seeing and being seen in the constitution of subjectivity, the governess's wish to be seen – a wish powerful enough to influence almost everything she says, does, and thinks, as manifested by the various permutations upon this wish that govern her narrative – is not itself gender-specific. Partly an index of her social invisibility, this wish expresses the desire for the recognition of the other that all subjects share, as well as a wish to see herself whole and in control. The erotic pressure of unrequited love intensifies this desire in the governess, but it too is something that both men and women suffer. Why, then, is the desire to be seen so problematic for the governess, and why does she repress it? And what have the checks upon this desire to do specifically with the situation of the middle-class woman of the nineteenth century, at least as she is (problematically) represented by the governess?

Freud explains that repression occurs when the satisfaction of an instinct becomes 'irreconcilable with other claims and intentions' and 'would, therefore, cause pleasure in one place and unpleasure in another' ('Repression', p. 147).[25] Elsewhere he elaborates slightly those 'other claims' as one's ethical or cultural ideals.[26] A wish to be seen would be subject to repression if it conflicted with 'other claims and intentions' such as one's acceptance of current cultural mores demanding self-effacement, a placing of oneself on the side of the *not-seen*.

The burdensome presence of such a cultural force operating upon women is articulated in the diary of an actual nineteenth-century woman James knew well, one whose 'case' has even been seen as the inspiration for the governess's story.[27] Alice James recorded in her diary for 14 December 1889 the following observation, offered without pretext or comment: 'The negro lad who prayed, when leading a revival, "Lord, make Thy servant conspicuous", isn't bad!'[28] Her tacit 'amen', with its mingled admiration for and condescension towards the black preacher, wryly protests against an imposed invisibility. Despite the vast social gulf separating her from the anonymous (and possibly apocryphal) black preacher, and though she herself was by her own account 'hopelessly relegated among the smug and the comfortable' (12 August 1889), Alice James evidently understood that invisibility can perpetuate power-lessness and marginality. In seconding the black man's desire for conspicuousness, she seems to respond not only to the social and cultural forces that rendered most women's work and achievements invisible, but also to an alignment with the unseen experienced more personally or intersubjectively (or more strictly so) as a demand for self-effacement, for an inconspicuousness willingly assumed as a part of one's self-presentation – worn, almost, like an article of clothing.

Thus elsewhere in her diary Alice James described herself as 'ab-sorbing into the bone that the better part is to clothe oneself in neutral tints, walk by still waters and possess one's soul in silence' (19 February 1890). Here she explicitly links the demand for in-conspicuousness with the cultural imperative enjoining women to suffer and be still. The references to clothing and neutral tints make clear that the inconspicuousness she protests is no metaphor, but pertains very literally to visual presence. Such moments in the diary articulate not only a code of conduct, but also a gendered code of visual relations. This code defines woman not as the object of the gaze, as most accounts of women and the visual might lead us to expect, but rather as she who offers to disappear before it. Internalised as a set of ethical norms, such a code would conflict with a wish to be seen, and perhaps result in the repression of that wish.[29]

III

In *Desire and Domestic Fiction* Nancy Armstrong offers extensive evidence for the existence of a code of conduct requiring feminine invisibility. Surveying eighteenth-century conduct books and some domestic novels of the eighteenth and first half of the nineteenth centuries, Armstrong discovers a shift in the attitude towards women that accompanied the middle class's accession to power. She argues that the middle classes, in order to distinguish themselves from the aristocracy and claim for themselves the moral high ground, constructed their sense of what made a woman desirable by emphasising 'depths' – characteristics such as moral uprightness, thrift, and heightened sensibility or emotional intensity – rather than 'surface', such as the aristocratic manners and sartorial finery by which upper-class women functioned as signs of wealth. As a corollary, the prevailing moral economy that the conduct books and novels together helped to consolidate made it a kind of 'crime' for a middle-class woman 'either [to] want to be on display or simply allow [herself] to be "seen ...".[30] According to Armstrong, 'It is a woman's participation in public spectacle that injures her, for as an object of display, she always loses value as a subject.' Though it is *public* spectacle and display that damage the woman in this account, the argument implies that the middle-class woman risks losing her value if she presents herself in any way as an object of visual pleasure. As such an object, she sacrifices 'the quality of subjectivity' that defines the desirable woman according to middle-class mores from the late eighteenth century through the nineteenth. ('Desirable', as Armstrong uses it, means above all both suitable and appealing as a wife.)[31]

Armstrong claims, then, that strong cultural forces obliged nineteenth-century women like James's sister and his fictional governess to renounce the scopic position by which women had previously been defined: that of object of the look, or spectacle. She argues that the ideal middle-class woman was instead retiring, inconspicuous, even invisible. Not only that, she embraced this 'invisibility' (the term is Armstrong's) precisely so that within the domestic sphere over which she presided, she could more effectively exercise the powers of supervision: '[S]he cannot be "seen" and still be vigilant'.[32] Later in her book Armstrong claims that Richardson's *Pamela* depicts a 'shift of the gaze from male to female', and that this shift 'changes the very nature of the gaze from voyeurism to supervision'.[33] Likewise, she finds in a conduct book written by Erasmus Darwin a call *not* for 'a woman who attracts the gaze as she did in an earlier culture, but [for] one who fulfils her role by disappearing into the woodwork to watch over the household'.[34] We might say that in the discourses of domesticity as Armstrong represents them, the ideal woman was valued for and defined by her failure or refusal to display the quality Mulvey calls 'to-be-looked-at-ness' and which Armstrong, using somewhat different terminology, attributes to the aristocratic woman against whom the middle-class woman was being defined. In Armstrong's narrative the newly created ideal woman, no longer the object of the look, became its bearer, but not by turning voyeurism back on men. Instead she was idealised as a moral presence whose *supervisory* gaze imposed order on the household and made possible 'the economic behaviour that ... ensures prosperity'.[35]

Armstrong's reading of conduct books and novels usefully historicises visual relations. But it does so at the cost of neutralising a tension between the psychical and the social forces that jointly construct the subject – that is, a tension between the intersubjective relations through which one's sense of identity, of self, is both produced and undermined, and a social order that produces the subject through other kinds of relations, such as those obtaining between individuals and institutions or the relations of social class. Critics pursuing a Marxian or Foucauldian model of the subject (Armstrong falls into the second category) and those privileging a psychoanalytic one seem often to be talking at cross-purposes because each wants to reduce the other to a version of itself – the socially-oriented critic to absorb psychical reality into the social, the psychoanalytic critic to explain the social as the psychical writ large.[36] The tension between these approaches may articulate a tension in subjectivity itself, or rather, may point to the foundation of subjectivity in forces that do not necessarily coincide with respect to their interests or their effects.

Looked at another way, the narrative logic Armstrong's argument implies – of a historically prior voyeuristic male gaze giving way to a supervisory female gaze – is too monologic. It excludes the resistances to what is socially mandated that are expressed (or repressed) in (unconscious) desire, an exclusion determined by Armstrong's preference for Foucault over psychoanalysis. (In this regard, the meaning of *desire* in her book as desirable in marriage – an entirely *licit* and social sense of desire – is symptomatic.) Moreover, it seems more likely that the earlier scopic regime that defined woman as the object of the gaze endured, if in an attenuated form, despite the dominance of the later one – a possibility that seems all the likelier when we consider the force of those earlier conventions in our own time. Social and medical discourses beginning in the mid-nineteenth century, particularly in the panic about prostitution that culminated in the Contagious Diseases Acts, continued to make women (mostly the working-class women against whom the domestic woman was defined) into the object of a gaze – now a clinical, disciplinary one, but one perhaps never entirely free of a libidinal, voyeuristic impulse.[37] Existing alongside or 'beneath' the dominant ethos of the inconspicuous but vigilant woman as a counterdiscourse, the older set of relations that defined woman as spectacle would surely come into conflict with that ethos. The conflict would be exacerbated by the fact that for women as for men, seeing oneself seen by others is necessary to the constitution of identity, though this (seeing oneself) being seen can probably never be disentangled from the web of gender relations in which it is caught.

The major works of nineteenth-century British fiction abound with evidence of a conflict between two definitions of ideal femininity as one of the main contradictions they seek to resolve. Charlotte Brontë addresses it in *Jane Eyre* – or rather, there smooths over a contradiction she will explore in her later fiction – by setting up Blanche Ingram as the spectacular woman and Jane herself as the retiringly vigilant one who ultimately triumphs over her flashier rival. Several crucial events in that novel, including the charades in which Jane participates only as spectator, emphasise that she wins her man because she knows how to position herself as the subject of a supervisory gaze who can even see in behalf of the master when Rochester is blinded and maimed. But by the time she writes *Villette*, Brontë seems less content with this simple division of women into object of display and subject of the gaze. Lucy Snowe's fascination with the actress Vashti, and her own brief foray onto the stage, articulate some dissatisfaction with the ideal inconspicuousness of the middle-class woman. Moreover, her peculiarly self-effacing narrative expresses formally a contradiction Brontë blithely ignored in writing *Jane Eyre*, a tension between self-revelation before some Reader and an insistence upon the value of feminine invisibility. One might read a similar narrative in George Eliot's *oeuvre*, beginning with a fairly simple denunciation of the woman-as-spectacle in *Adam Bede's* Hetty Sorrel (though Dinah's preaching, a kind of performance, complicates the equation), and moving towards a much more complex treatment of the problem in *Daniel Deronda*. There, a tension between two versions of the desirable woman – one represented as a cynosure, an object of visual display, and one who refuses that definition – is expressed as an almost agonistic struggle between the novel's heroine and her rival. This struggle pits the limelight-seeking Gwendolen Harleth against Mirah Lapidoth, a singer and actress who shuns the stage to which she was bred for the more domestic venues of the family and the genteel drawing room where she continues to perform privately. Mirah wins the love of the hero and the novel's explicit approbation, but the history of the novel's reception reveals that readers have found Eliot's flamboyant heroine the more attractive of the two.[38] In Dickens, paired female figures like Esther Summerson and Lady Dedlock in *Bleak House* or Dora Spenlow and Agnes Wickfield in *David Copperfield* make even clearer a split between the woman as the object of a libidinal look and the subject of supervision, and also reveal the continued fascination and desirability, in the male imagination, of the first.

IV

The Turn of the Screw does not develop a contrast or sexual rivalry between two female characters to express the incompatibility between two ways of defining women, as do most of the novels mentioned above. Rather, it explores what we might call a crisis of scopic positioning as a conflict besetting a single character, the governess. Unlike most of the inconspicuous heroines in Brontë, Eliot, and Dickens, and rather more like Alice James, the governess in James's tale registers some discontent with her inconspicuousness. 'I now saw that I had been asked for a service admirable and difficult', she writes after recording her second encounter with Quint; 'and there would be a greatness in letting it be seen – oh in the right quarter!' (p. 28). She recalls feeling that to be seen thus at her 'extraordinary flight of heroism' might enable her to 'succeed where many another girl might have failed' (p. 28). Yet as the events in her narrative unfold, she becomes less concerned with being seen – by the master or anyone else – than with maintaining an untiring surveillance over her two charges. This surveillance even becomes part of her 'extraordinary flight of heroism'. Ostensibly the means by which she hopes to 'save' the children from the torments of the damned, it expresses her determination to install herself in the subject-position dictated by nineteenth-century bourgeois society as the one appropriate to the properly domestic woman.

If we provisionally 'decide' what *The Turn of the Screw* makes undecidable and read the ghosts as hallucinations, they highlight the psychical consequences of the crisis in which the governess is caught. The nightmarish apparitions she encounters – particularly Peter Quint, who repeatedly 'fixes' her with his aggressive, bold stare – may perhaps be understood as ironic and self-punishing pro-jections answering to an unacceptable desire, on the part of a genteel woman who finds herself cast as a kind of servant, to be conspicuous.[39]

Quint in particular would seem then a projected self-punishment not so much for her desire for the master, which she admits, however elliptically, but more specifically for the way this desire manifests itself in the one she reveals more obliquely, the desire to be seen, to experience the pleasure of being looked at. Because this desire coexists uneasily with the domestic ideal that constructs the proper lady (and desirable woman) as vigilant but inconspicuous, as well as free from unambiguously erotic desire if she is young, un-married, and inexperienced, it is incompatible with the ethical norms by which the governess evaluates herself and constructs herself as a potentially desirable woman. In other words, this desire is ripe for repression – and for symptomatic unconscious expres-sion in the form of hallucinations.

But whether we interpret Quint as a hallucination or a 'real' ghost, the effect of his appearance is the same, and entirely consist-ent with the ideal of the invisible but vigilant woman. It makes her recoil from being seen, and intensifies her supervision of the chil-dren. It is as though the governess's earnest, conscious desire to be the ideal domestic woman (the better to please her employer and perhaps gain his love) forces her into a sharper, more stringent sur-veillance. Such surveillance was, moreover, the province of the gov-erness even more than of the wife and mother, the 'real' domestic woman. According to a popular mid-century treatise on the gov-erness, 'the eye of the governess must be fixed on her pupils from morning till night, every day of her existence: her duty is not confined to the school-room, nor to mere lessons on the subjects of study: it extends to every occupation – almost to every word and gesture.'[40] Faced with such an onus, it is not surprising that James's governess is at least as ambivalent about her supervisory role as she is about being the object of a man's look.

Her response to Miss Jessel reveals her ambivalence about her supervisory role. Reporting her sighting of her predecessor to Mrs Grose, the governess says: 'She gave me never a glance. She only fixed the child.' To Mrs Grose's uncomprehending repetition of the word *fixed*, the governess adds for her further enlightenment, 'Ah with such awful eyes! ... With a determination – ... a kind of fury of intention' (p. 32). Miss Jessel's 'fixing' of Flora seems a malign parody of the governess's own avowed intention '[t]o watch, teach, "form" little Flora' (p. 8). Even the word 'fix', emphasised by Mrs Grose's repetition of it, seems analogous to the more benign 'form', emphasised by the quotation marks with which the governess sets it off.[41]

The governess herself unwittingly acknowledges a treacherous similarity between Miss Jessel's 'fixing' of Flora and her own intention to watch and form her. She claims that when she describes Miss Jessel's 'awful eyes' to Mrs Grose, the housekeeper 'stared at mine as if they might really have resembled them' (p. 32). Whether Miss Jessel is a 'real' ghost or an hallucination, the governess unconsciously identifies with her, and the identification is negative. Invisible to everyone but the governess, Miss Jessel as apparition monstrously exaggerates not only the governess's own social invisibility but also the unremitting surveillance that all governesses were expected to exercise, and that James's governess herself sought to practise. At the same time, Miss Jessel in her character as the governess's 'vile predecessor' (p. 59) – the 'infamous' woman who in life responded to her own sequestration at Bly by succumbing to the advances of Peter Quint – represents the temptation of refusing the burdens of domestic surveillance, and pursuing instead the recognition of oneself as a sexual being.

The governess, then, occupies a stress-point between two different scopic positions. Her role as domestic overseer requires that she assume a supervisory stance that she must not relax, at the same time denying her participation in the libidinal economy of seeing and being seen. Yet she is already defined by this economy, having internalised its structure and effects as part of her own self-definition. She has internalised as well a psychosocial structure at odds with the imperative towards female inconspicuousness – an older, persistent, still powerful set of visual relations that define woman as the object of a libidinal look. Caught between two definitions of ideal femininity – one valuing the inconspicuous but vigilant woman, the other representing the desirable woman as an object of visual pleasure – she consciously chooses the former. But she cannot divest herself of her unconscious desire to be seen, which influences her insistent seeing and possibly – if the ghosts are hallucinations – the content of what she sees.

One of the governess's remarks about her situation at Bly neatly expresses the contradiction in which she is caught. She concludes, after one of her consultations with Mrs Grose, that 'whether the children really saw or not – since, that is, it was not yet definitely proved – I greatly preferred, as a safeguard, the fulness of my own exposure' (p. 52). In its context, the 'exposure' she is willing to endure is her exposure to the ghosts, to the supernatural, to knowledge of 'the very worst that was to be known', as though they were a kind of infection (p. 52). But it might be possible to hear in her willingness to endure such 'exposure' a disguised expression of her desire to be seen, a wish that she could best exercise her supervisory duties and prevent the children from seeing the ghosts by in some way 'exposing herself'.

What she exposes herself to, though, turns out to be a reverse supervision, one that unsettles her surveillance of her two charges by deflecting her own supervision back upon herself. In fact, the requirement that she spend so much of her time confined to the children and the domestic sphere – an exaggerated version of what was expected of the domestic woman who was a wife and mother rather than a paid servant – functions as a mode of social control that works smoothly in the absence of any other supervisor. It produces a structure of self-regulation that ensures no untoward behaviour on the part of the woman unless she is willing to compromise the children as well, as Miss Jessel evidently was.

As we might expect in a Jamesian text, the imprisonment of the 'gaoler' herself within this self-enclosed system is suggested in *The Turn of the Screw* by a verbal ambiguity. The governess refers to passing several days 'in constant sight of my pupils' (p. 38). The context suggests that she means that Miles and Flora remained constantly in *her* sight; as she tells us, she was 'careful almost never to be out of' their company (p. 39). But she reveals that in retrospect, she saw herself as fully scrutinised by them – as much in *their* sight – as she knows them to be in her own. Of their frequent requests for whatever autobiographical anecdotes she can supply, she remarks that 'nothing else perhaps, when I thought of such occasions afterwards, gave me so the suspicion of being watched from under cover' (p. 51). Though she compares herself to 'a gaoler with an eye to possible surprises and escapes' (p. 55), it is she who contemplates running away, in order not to have to explain her absence from church – an absence occasioned by her alarmed sense that Miles has bested her in a recent bid for power. She imagines her pupils chastising her for her absence: 'What *did* you do, you naughty bad thing? Why in the world, to worry us so – and take our thoughts off too, don't you know? – did you desert us at the very door?' (p. 58). What horrifies her most in this imagined scene in which the disciplinary roles have been reversed is the children's 'false little lovely eyes' – the falsity of their pretended innocence as, in their precocious knowledge, they scrutinise the conduct of the person supposedly charged with supervising their own.

V

Visual relations govern not only the content of *The Turn of the Screw* but also its enunciation. The governess's first-person narration ensures that the events in her story and her struggle to contend with them are presented without recourse to some external source of privileged knowledge. Such knowledge, though it would be revealed in the text discursively, would nevertheless imply a transcendent gaze: one capable (through the conventions of focalisation) of seeing 'inside' the governess and knowing what she is thinking. James's use of homodiegetic first-person narration (the governess as teller of her own story) amounts to a refusal to endorse such a transcendent, disembodied gaze; so too does his appropriation of the romance conventions of framing, the word-for-word repetition of the same story by other tellers whose voices raise the possibility of critical distance, of alternative and possibly privileged 'points of view', without ever providing one. Instead, as the exchange of erotically-charged glances between characters in the narrative frame suggests, James seems to insist through the form of his tale that such a privileged, transcendent gaze has no objective existence; there are only partial, embodied *looks*.

Nevertheless, the governess's own self-exposure through her confessional narrative makes her easily appropriated as an object of a critical gaze, a relentless scrutiny that seeks to expose the governess more fully than she confessionally exposes herself. Edmund Wilson's famous reading of the tale, which decisively conjures away the ghosts as the neurotic symptoms of a 'thwarted Anglo-Saxon spinster', tinged this scrutiny almost from the beginning with a kind of hermeneutical voyeurism – a search for the 'truth' about the governess and the discovery that it lies in her sexuality.[42] Even where the governess's sexuality is not gleefully unveiled, the tendency is often for readers to sit in judgement upon her and declare her guilty: 'The real Evil is the supposedly innocent gaze which perceives in the world nothing but Evil, as in *The Turn of the Screw* by

Henry James, in which the real Evil is, of course, the gaze of the storyteller (the young governess) herself. ...' [43] What *The Turn of the Screw* reveals, though, is not so much the evil of any gaze as the complicated knot of visual relations in which the nineteenth-century middle-class woman might find herself caught.

From *Novel: A Forum on Fiction*, 26: 1 (1992), 43–63.

NOTES

[Beth Newman's essay presents a historical feminist examination of the gaze, governesses and female identity in *The Turn of the Screw*. First differentiating between 'look' and 'gaze', she takes Lacanian theorising of the 'mirror stage' as her starting point for a thoroughgoing analysis of the gendered code of visual relations perceived to underlie *The Turn of the Screw*. To this psychoanalytical slant Newman adds a Foucault-based historicised approach to visuality, drawing from and taking issue with Nancy Armstrong's *Desire and Domestic Fiction* (Oxford, 1987), in her exploration of the libidinal economy of seeing and being seen in this striking example of late nineteenth-century fiction. Ed.]

1.   Jacques Lacan, *The Four Fundamental Concepts of Psychoanalysis*, ed. Jacques-Alain Miller, trans. Alan Sheridan (New York), 1981, p. 75.

2.   Toni Morrison, *Beloved* (New York), 1987, p. 118.

3.   Laura Mulvey, 'Visual Pleasure and Narrative Cinema', *Screen*, 16 (1975), 6–18.

4.   Foucault discusses 'panopticism' in *Discipline and Punish: The Birth of the Prison*, trans. Alan Sheridan (New York, 1979), pp. 195–228; and the 'clinical gaze' in *The Birth of the Clinic: An Archeology of Medical Perception*, trans. Alan Sheridan (New York), especially pp. 107–23.

5.   See, for example, Stephen Heath, 'Difference', *Screen*, 19 (1978), 88–92; and Linda Williams, 'When the Woman Looks', in *Re-vision: Essays in Feminist Film Criticism*, ed. Mary Anne Doane et al. (Frederick, MD, 1984), pp. 83–99. I have argued elsewhere that *Wuthering Heights* represents the structures of looking whereby a woman's returning look is perceived – wrongly, in the novel's estimation – as threatening to male subjectivity: see 'The Situation of the Looker-On: Gender, Narration and Gaze in *Wuthering Heights*', *PMLA*, 105 (1990), 1029–41.

6.   Kaja Silverman, 'Fassbinder and Lacan: A Reconsideration of Gaze, Look and Image', *Camera Obscura*, 19 (1989), 59.

7. Shoshana Felman, for example, discusses the 'seductive *play of glances*' in her famous 'Turning the Screw of Interpretation', *Literature and Psychoanalysis: The Question of Reading: Otherwise*, ed. Shoshana Felman (Baltimore, MD, 1982), pp. 131–2. More recently, Terry Heller, *The Turn of the Screw: Bewildered Vision* (Boston, 1989) considers the importance of the visual in *The Turn of the Screw*, often in ways similar to my own consideration of the same issues.

8. I specify 'professional' readers because my experience in the classroom has taught me that the assumptions made by literary critics in this regard may not be shared by the general reading public (whatever that may be). Students of mine several years ago all assumed that the unnamed narrator of James's tale was female. My attempts as a knowing, 'jaded' reader (as James puts it in the tale's preface) to persuade them that the narrator was male, and the flirtation between 'him' and Douglas therefore subtly homoerotic, were undermined by my students' arguing persuasively that I had no reason to assume a male narrator other than the absence of feminine markers. Recently critics have made similar arguments; see e.g. Michael J. H. Taylor, 'A Note on The First Narrator *The Turn of the Screw*', *American Literature*, 53 (1982), 717–22. Linda Kauffman similarly considers in her chapter on *The Turn of the Screw* 'the ways in which the tale is transformed if one reads *as if* [the unnamed narrator] were female': *Discourses of Desire: Gender, Genre and Epistolary Fictions* (Ithaca, NY, 1986), p. 230; and Benjamin Newman, though aware of the lack of textual markers indicating the narrator's gender, assumes that the narrator is female because 'Everything fits just right if she is': *Searching for the Figure in the Carpet in the Tales of Henry James: Reflections of an Ordinary Reader* (New York, 1987), p. 92. 'Everything' in the context provided by this self-styled 'ordinary reader' refers to the narrator's apparent intimacy with Douglas.

9. Henry James, *The Turn of the Screw*, ed. Robert Kimbrough (New York, 1966), the Norton Critical Edition, p. 3. Subsequent citations refer to this edition and will appear in the text.

10. For a discussion of the relations of seeing as they apply to homoerotic currents in James's fiction (especially *The Wings of the Dove*), see Michael Moon, 'Sexuality and Visual Terrorism in *The Wings of the Dove*', *Criticism*, 28 (1986), 427–43.

11. The salient exception is a quotation from *Coward Conscience*, an 1879 novel by Frederick W. Robinson. It reads: 'Ursula ... "fixed" Mrs Coombes with a steady, searching stare'. The quotation marks around 'fixed' register some discomfort with the usage.

12. Lacan, 'The mirror stage as formative of the function of the I as revealed in psychoanalytic experience', *Ecrits: A Selection*, trans. Alan Sheridan (New York, 1977), pp. 2–4. The 'mirror stage' has been

invoked in relation to this scene in Christine Brooke-Rose, *A Rhetoric of the Unreal: Studies in Narrative and Structure, Especially of the Fantastic* (Cambridge, 1981), p. 161, and in Heller, *Bewildered Vision*, pp. 43–8. The governess's ambivalent confrontations with the mirror may in this light be a telling convention of governess fiction. For example, when the title figure of Anne Brontë's *Agnes Grey* (Harmondsworth, 1988) confronts herself in the mirror on arriving at the home of the Bloomfield family, her first employers, she too experiences a sense of physical insufficiency. The terms of this experience seem more 'superficial' (that is, more explicitly concerned with the accidents of her dress than with something like 'self' or 'being'), but may register a similar crisis of identity in response to felt social inferiority: 'I was somewhat dismayed at my appearance on looking in the glass ... the cold wind had swelled and reddened my hands, uncurled and entangled my hair, and dyed my face of a pale purple; add to this my collar was horribly crumpled, my frock splashed with mud, my feet clad in stout new boots, and as the trunks were not brought up, there was no remedy, so ... I proceeded to clomp down the two flights of stairs ... and ... found my way into the room where Mrs Bloomfield awaited me' (p. 74).

13. Her metaphor of being 'strangely at the helm' of a drifting ship (p. 10) even suggests the 'motor incapacity' of the infant who jubilantly confronts his/her image in the mirror in Lacan's account: 'The mirror stage', p. 2.

14. Ibid.

15. Ibid.

16. Ibid., pp. 1, 2.

17. Ibid., p. 2. The first insertion of French (in parentheses) is Sheridan's; the one in square brackets is mine. *Figer*, the word 'fixes' here translates, means to clot, congeal, or freeze. Perhaps what all these words (including 'fix') mean, in this context, is 'reify'.

18. Ibid.

19. Ibid., p. 4.

20. One could say of *The Turn of the Screw* what Kaja Silverman says of Fassbinder's films: 'subjectivity is ... shown to depend upon a visual agency which remains insistently outside' (Silverman, 'Fassbinder and Lacan', p. 57).

21. M. Jeanne Peterson, 'The Victorian Governess: Status Incongruence in Family and Society', in *Suffer and Be Still: Women in the Victorian Age*, ed. Martha Vicinus (Bloomington, IL, 1972), pp. 3–19.

22. For the argument about the proximity in the mid-century discourse of the governess to the working-class woman, the lunatic and the fallen

woman, see Mary Poovey, 'The Governess and *Jane Eyre*', *Uneven Developments: The Ideological Work of Gender in Mid-Victorian England* (Chicago, 1988), pp. 146–63.

23. Recent remarks on the relationships between *Jane Eyre* and *The Turn of the Screw* include Kauffman, *Discourses of Desire*, 209–11; and Alice Petry, 'Jamesian Parody, *Jane Eyre*, and *The Turn of the Screw*', *Modern Language Studies*, 13 (1983), 61–78.

24. Heller, *Bewildered Vision* (p. 45) usefully discusses the governess's need for approving reflections herself not only from the inhabitants of Bly but also from Douglas, and makes this need the motivating force behind her storytelling.

25. 'Repression', p. 147: seeing and being seen function as aspects of an 'instinct' (*treib*) Freud discusses as scopophilia [*Schaulust*] in *Three Essays in the Theory of Sexuality*, *The Standard Edition of the Complete Psychological Works of Sigmund Freud*, ed. and trans. James Strachey (London, 1955), vol. 7, pp. 156–7, 169. Lacan renames this drive or instinct the 'scopic drive' (*Four Fundamental Concepts*, pp. 180–4). For him the object of this drive has not the body or body-parts but the gaze itself – a structure of 'seeingness' or '*voyure*' (p. 82) – as its sought-for object, as that which the subject (unconsciously) imagines will close a hole in being. I am arguing not that the entire scopic drive is repressed in the governess, but that the wish it produces of being seen undergoes repression.

26. Freud, 'On Narcissism', 7, p. 43.

27. See Oscar Cargill, '*The Turn of the Screw* and Alice James' (1963), reprinted in *The Turn of the Screw* (Norton Critical Edition), pp. 145–65.

28. *The Diary of Alice James*, ed. Leon Edel (Harmondsworth, 1982).

29. In strictly Freudian terms, repression of a wish often depends upon other factors such as infantile wishes and memories of the kind we are not usually granted in literary texts. But my intention here is not to 'psychoanalyse' the governess – though I must plead guilty to doing that – but rather to see the governess as a figure representing larger cultural patterns. And though a wide social gulf separates this poor parson's daughter from the far more socially privileged Alice James, with the ascendancy of the middle classes and their values, both would be to some degree governed by the same social codes.

30. Nancy Armstrong, *Desire and Domestic Fiction: A Political History of the Novel* (Oxford, 1987), p. 77.

31. Ibid., pp. 76–7.

32. Ibid., p. 77.

33. Ibid., p. 278, note 42.

34. Ibid., p. 80.

35. Ibid., p. 81. I should emphasise that Armstrong's point about the shift in the nature of the gaze is only one point in a much larger, and to my mind very persuasive, argument about the history of the novel and the construction of femininity. I seize upon it nonetheless, and not only because of its usefulness for my own argument. Armstrong's reading of the gaze (a misreading, as I argue below) is related to a problem with the book's larger argument about the power of the domestic woman. In stressing 'the particular power that our culture does give to middle-class women' in preference to extending 'the rhetoric of victimisation' (which she is careful, nevertheless, not to reject entirely), Armstrong tends to elide the ways in which this very limited power ultimately served the interests of the male head of the household. (It was limited, for example, by legal convention of *couverture* that made married women non-persons legally and therefore powerless in their invisibility.)

36. I am adapting an observation made by Joan Copjec, in 'Cutting Up', *Between Feminism and Psychoanalysis*, ed. Teresa Brennan (New York, 1989). Addressing the difficulty, especially for feminism, of 'articulating the relation between psychoanalysis and politics', she writes: 'Too often these difficulties entail either the elimination of psychical reality, its virtual absorption by the social, or the elimination of social reality, which is conceived merely as a realisation of a given psychical relation between men and women. Each alternative foredooms feminist analysis, which depends on the existence of a psychical semi-independence from patriarchal structures' (p. 244). The 'elimination of psychical reality', its 'absorption' by the social, is precisely what limits Armstrong's account of the gaze in *Desire and Domestic Fiction*.

37. See Jacqueline Rose, 'George Eliot and the Spectacle of Woman', *Sexuality in the Field of Vision* (London, 1986), on the 'sexual fantasy' underwriting the Contagious Diseases Acts of the 1860s, a fantasy that involved 'the relentless and punishing scrutiny of the woman' (pp. 111–12).

38. James knew *Daniel Deronda* well; it is often regarded as the precursor text for *The Portrait of a Lady*, another novel about a naïve young woman who makes a disastrous marriage to a worldly and world-weary man. More to the purpose, it inspired a commentary in dialogue form that registers James's awareness of Eliot's interest in the relations of seeing. See Henry James, 'Daniel Deronda: A Conversation', *Partial Portraits* (New York, 1911). Toward the end of the conversation the following remarks are exchanged:

Pulcheria: She talks too much about the 'dynamic quality' of people's eyes. When she uses such a phrase as that in the first sentence in her book she is not a great literary genius, because she shows a want of tact. There can't be a worse limitation.

Constantius: The 'dynamic quality' of Gwendolen's glance has made a tour of the world.

(p. 82)

The 'dynamic quality' of Gwendolen's 'glance', the topic of the opening paragraph of *Daniel Deronda*, makes her beauty disturbing to the spectator (Daniel himself), who raises the question, 'Why was the wish to look again felt as coercion and not as a longing in which the whole being consents?' (p. 35). The answer suggested by the opening sentence is that her dynamic glance, her active looking, spoils the spectacle of her beauty by making her both subject and object of the look; presumably she ought to settle herself on one side or the other.

39. The argument that the text makes it impossible to determine whether or not the ghosts are real was made almost simultaneously by Felman and Brooke-Rose. More recently, some critics have sought to historicise the notions of undecidability and indeterminacy as concepts produced in a specific critical moment. See John Carlos Rowe, *The Theoretical Dimensions of Henry James* (London, 1985); Vincent Pecora, 'Of Games and Governesses', *Perspectives on Contemporary Literature*, 11 (1985), 28–36; and Elliot Schrero, 'Exposure in *The Turn of the Screw*', *Modern Philology*, 78 (1981), 261–74. On the possibility that the ghosts *are* hallucinations, cf. Heller, *Bewildered Vision* (p. 97): 'What if we interpret the ghosts as unconscious answers to [the governess's] conscious desire to be seen?' He stresses the governess's fragmentation 'under the pressure of the uncle's refusal to look at or hear her' (p. 99). I differ from Heller in regarding the desire to be seen as unconscious, and in calling attention to the interplay of this individual, psychical pressure with a social and historical one: the imperative towards inconspicuousness for middle-class women.

40. Sir George Stephen, *The Governess*, quoted in Schrero, 'Exposure', pp. 269–70. Schrero quotes this passage to argue that the governess, far from being the obsessional neurotic of much twentieth-century criticism on *The Turn of the Screw*, was simply doing her job as it was understood at mid-century as well as by James's contemporaries. While I am sympathetic with Schrero's impulse to get the governess off the couch, so to speak, and thus out from under a critical/clinical gaze, I cannot agree with his larger argument. He argues that the notion of 'undecidability' is an imposition onto James's tale by late twentieth-century readers ignorant of the tale's social and historical

context. To this end he recontextualises the tale in terms of middle-class fears about the presumably corrupting influences on children of working-class domestic servants and the atmosphere of sexual experimentation at public schools (such as the one from which Miles is expelled). The context Schrero provides is illuminating, but to push his anti-deconstructive arguments to the extreme that he does he must ignore the well-known ambiguities of James's writing and assume a single, identifiable intention governing the meaning of the tale.

41. In fact, one definition of 'fix', according to the *OED*, is 'To settle or determine the form of, give permanent form to', though the word is used this way only with relation to language or literature: e.g. fixing a version of a text, fixing the language, etc.

42. Edmund Wilson, 'The Ambiguity of Henry James', *The Triple Thinkers: Ten Essays on Literature* (New York, 1938), p. 132.

43. Slavoj Zizek, *The Sublime Object of Ideology* (London, 1989), p. 27.

7

Gender, History and Modernism in *The Turn of the Screw*

MARIANNE DeKOVEN

James's parallel distrust of the 'revolutionary horizon' was clear by 1886, the year he published *The Princess Casamassima* and *The Bostonians*.[1] In *The Turn of the Screw*, issues of female power, sexuality, and autonomy and issues of class inequality are muted but crucial. They are also linked. In the 1908 New York Edition Preface to *The Turn of the Screw*, an extended metaphor that could have been taken straight from Theweleit[2] uses water to represent the impossible dialectic of unleashing and at the same time restraining the imagination. This metaphor serves as an apt introduction to my argument here:

> Nothing is so easy as improvisation, the running on and on of invention; it is sadly compromised, however, from the moment its stream breaks bounds and gets into flood. Then the waters may spread indeed, gathering houses and herds and crops and cities into their arms and wrenching off, for our amusement, the whole face of the land – only violating by the same stroke our sense of the course of the channel, which is our sense of the uses of a stream and the virtue of a story. Improvisation, as in the Arabian Nights, may keep on terms with encountered objects by sweeping them in and floating them on its breast; but the great effect it so loses – that of keeping on terms with itself.[3]

Note the flood's femininity, both in its implied association with Scheherezade and in 'floating them on its breast', and its concomitant suggestiveness of revolution. Again, the feminine revolutionary horizon promises/threatens to write a wholly new story, which is precisely how James describes *The Turn of the Screw* elsewhere in the Preface: 'The thing had for me the immense merit of allowing the imagination absolute freedom of hand, of inviting it to act on a perfectly clear field, with no "outside" control involved, no pattern of the usual or the true or the terrible "pleasant" (save always of course the high pleasantry of one's own form) to consort with.'[4]

This narrative, says James, must be at once totally free and strictly restrained; subsequently, the critical history of *The Turn of the Screw* has made it a locus classicus of 'ambiguity'.[5] The 1934 essay by Edmund Wilson that instituted the interpretive controversy that still rages in relation to his essay almost sixty years later is entitled 'The Ambiguity of Henry James'.[6] The controversy of course concerns whether it is the protagonist or the children who are 'guilty', whether the ghosts are 'real' or projections, as Wilson argues, of the protagonist's repressed sexuality.

This controversy has spawned the remarkable terms 'apparitionist' and 'antiapparitionist', and on several counts, terminological self-consciousness is important in approaching criticism of this story. By convention, the character I have been calling the 'narrator' or the 'protagonist' is referred to as the 'Governess'. The framing narrator who introduces the tale is referred to as '*the* narrator' or the 'I' (we consider Marlow, not the framing narrator, *the* narrator of *Heart of Darkness*). Evidently, such a view fixes the protagonist in, and defines her by, her subordinate class-gender status, while it confers on the male framer the privileged status of centred subjectivity, of reader-identified selfhood. James, however, makes *her* the focal narrative agency, the organising Jamesian consciousness. One might argue that James emphasises so explicitly the authorial prowess of the protagonist – 'Douglas … had begun to read with a fine clearness that was like a rendering to the ear of the beauty of his author's hand' (p. 14) – that he has made some of his readers uncomfortable enough to reascribe his authorisation.[7]

Much of the 'antiapparitionist' criticism is highly critical of the 'Governess', frequently in a way that invokes misogynist stereotypes, emphasising her 'vanity', her pushiness, her delusional sexual frustration (like the 'old maid' who is imagined to imagine rapists), her supposedly aggrandised notion of her position at Bly.[8] If the ghosts are not 'real', then one must feel a combination of pity and contempt for the hysterical, repressed, deluded and deluding

'Governess'. One must also ultimately judge her guilty at least of tormenting innocent children, at most of murder. (But what can one expect of a poor, badly educated country parson's daughter?) James's strong statements on behalf of his protagonist's strength, intellect, and probity, and of the 'reality' of his ghosts, are easily dismissed by these 'antiapparitionists'. (I am not suggesting, of course, that his statements be given either unquestioning credence or the unquestioned authority of 'authorial intention'; rather, that such easy dismissal of them becomes readable as an act of repression.)

The debate over *The Turn of the Screw* reproduces the hierarchical either/or paradigm that has covered and distorted modernist ambivalence. *The Turn of the Screw* moves into a realm beyond ambiguity, a realm of pure irresolvable contradictoriness, where powerful evidence of the ghosts' reality *coexists* in the text with equally powerful evidence of their unreality.[9] As Leo Bersani says, in *A Future for Astyanax*, 'the very question of what is "true" is made irrelevant ... the questions of the ghosts' reality and of the governess's repressions are unanswerable.'[10]

Bersani also claims that those questions are unanswerable 'because *The Turn of the Screw* raises no questions at all'.[11] Bersani's emphasis is on the power of the Jamesian consciousness to generate narrative virtually unaided by standard fictional impedimenta. The protagonist is the Jamesian character par excellence, who, as assimilated to Jamesian authorship, 'released from the obligation of having to operate within a clearly and distinctly given world of fictional events, assumes the function of novelising.'[12] Bersani gives her almost unlimited power, more even than she claims for herself, but in doing so he suppresses the 'questions' of gender and class that this text clearly 'raises'.

Reading *The Turn of the Screw* in conjunction with 'The Yellow Wallpaper' and in relation to Jamesian ambivalence concerning the concomitant claims to power and equality of women and of the 'lower orders' yields no 'definitive' reading of the text – needless to say, and particularly here, there is no such thing – nor is it intended to replace psychoanalytic, epistemological, or deconstructive readings.[13] But such a reading does constitute the text in suggestive ways not otherwise apparent (all that any reading can finally hope to do).

James postulates, in this story, a protagonist disadvantaged by gender and class, who nonetheless rises determinedly to the frightening challenge posed by the class advantage of both 'master' and children and the absolute hereditary cultural proprietorship represented by Miles, the 'little gentleman', heir to the haunted ancestral house. These children need not be seen as the helpless innocents they appear when class issues are elided from a reading of this text. In fact, one might argue that if they were not lowered, as it were, nearer their governess's status by their age, there would be no story for this protagonist – no possibility of such a poignantly valiant self-assertion on her part. The gulf would be too great.

The protagonist displaces her erotic engagement with the unreachable 'master' onto his house and its inhabitants, his other dependants, as James concomitantly displaces the master's chilling power over the narrative and the protagonist to the same location.[14] The plot is generated by the protagonist's battle to bridge, by an eroticised self-assertion, the distance the master has imposed between her and his world of hereditary masculine upper-class privilege. Peter Quint and Miss Jessel always appear to the protagonist in relation to episodes or situations that make this self-assertion problematic. I would argue that they are figures of her fear of, and James's ambivalence about, such a gender- and class-specific claim to power.

As figures, their particularity constitutes a multiple or overdetermined representation. Like the 'governess' and the beautiful, angelic-demonic orphan children, they are stock types of Victorian melodramatic fiction. Peter Quint, with full name but no title, is the licentious, drunken, presumptuous seducer, with red hair and a bold expression. Miss Jessel, with no first name but the 'Miss' of her own governess position, is the tragic, doomed, darkly beautiful female victim-monster.[15] They are apparitions of the Victorian past of narrative and political possibility. Quite literally, they represent the past of this narrative: the dark secret of this haunted house, the limits against which the protagonist attempts to define a new order of narrative and social power, where the consciousness and *vision* of a poor, badly educated woman of undistinguished birth can shape a fiction that defies both 'the master's' power and the spectres of Victorian sexual and narrative scenarios (in fact, the narrative is set at midcentury). The apparitions simply haunt the protagonist's acts of self-assertion. She is at war with them for control of the children, the future.

She first sees Peter Quint when she is in the act of claiming various prerogatives of power. Issues of power are frequently

figured for her by images of water: At the end of the first chapter, in
'possession' of Bly, she says she 'had the fancy' that she, the children, Mrs Grose, and the other servants are 'almost as lost as a
handful of passengers in a great drifting ship. Well, I was, strangely,
at the helm!' (p. 18). She represents her position here in a telling
paradox: she is 'at the helm' of a 'drifting' ship. She has all power;
she has no power.

In the sequence leading up to her first encounter with Quint, she
says that the summer after Miles returns from school is 'the first
time, in a manner, that I had known space and air and freedom'
(p. 24), but then compares her charges to 'little grandees, princes of
the blood' (p. 25), as if reminding herself of their actual position
relative to her. In these long summer days, she allows herself 'what
I used to call *my own hour*, the hour when, for my pupils, tea-time
and bed-time having come and gone, I had, before my final retire-
ment, a small interval alone. Much as I liked my companions, this
hour was the thing in the day I liked most. ... I could take a turn
into the grounds and enjoy, *almost with a sense of property* that
amused and flattered me, the beauty and dignity of the place'
(p. 25, italics added).

She strolls through the estate, feeling that she possesses it, possesses herself, possesses at least a small piece of time. As she strolls,
she thinks with complacency, even self-flattery (and her language
here is used against her by some 'antiapparitionists'), of her success
in fulfilling the requirements of the absent master for whose sake
she is undertaking her difficult assignments, the man 'to whose
pressure I had responded' (p. 25). Precisely in her moment of claiming power, she thinks erotically of her absolute subordination to
him. She concludes that she is '*a remarkable* young woman' – a
very ambiguous word that is used repeatedly to describe the children, a word that encompasses James's simultaneous approval and
disapproval of her claims.

'Plump, one afternoon, in the middle of my very hour', just as she
is fantasising that the master will suddenly appear to her, smiling
and approving, his knowledge of her successful sacrifices for him
shining in his handsome face, she sees instead Peter Quint, the embodiment not only of the male sexual aggression she is both suppressing and representing in her benign fantasy of the master's
approval, but also of the melodramatic fictional scenario and the
Victorian scenario of gender relations that she is attempting to
rewrite and redress in her claims to authorship, power, autonomy,

even a sort of equality with the master, figured for her by her fantasy of their mutual understanding.

Just when she thinks she will encounter the master at mutual eye-level, the double of his questionable and sinister power appears in a position of *illegitimate* superiority. The symbolic significance of Peter Quint's location, or the protagonist's placing of him, is almost parodically overloaded. He is standing high above her in a tower, specifically the 'old' tower (there are two towers, 'old' and 'new'); he 'fixes' her with a bold 'scrutiny', he is 'very erect'.[16] He becomes almost a textbook illustration of phallic symbolism, and as a phallus he is clearly invested with power and proprietorship. The overdone quality of this symbolism, like the characterisation and behaviour of the master whom Quint hideously duplicates, is in line with the 'old tower' itself – the bankrupt conventions of the fiction and society dominated by such an extreme of male power.

Most tellingly, with the statement 'I saw him as I see the letters I form on this page' (p. 28), James reminds us that the protagonist is the authorial sensibility, and also literally the author of the manuscript that *is* the story. At the same time, her stature as author is undermined, along with the other power and freedom she claims, by this emanation of the killing 'old' story from which hers must be wrested. The apparition of Quint, both punishing and monitory, appears like an earlier version in a palimpsest, threatening to blot out the narrative she is trying to write.

The first encounter with Quint establishes a structure opposite to that of 'The Yellow Wallpaper', where apparitions were generated by the narrator's self-repression. The second encounter with Quint establishes a counter-structure within *The Turn of the Screw* similar to the structure of 'The Yellow Wallpaper'. The situation of this encounter is precisely opposite to that of the first. Rather than feeling her freedom and power, the narrator is feeling oppressed, troubled by the mystery of Miles's dismissal from school – the painful challenge to which she is not at all sure she can rise – and by reminders of her origin, her past, rather than feeling elevated by fantasies of her empowering present or gratifying future: 'I was in receipt in these days of disturbing letters from home, where things were not going well' (p. 31).

As in 'The Yellow Wallpaper', it is rain – masculine water overwhelming and permeating the atmosphere – that precipitates this development: 'There was a Sunday – to get on – when it rained with such force and for so many hours that there could be no procession to church' (p. 31). Church is a locus, of course, of convention, tradition, the old, established hierarchies of class and gender. Deluging rain prevents the orderly *procession* to church, but only temporarily, long enough to enact for the protagonist the agon of her rebellion against orderly procession. The rain stops; they are on their way to evening service; she has forgotten her gloves – left them in 'that cold, clean *temple* of mahogany and brass, the "grown-up" dining room' (pp. 31–2), italics added). This dining room, 'temple' of legitimate authority, becomes the very important setting of the protagonist's final struggle. Here it is the setting of her humility: rather than presiding in dignity over the formal Sunday dining room tea, she had been enacting her lowly status by sewing her (worn-out?) gloves: 'I remembered a pair of gloves that had required three stitches and that had received them – with a publicity perhaps not edifying – while I sat with the children at their tea' (p. 31). Reminded of her 'perhaps not edifying' position, as she is about to join the procession to church, she sees Quint through the dining room window: 'One step into the room had sufficed; my vision was instantaneous; it was all there' (p. 32). Her position – 'it was all there' – is revealed to her in a moment of 'instantaneous vision'. Quint, embodiment of that position, appears to her 'with a *nearness* that represented a forward stride in our intercourse' (p. 32, italics added): instead of striking us as the master's dark double, he now strikes us as hers. Like her, he is now positioned as the excluded, in the classic posture of the disenfranchised, outside the window looking in. His bold stare through the window is now a challenge to constituted authority identical to her challenge. He figures her fear of, and uncertainty about, her claim, that is, James's own ambivalence about it.

With hindsight, we can now see him as having been her double, as well as the master's, in the first encounter too. He appeared then in a position of threatening, illegitimate proprietorship just when she was feeling the fullness of her own, illegitimate(?) claim to equality and proprietorship. In the first encounter, the sight of Quint undermined her too-easy, self-flattering sense of successful mastery. In the second encounter, the consolidation of her knowledge of her marginality, the falseness of her claim to be an insider – to see Quint looking in from outside the window is to see it all clearly – brings to her a new knowledge: 'On the spot there came to me the added shock of a certitude that it was not for me he had come there. He had come for someone else' (p. 32).

She disavows her direct connection to Quint, even as she literally puts herself in his position: she immediately runs outside to stand just where he had stood, looking through the window. Mrs Grose comes into the dining room, sees her there, and is terrified in her turn (the hierarchical 'procession' of intimidation). Her decision that Quint has 'come for someone else' is just as much an act of identification with him as it is a denial of that identification. Like Quint, she has 'come for someone else': come to Bly for the master's sake and for service to the children. But 'come for' is of course also a statement of a sinister desire to take possession. The object of that desire, the 'someone else', now becomes Miles, the inheritor of patriarchal upper-class authority, power, autonomy, legitimacy. Miles's name reminds us of that echt-masculine stock character, *Miles Gloriosus*. He is, of course, usually 'little Miles', putting him within her reach. Flora's name evokes a feminine vegetation goddess, an evocation reinforced by her association with water and plants. The first initials of the two names, *M* and *F*, make them together an allegory of gender.

The narrator's new knowledge, the displacement or focusing of her struggle for power onto possession of Miles, strengthens her shaken resolve: 'The flash of this knowledge – for it was knowledge in the midst of dread – produced in me the most extraordinary effect, started, as I stood there, a sudden vibration of duty and courage' (p. 32). This 'vibration of duty and courage,' courage acceptable because imagined as being in the service of duty rather than ambition, focuses itself, in subsequent conversation with Mrs Grose (whose name wonderfully exonerates her from all trials of consciousness) as a determination to assert her power in order to 'save' the children – a goal not questionable, troubling, frightening, as her desire to be generally in charge of Bly evidently was. Her fantasy of noble self-sacrifice, with the master, one imagines, always in mind as admiring audience and instigator, puts her right back in the masochistic Victorian feminine scenario: 'I had an absolute certainty that I should see again what I had already seen, but something within me said that by offering myself bravely as the sole subject of such experience, by accepting, by inviting, by surmounting it all, I should serve as an expiatory victim and guard the tranquillity of my companions. The children, in especial, I should thus fence about and absolutely save' (p. 39).

But the desire for power leaks through the many cracks in this safe masochistic fantasy. She will continue to 'see': to be the sole governing consciousness ('sole subject of such experience'). She will offer herself 'bravely'; she will invite, surmount, and guard: verbs of active power. She will 'fence about and absolutely save' the children: a vision of absolute control, asserted more safely in the service of her ostensible repudiation of self-assertion.

She is now ready to meet the double of her (partial) acceptance of the Victorian feminine position. Her vision of noble self-sacrifice generates the apparition of the doomed, tragic, ruined former governess. Her first and last encounters with Miss Jessel take place across a body of water, the small lake or pond of the estate. Like the first two encounters with Quint, they reverse the relative positions of protagonist and apparition. In the first encounter, Miss Jessel appears to the protagonist with the body of water and Flora herself, her back turned to the site of the apparition, between them.

This encounter is preceded by a consolidation for the protagonist of her position of power gotten paradoxically by self-sacrifice. Masochism is always an obverse form of power, of course, but here the 'secondary benefit' is foregrounded emphatically: 'I was in these days literally able to find a joy in the extraordinary flight of heroism the occasion demanded of me. I now saw that I had been asked for a service admirable and difficult; and there would be a greatness in letting it be seen – oh, in the right quarter! – that I could succeed where many another girl might have failed' (p. 42). She delivers herself over to the children, she 'walk[s] in a world of their invention' (p. 43), and they make her, in their fantasy games, 'some remarkable person' of 'superior ... exalted stamp' (p. 43).

The protagonist is playing some such game with Flora, 'on the edge of the lake', which, in the game, is the 'Sea of Azof': a wonderful figure of putative or hypothetical possession. They are sitting where the 'old trees, the thick shrubbery, made a great and pleasant shade': overgrown, shady verdure, the world of 'Flora', adjacent to a body of water; precisely the site of female freedom and eroticised empowerment imagined by Gilman in 'The Yellow Wallpaper'. She is again sewing, reminding us of her position in her last encounter with Quint.

The language in which she afterward describes to Mrs Grose the appearance of Miss Jessel is straight from the melodramatic mode into which she has temporarily lapsed: 'a figure of ... unmistakable horror and evil: a woman in black, pale and dreadful – with such an air also, and such a face!' (p. 46). But during the encounter itself, what she focuses on, and describes calmly, with restraint, is Flora's activity:

> She had picked up a small flat piece of wood, which happened to have in it a little hole that had evidently suggested to her the idea of sticking in another fragment that might figure as a mast and make the thing a boat. This second morsel, as I watched her, she was very markedly and intently attempting to tighten in its place. My apprehension of what she was doing sustained me so that after some seconds I felt I was ready for more. Then I again shifted my eyes – I faced what I had to face.
>
> (p. 45)

Flora's action suggests 'the turn of the screw' – that multifarious figure of aggressive sexuality, associated with children, that governs the text. Peter Quint and Miss Jessel are damnable seducer and damned seduced; in turn they become seducers of the children. The protagonist's struggle is with her own 'illicit' desire for the master and for mastery, displaced onto his future heirs and haunted by his past retainers. Flora's neat objective correlative of the sexual consummation that would provide a 'boat' – a means of actually embarking on the dangerous waters of these desires without being overwhelmed by them – gives the protagonist the courage to face, and face down by splitting the image off from herself, the embodiment of her own inscription in melodrama.

The encounter with Miss Jessel marks the end of the first movement of the story. The protagonist has detached from herself, as apparitions, the threatening aspects of her claims to power, autonomy, sexual self-expression. Peter Quint, the seducer, is 'no gentleman';[17] he is an illegitimate usurper of the master's position, even to the point of appearing to the protagonist in the master's stolen clothes. Miss Jessel, a 'lady' – respectable like the protagonist – has been dragged down to Peter Quint's class level by her sexuality.

In the middle section of the book, once the protagonist has decided that the children 'know'– that they are Quint's and Miss Jessel's accomplices – she sees Quint *below* her on the stairs, faces him 'in our common intensity' (p. 59), and feels no fear. She has joined him in the quest for socially and sexually illegitimate power, even as the overt version of that quest takes a noble, self-sacrificing, orthodox form: 'dread had unmistakably quitted me and ... there was nothing in me there that didn't meet and measure him' (p. 59).

Miss Jessel appears to her as only pathetic, sitting, again on the staircase *below* the protagonist – these issues of relative positioning are crucial – and then sitting wretchedly at the nursery table. She becomes an expression of the protagonist's own increasing wretchedness at her total abandonment by the master. Miss Jessel seems at first to be a servant 'writing a letter to her sweetheart' as she sits at the nursery table – a displacement and reversal, as well as an echo (servant) of the protagonist's own hopeless erotic position. She cannot bring herself to write to the master; when she does at last, the letter is stolen by Miles, the heir.

The despair she feels at her decision that the children 'know' – that they are demonic rather than angelic, though potentially savable – enables her to redouble her efforts at control. She will enclose them, win them over, possess them. Her impulse toward self-assertion has found a socially, fictionally, and theologically acceptable channel, but a channel that *James* presents as having become sinister and frightening just when the apparitions have become so much less so.

In fact, the apparitions cease for the moment to appear. The climactic episode of this section begins with the protagonist discovering Flora looking out of the window. She assumes Flora is communing with Miss Jessel, but the girl is in fact looking at Miles, who has gone outside and is looking at some point on the tower above the grand, stately, chillingly empty (master?) bedroom that the protagonist has decided is the best vantage point for her to observe an apparition on the lawn that she thinks will be Miss Jessel. The protagonist is literally not positioned at this moment to see what Miles is looking at on the tower, though she assumes it is Quint. This episode enacts the futility of the protagonist's position: she cannot inhabit the master bedroom legitimately; she is not entitled to encounter the children directly – they are looking elsewhere. Although hers is the authorial consciousness, the only consciousness capable of vision, that vision can only be partial and misdirected, compromised as it is both by the illegitimacy of her claims and by her capitulation to her fear of that illegitimacy.

The narrative turning point comes in the appropriately gothic churchyard, on another aborted procession to church. Miles asserts, against the protagonist's assertion of power over him, his ineluctable class and gender rights, rights that would inevitably be reasserted once the protagonist acceded to the domain in which they hold sway by redefining her struggle within such orthodox narrative-political boundaries. It is not James who elides or even suppresses issues of class and gender privilege in this text: 'Turned out for Sunday by his uncle's tailor ... Miles's whole title to independence, the rights of his sex and situation, were so stamped upon him that if he had suddenly struck for freedom I should have had nothing to say' (p. 77). On Sunday, on his way to church, legitimately apparelled in his own version of his uncle's clothes, his title and his rights, if openly claimed, would obliterate hers. They would in fact silence her, terminating her continuing effort, however compromised, to write a different story.

In the final movement of the text, the now openly acknowledged power struggle between the protagonist and the children is organised around two culminating episodes, the first involving Flora and the closing episode, of course, Miles. In these two episodes, first Mrs Grose and then Miles himself fail to see, respectively, Miss Jessel and Quint, leaving the protagonist entirely alone, except for Mrs Grose's crucial continuing faith in her vision. ('It is certain my conviction gains infinitely, the moment another soul will believe in it', says Novalis in Conrad's epigraph to *Lord Jim*.)

The penultimate episode releases the protagonist from both the earth-bound, non-visionary, traditionally female world of motherly 'Mrs Grose' and also from the melodramatic plot within which she has self-defeatingly cast herself as noble, piteous heroine. This episode is saturated with water: there has been a storm the previous night (in which the protagonist has confronted Miles, inconclusively, with his guilty 'knowledge'); the afternoon is 'damp and grey' (p. 94). On this rainy day, Miles beguiles the protagonist with music, drawing her into his privileged world of high culture and accomplishment. Flora meanwhile 'escapes' to the lake; at last missing her, the protagonist annexes Mrs Grose and goes to look for her. She opens the first of the two chapters that narrate this episode with a digression on 'sheets of water':

> We went straight to the lake, as it was called at Bly, and I dare say rightly called, though I reflect that it may in fact have been a sheet of water less remarkable than it appeared to my untravelled eyes. My acquaintance with sheets of water was small, and the pool of Bly, at all events on the few occasions of my consenting, under the protection of my pupils, to affront its surface in the old flat-bottomed boat moored there for our use, had impressed me both with its extent and its agitation.
>
> (pp. 94–5)

Throughout the text, the protagonist's overall situation is described in water imagery, particularly as 'depths' to be 'sounded' or 'plunged' into (recall the 'great drifting ship' of which she is 'strangely at the helm' of the first chapter). The emphasis here is on the protagonist's inexperienced vision – her 'untravelled' eyes – and the shallowness of the water (a 'sheet' is a flat surface, suggesting, moreover, both beds and shrouds), an emphasis that is reiterated a paragraph later: 'the depth is, I believe, nowhere very great' (p. 95). It is also important to note the intimidating, threatening quality of the pool, despite its shallowness: 'its extent and agitation'. The female element is hostile; it is shallow but unfamiliar and threatening; it is aggrandised by the terminology of Bly, made a 'lake' rather than the mere 'pool' it really is. The protagonist is simultaneously intimidated by and contemptuous of it. I would argue that, at this point in the text, the negative component of James's ambivalence toward the feminine – his fear and contempt of female sexuality, in particular – is mobilised on behalf of the protagonist's coming battle with the social and narrative conventions of the feminine that, during the middle section of the story, have worked against her vision and her new narrative of power.

The protagonist's subsequent description of the 'pond' (a compromise between 'lake' and 'pool') confirms it as, at this moment of the text, a figure of female sexuality: 'The pond, oblong in shape, had a width so scant compared to its length that, with its ends out of view, it might have been taken for a scant river' (p. 96). In this fairly explicit vaginal image, the repetition of the word 'scant' signals a defence, by belittlement, against the clearly threatening quality of what is called in the very next sentence 'the empty expanse'.

Fairly dragging Mrs Grose behind her, the protagonist must skirt the rough perimeter of the pond, since Flora has taken the homely, reassuring 'old flat-bottomed boat', leaving the two women with no means to cross the hostile body of water. (The protagonist immediately knows that Flora has gone to the spot across the pond where Miss Jessel first appeared: see n. 9.) The protagonist's valour in the face of the threatening watery oblong and its surrounding tangle of nearly impenetrable vegetation is asserted here in her fortitude at braving the 'ground much broken' and the 'path choked with overgrowth' (p. 96), just as it is earlier, when she tells Mrs Grose they are going to look for Flora at the lake: '"You're going to the water, Miss? – you think she's *in* –?" "She may be, though the depth is, I believe, nowhere very great"' (p. 95). James is establishing the protagonist's ability to overcome what he represents as the watery grave of feminine superficiality, which he again, associates here with the dangers of female sexuality and the inability to *see* that Mrs Grose and Flora demonstrate in this episode – as we know from Irigaray, vision is masculine, blank watery embodiment feminine.[18]

What they are unable to see (or, in the case of Flora, what she perhaps refuses to acknowledge the sight of) is the alternative femininity that Miss Jessel has come to represent. While Flora was a figure simultaneously of a bankrupt Victorian narrative and also of a potentially new future, she had been allied with Miss Jessel. During this episode she openly repudiates both the vision of Miss Jessel and also the real presence of the protagonist, aligning herself instead entirely with Mrs Grose. James figures the bankruptcy of her mode of femininity by mocking her mythological name – as the protagonist and Mrs Grose approach her, where she stands 'on the grass' in a 'copse', she 'stoop[s]' to pick 'quite as if it were all she was there for – a big, ugly spray of withered fern' (p. 97). Her 'floral' loveliness has 'withered', become 'ugly'; moreover, it is now 'all she is there for' – she no longer offers the protagonist anything of worth.

The word 'ugly' is important, signalling the end of the protagonist's enchantment with Flora's Victorian angelic-demonic-melodramatic beauty. Flora first becomes 'old', a description of her that is repeated several times during the course of the episode. She has become, literally, the embodiment of the 'old' order, like the 'old' tower. As she turns toward Mrs Grose and against the protagonist and the vision she offers, looking at the protagonist with 'an expression of hard, still gravity, an expression ... that appeared to read and accuse and judge me', 'united' with Mrs Grose 'in pained opposition to me', Flora becomes to the protagonist not only 'ugly' but 'common': 'I prayed God to forgive me for seeming to see that, as she stood there holding tight to our friend's dress, her incomparable childish beauty had suddenly failed, had quite vanished. I've said it already – she was literally, she was hideously hard; she had turned common and almost ugly' (p. 101). Flora's speech repudiating the protagonist 'might have been that of a vulgarly pert little girl in the street' (p. 101). The beautiful fairy princess (one thinks of the fantasy games they play in the middle section of the book) has turned into a plain, vulgar commoner, fit only to be carried off by

Mrs Grose. The negative component of James's ambivalence about the 'revolutionary horizon' of redress of class inequity – his contempt for the lower orders – is mobilised here concomitantly with the negative component of his ambivalence toward women's new claims to equality. They are both deployed in the service of the protagonist, a relatively lowly woman, who is to be exempted from the negative judgement against women and the lower orders because of her saving power of consciousness, the writer's power of authorship, that power so prized by the modernists as the hope of redemption from cultural bankruptcy, the vision she has attained in the course of this story.

That vision, embodied in this episode as Miss Jessel, presents itself to her again across water; the female element of water both separates and unites the two women. The language of identification between the protagonist and Miss Jessel is heavily emphasised here: she appears just where the protagonist had sat with Flora in the first encounter; in insisting that Flora sees Miss Jessel, the protagonist says, 'you see her as well as you see me!' (p. 99). The protagonist's first reaction to the sight of Miss Jessel 'on the opposite bank' is a 'thrill of joy': 'she was there, and I was justified' (p. 98).

Miss Jessel is no shining figure of triumphant femininity, however. The protagonist establishes in her vision of Miss Jessel simultaneously her own power and her own 'evil'. To repudiate the conventional feminine is not at all, in this incipiently modernist text, to be free of it; quite the contrary, as Gilman's protagonist has already poignantly taught us. Where Gilman's protagonist pays the price of madness for capitulation to patriarchal authority, James's protagonist pays the price of 'damnation' for defiance of it.

Miss Jessel is a 'pale and ravenous demon' (p. 99), suggesting now vampirism rather than melodramatic victimhood. She rises 'erect on the spot my friend and I had lately quitted', a figure of masculinised power, 'and there was not, in all the long reach of her desire, an inch of her evil that fell short' (p. 99). An 'erect', potent, efficacious figure of 'evil desire', she simultaneously embodies and makes hideous the protagonist's libidinal and social ambitions. The phrase 'she's as big as a blazing fire' (p. 100) suggests, obviously, uncontrolled, destructive desire, damnation, and also the antithesis of water: to repudiate the feminine is to become a hideous, destructive, damned version of the masculine.[19]

When the protagonist turns 'to communicate again' with Miss Jessel, she is 'as vividly there for my disaster' as she is 'not there for my service' (p. 101). Nonetheless, she had felt a 'thrill of joy' at seeing her, and she sends her an 'inarticulate message of gratitude' (p. 99). The joy and gratitude are ostensibly for the 'service' the protagonist thinks Miss Jessel will render by finally showing herself to Mrs Grose and to Flora in her presence, thereby confirming the protagonist in her increasingly desperate control over the children. Similarly, the 'disaster' is presumably Mrs Grose's failure to see and Flora's failure, or refusal, to acknowledge the sight. But this language focuses, apart from, and in conjunction with, this issue, the paradox of the protagonist's situation: this appearance of Miss Jessel *is* simultaneously the protagonist's triumph and her disaster. The protagonist says, without explanation, precisely that. Mrs Grose's failure to see Miss Jessel, followed immediately by her annexation of Flora, marking the end of the protagonist's compromise with the old plots, produces this remarkable passage:

> with this hard blow of the proof that her [Mrs Grose's] eyes were hopelessly sealed I felt my own situation horribly crumble. I felt – I saw – my livid predecessor press, from her position, on my defeat, and I was conscious, more than all, of what I should have from this instant to deal with in the astounding little attitude of Flora. Into this attitude Mrs Grose immediately and violently entered, breaking, even while there pierced through my sense of ruin *a prodigious private triumph*, into breathless reassurance.
>
> (p. 100, italics added)

Through her sense of the 'ruin' of the painfully achieved status quo of the middle section of the book, a ruin marked by her separation from Mrs Grose and Flora, newly allied within the conventional feminine, pierces the 'prodigious private triumph' of her full allegiance with Miss Jessel, explicable only as the triumph of her emergence from that compromise into a fully realised, and fully damned, claim to power.

The crisis in this episode had been brought on by the protagonist's allowing herself at long last to utter Miss Jessel's name to Flora, thereby literally summoning her presence. When Flora asks her 'And where's Miles?' she responds: 'There was something in the small valour of it that quite finished me: these three words from her were, in a flash like the glitter of a drawn blade, the jostle of the cup that my hand, for weeks and weeks, had held high and full to the brim and that now, even before speaking, I felt overflow in a deluge' (p. 98). Drawn blade and overflowing cup: heavily

conventional symbols of the masculine and the feminine – the masculine invoked by the name of Miles, the feminine cup overflowing
in a deluge at the summoning of Miss Jessel. After Mrs Grose
whisks away the transformed Flora, who does not appear again in
the narrative, the protagonist swoons. When she comes to, she is on
the ground, aware only of 'an odorous dampness and roughness'
(p. 101). She gets up and sees 'the grey pool and its blank, haunted
edge' (p. 102): clearly (to me) a figure of antifemale sexual disgust.
The deluge has receded, leaving in its damp, blank residue a fore-
shadow of the protagonist's empty triumph, avatar of a damned
empowered maternal feminine, over the heir.

Mrs Grose and Flora fly to London and, presumably, the master's
protection, reintegrated into the order he represents. The protagonist assumes full command: 'It was precisely, in short, by just
clutching the helm that I avoided total wreck; and I daresay that, to
bear up at all, I became, that morning, very grand and very dry'
(p. 109). Far from finding herself 'strangely at the helm' of a 'great
drifting ship', she is 'clutching the helm' of a ship on the point of
'total wreck'. Saving the ship by means of such desperate but firm
and determined self-assertion keeps her 'very dry' and also makes
her 'very grand'. She becomes the lady of the house, taking meals
with Miles, who has assumed almost fully the position of the
master: with evident erotic displacement, she compares their em-
barrassed silence in the presence of the maid to that of 'some young
couple who, on their wedding-journey, at the inn, feel shy in the
presence of the waiter' (p. 112).

These silent meals are eaten in that crucial formal dining room.
(In case we have forgotten, the protagonist reminds us of its
significance: 'I had been waiting for him [Miles] in the ponderous
pomp of the room outside of the window of which I had had from
Mrs Grose, that first scared Sunday, my flash of something it would
scarce have done to call light' [p. 110].) She renounces the 'fiction
that I had anything more to teach him' (p. 110) – he has attained to
the rights of his gentlemanly status. It is with a young man, a gentleman and putative proprietor, not an orphaned child, that she has
her final contest.

The final episode is a fight to the death in the ring of the formal,
traditional, domestic interior, with the illegitimate claim to power
represented by Quint again relegated to marginality, positioned
outside looking in through the window. The language of this
episode is highly eroticised, and characterised by an intensification

of water imagery. The protagonist begins by eliciting from Miles a reluctant 'surrender', yielded up with 'the finest little quiver of resentful passion' (p. 115): an acknowledgement that there is something for him to confess. This surrender thrills her: 'I can't begin to express the effect upon me of an implication of surrender even so faint. It was as if what I had yearned for had come at last only to astonish me' (p. 115). She is delighted that he seems to be afraid of her, which is 'perhaps the best thing to make him' (p. 115). She describes herself as 'nearly reaching port' (p. 115), dry and in command.

Fortified by these successes, she works herself up to asking Miles whether he stole the letter she finally wrote to the master from the hall table the previous day, an act that officially confirms his 'evil', but also serves to place him literally in the master's position, the usurping but nonetheless functional recipient of the protagonist's letter to the master. As soon as she asks this question, Peter Quint appears at the window, embodiment of the illegitimacy not of Miles's theft of the master's right, because he is its legitimate heir, but rather the illegitimacy of the protagonist's claims. Only she can see Quint now: it is clear to her, and James confirms for the reader (by having Miles ask whether Miss Jessel is at the window) that Miles cannot see him. She is alone with Quint in the presence of Miles, just as she was alone with Miss Jessel in the presence of Mrs Grose and Flora.

Quint no longer offers a bold, challenging stare. His is now the 'white face of damnation' (p. 116), now that the protagonist has asserted mastery, taken on not just Flora but Miles himself, and is to be damned for it. The sight of Quint reconfirms her in her self-assertion: she is going to play the drama out to the end. She experiences her self-assertion sexually, 'enfold[ing]' Miles 'with a moan of joy' (p. 117). Her 'quickened courage' brings her a 'success' that is measured by the severing of 'communication' between Miles and Quint, itself again a measure to her of her empowerment as authorial consciousness, the only one who *sees*. With the damned, outcast usurper Quint as her dark double, she has taken command: 'I felt that the cause was mine and that I should surely get *all*' (p. 118; note the ambiguity of 'cause' and of the emphasised 'all', also the grammatical ambiguity of 'should').

She turns on Miles to press home her victory, shaking him, 'but it was for pure tenderness' (p. 118), to get from him a full confession, a total 'surrender'. Miles is suddenly submerged: 'He looked in vague pain all round the top of the room and drew his breath, two or three times over, as if with difficulty. He might have been standing at the bottom of the sea and raising his eyes to some faint green twilight' (p. 119). The protagonist is no longer at the helm of her ship, dry, near port. His 'surrender' (repeated again) and her 'victory' bring her for the first time into the water, the 'sea', first floating on the surface and then foundering in bottomlessness with Miles: 'I seemed to float not into clearness, but into a darker obscure, and within a minute there had come to me out of my very pity the appalling alarm of his being perhaps innocent. It was for the instant confounding and bottomless, for if he *were* innocent, what then on earth was *I*?' (p. 119). She is precisely *not* 'on earth', and there is no longer even any ship whose helm she can clutch. 'It', the consequence of her self-assertion, is 'confounding and bottomless'. The wreck has come, she is going down. The sea bordered by the 'revolutionary' class and gender 'horizon', across which she had hoped to steer her authorial ship to the port of a new social and narrative order, has become 'confounding and bottomless', enforcing its threat rather than yielding up its promise. Her victory is complete – she 'dispossesses' the gentleman-proprietor-heir – but she can do so only by killing him. If he is innocent, legitimate, then what on earth is she: doomed either to marginality and illegitimacy or to damnation. In 'The Yellow Wallpaper', a female-signed text fearing what it desires, female capitulation is damnation; in *The Turn of the Screw*, a male-signed text desiring what it fears, female (and subaltern) victory is damnation.

From Marianne DeKoven, *Rich and Strange: Gender, History, Modernism* (Princeton, NJ, 1991), pp. 47–63; 227–9.

NOTES

[Marianne DeKoven's essay is taken from her chapter entitled 'A Different Story: "The Yellow Wallpaper" and *The Turn of the Screw*', in which she reads James alongside the story by Charlotte Perkins Gilman (of 1892). We print the portion dealing with *The Turn of the Screw*, in which she takes a historical feminist approach to the issues of gendered power relations and modernism. DeKoven here engages with the Jamesian fear of (in contrast to Gilman's desire for) the 'revolutionary horizon' of emergent feminism and socialism in Victorian England. The two texts, interpreted as incipiently modernist expressions of ambivalence, feature a female protagonist's domination by a distant authoritarian male figure who, in initiating the narra-

tive, motivates her psychological struggle. In both texts the female protagonist narrates her own attempt to write a different story. Ed.]

1. [The phrase 'revolutionary horizon' is used several times in this
    chapter of DeKoven's book. The following note is given (p. 39) at
    the first mention. Ed.] See Gilman's socialist-feminist *Women and
    Economics* (1898; reprint, New York, 1966), and her feminist
    utopian novel *Herland* (1915; reprint, New York, 1979). See James's
    anti-feminist novel *The Bostonians* (1886; reprint, Harmondsworth,
    1966) and his anti-socialist, anti-monarchist novel *The Princess
    Casamassima* (1886; reprint, Harmondsworth, 1977).

2. [Klaus Theweleit, author of *Male Fantasies* (Minneapolis, 1987),
    originally published as *Männerphantasien* (Frankfurt, 1977–8):
    referred to elsewhere in DeKoven's study. Ed.]

3. Henry James, 'The New York Preface', quoted from *The Turn of the
    Screw*, ed. Robert Kimbrough (New York, 1966: the Norton Critical
    Edition), p. 119.

4. Ibid., p. 118.

5. For an account of this critical history, and particularly of the 'appari-
    tionist' versus 'antiapparitionist' debate, see Charles Thomas
    Samuels, *The Ambiguity of Henry James* (Urbana, IL, 1971). See also
    Shoshana Felman, 'Henry James: Madness and the Risks of Practice
    (Turning the Screw of Interpretation)', *Writing and Madness*, trans.
    Martha Noel Evans et al. (Ithaca, NY, 1985), pp. 141–247; and John
    Carlos Rowe, *The Theoretical Dimensions of Henry James* (Madison,
    Wl, 1984) [see essay 3. Ed.]. As Shlomith Rimmon says in *The
    Concept of Ambiguity* (Chicago, 1977): '*The Turn of the Screw* has
    been so firmly linked with ambiguity that even people who have not
    read it know that it is somehow supposed to be ambiguous' (p. 116).

6. Edmund Wilson, 'The Ambiguity of Henry James' (1934) reprinted in
    A Casebook on Henry James's The Turn of the Screw, ed. Gerald
    Willen (New York, 1960), pp. 115–53.

7. Henry James, *The Turn of the Screw and Other Stories*
    (Harmondsworth, 1969), pp. 7–121. Subsequent quotations from this
    source will hereafter be cited parenthetically in the text by page
    number.

8. See for example, Samuels, *The Ambiguity*, p. 13 (he accuses her of
    'vanity'). He also calls her 'a snob and a prude, conceited and self-
    justifying' (p. 16), 'murderously ruthless in expression of her ideals'
    (p. 20), and attacks her 'moral pretensions and class envy' (p. 21).
    Thomas M. Cranfill and Robert L. Clark, Jr, in *An Anatomy of The
    Turn of the Screw* (Austin, TX, 1965), portray her in almost hysteri-

cal terms as a sort of monstrous Big Nurse, referring to her 'concentration-camp surveillance' (p. 158).

9. The evidence against the apparitions' existence is that no one else beside the narrator sees them and that Mrs Grose and Flora in one episode, and Miles in another, explicitly fail to see them while they are appearing to the narrator. The evidence in favour of their existence is, first, that the narrator sees them in appropriate embodiment before she finds out from Mrs Grose who they are or what they should look like. She describes Peter Quint so accurately after her first encounter with him that Mrs Grose immediately knows it is he (pp. 36–7). (I would say that is the strongest piece of evidence in the text on either side of the debate.) Also, Flora does go to the spot across the pond where Miss Jessel first appeared to the narrator (p. 95). Finally, Miles, when he fails to see Peter Quint in the final episode, asks whether it is Miss Jessel at the window (pp. 120–1).

    That James himself was a convinced apparitionist is quite clear in the Preface: 'I recognise again, that Peter Quint and Miss Jessel are not "ghosts" at all, as we now know the ghost, but goblins, elves, imps, demons as loosely constructed as those of the old trials for witchcraft' ('The New York Preface', see note 3 above, p. 122).

10. Leo Bersani, *A Future for Astyanax: Character and Desire in Literature* (Boston, 1976), p. 139.

11. Ibid.

12. Ibid., p. 140.

13. Not, of course, an exhaustive list of contemporary critical approaches to James. As Richard A. Hocks says in *American Literary Scholarship 1986* (Durham, NC, 1988, p. 93): 'Like a huge magnet James continues to attract massive scholarship of every stripe and hue, from Adeline Tintner's "old-fashioned" source/analogue studies (a banner year, even for her) to the most theoretical day-after-tomorrow analysis. I detect a new thematic interest in James's "aestheticising of capitalism", as James Cox puts it, and more new psychoanalytic readings abound.'

14. See Felman and Rowe on the significance of the master's power. For a Foucauldian reading of issues of power in James, see Mark Seltzer, *Henry James and the Art of Power* (Ithaca, NY, 1984).

15. See Nina Auerbach, *Woman and the Demon: The Life of a Victorian Myth* (Cambridge, MA, 1982).

16. The evidence that Quint appears to the narrator on the old tower comes during her conversation with Mrs Grose following her second confrontation with him: '"Have you seen him before?" "Yes – once. On the old tower"' (p. 34).

17. This particular fact about Peter Quint is emphasised by reiteration: 'She thought a minute. "Was he a gentleman?" I found I had no need to think. "No." She gazed in deeper wonder. "No"' (p. 35). Again: '"He's tall, active, erect", I continued, "but never – no, never! – a gentleman"' (p. 36).

18. [Luce Irigaray: French feminist critic concerned with 'writing the female body' in such studies as *This Sex Which Is Not One*, trans. Catherine Porter with Carolyn Burke (Ithaca, NY, 1985), and referred to elsewhere in DeKoven's book. Ed.]

19. Miss Jessel is very close here to the 'blazing' Victorian madwoman, type of displaced feminist rage, discussed by Sandra Gilbert and Susan Gubar in *The Madwoman in the Attic: The Woman Writer and the Nineteenth-Century Literary Imagination* (New Haven, CT, 1979). Bertha Rochester of *Jane Eyre* is the locus classicus of this phenomenon. James's depiction of Miss Jessel in this scene is very similar (and perhaps indebted) to Brontë's of Bertha. *Jane Eyre* echoes through this tale of an ambitious governess as it does through 'The Yellow Wallpaper'.

8

'The Hideous Obscure': *The Turn of the Screw* and Oscar Wilde

RONALD KNOWLES

'The story *won't* tell, ... not in any literal, vulgar way', writes Henry James in the opening frame of his most famous tale.[1] Douglas is the speaker in the narratorial nest of Chinese boxes, but from a literal and vulgar point of view, developing from an anecdote, everything is indeed created by James's imagination, 'the imagination unassisted, unassociated – playing the game, making the score, in the phrase of our sporting day, off its own bat', as he claims in his later Preface.[2] Games have rules and in the ghost story mystery and mystification usually go hand in hand. Thus the reader can play the game – are Miss Jessel and Peter Quint 'real' ghosts, or hallucinations in the disintegrating mind of the governess? Is evil metaphysical and external, or psychological and internal, or both, the governess finally possessed by the Evil One?[3] What happens if the game is not played? A difficult question arises here, since James delights in activating the reader's literary credentials by planting fairly obvious red herrings, like allusions to Mrs Radcliffe's *The Mysteries of Udolpho* and Henry Fielding's *Amelia*, or suggesting analogies with Charlotte Brontë's *Jane Eyre*. Critics play the game and follow up the clues.[4] Between the 1890s and the 1990s, however, the goalposts have shifted, and the 'hideous obscure' as James calls it can be identified and named as something other than what may be immediately suggested in the story. Generally speak-

164

ing, the conventional rules of games remain constant, whereas the rules of conventional society can change completely. To be 'literal' and 'vulgar' now is perhaps to speak quite free from the censorship which prevailed then?

The Turn of the Screw attempts to provide a ghostly story for the Christmas season, but in fact puts Victorian society on trial, with Henry James as both defender and unwitting prosecutor. The origin of the tale was an anecdote. That anecdote was told James a week after the failure of his play *Guy Domville*. Three months after this the sequence of trials began which led to the public disgrace and imprisonment of Oscar Wilde. James dictated the tale a few months after Wilde's release in 1897. In these years it is recognised that in psychological terms James himself underwent something of a breakdown – 'the black abyss' as Leon Edel calls it, borrowing a phrase of James's – although the integrated man of society maintained his role as gentleman and man of letters.[5] The shame of public exposure when James was hooted off the stage was bad enough, but the public spectacle of Wilde's homosexual transgression shook James, as his one letter concerning Wilde's arrest testifies. This essay will argue that there is a complex relationship between the careers of Wilde and James, both as artists and as men of upper-class society, reflected within the story. The complexity consists in a compound dialectic with several permutations. The most powerful one is that between good and evil, and the angelic and the demonic, explicitly referred to in the story and implicitly related to Wilde's and James's lives. Then there is the relationship between the male author and the female narrator: one the integrated artist (James), the other the female author and disintegrating hysteric (the governess). Further, we have the dialectic between past and present. The story is set in the 1840s. James in his fifties resurrects his childhood. Internal dialectical movements, such as that between Miss Jessel and the governess, could be dwelt on but more important is the exterior dialectical relationship between the story and contemporary society: in brief, that between homosexuality and heterosexuality. Homosexuality, it will be argued, is the unnamable, 'the hideous obscure' that, with the advent of the Wilde trials, returned to haunt James's imagination, just when he was made aware of the ghosts who return to haunt two small children. The following procedure will be firstly to touch on the social circumstances and then to develop the argument by examining James's text.

Henry James chose to go to the Haymarket Theatre to see Wilde's *An Ideal Husband* on the first night (5 January 1895) of his own play *Guy Domville* at the St James's Theatre. By the close of his play James had returned to the theatre and was led on stage to the applause of his friends in the orchestra, but to the 'jeers, hisses' and 'catcalls' of the gallery 'roughs'. As Edel puts it, 'He had been hooted by a brutal mob as if he were some old-time criminal led through the streets for execution' (Edel, pp. 420, 425). After a brief run, James's play was taken off and replaced by *The Importance of Being Earnest*. James was exposed to ignominy as a bad playwright, not as a homosexual. The reverse was to happen to Wilde, the acclaimed dramatist who was to be vilified in the persecution of the streets.

Five days after the opening of *Guy Domville* James visited Edward White Benson, the Archbishop of Canterbury, who related the anecdote of the spirits of bad servants appearing to two small children in some remote country house to tempt them to destruction. James entered the story in his notebook. There is no mention of a governess.[6] Within a few months Wilde was charged with homosexual offences under the 1885 Criminal Law Amendment Act. Bail was refused and Wilde was sent to Holloway jail. Two days later, on 8 April, James wrote to Edmund Gosse. The language is important for *The Turn of the Screw*, thus a full quotation is warranted:

> Yes, too, it has been, it is, hideously, atrociously dramatic and really interesting – so far as one can say that of a thing of which the interest is qualified by such a sickening horribility. It is the squalid gratuitousness of it all – of the mere exposure – that blurs the spectacle. But the *fall* – from nearly twenty years of a really unique kind of 'brilliant' conspicuity (wit, 'art', conversation – 'one of our two or three dramatists, etc.') to that sordid prison-cell and this gulf of obscenity over which the ghoulish public hangs and gloats – it is beyond any utterance of irony or any pang of compassion! He was never in the smallest degree interesting to me – but this hideous human history has made him so, in a manner.[7]

The 'gulf of obscenity' had separated James on stage from the 'ghoulish public' in the gallery of St James's who also hung there, gloating at his exposure. The word 'hideous' has a particular importance for the course of the three Wilde trials, both in court and in the press over the following four weeks up to Wilde's conviction on 25 May and sentence of two years hard labour. When Wilde was arrested several hundred men fled in panic across the channel to France, fearing a like fate. Panic of another sort must have seized Henry James. For Fred Kaplan, following a contemporary theorist, 'the insidious sexual element in the story ... resonates as artistic rendering of homosexual panic'.[8]

For Eve Kosofsky Sedgwick, 'homosexual panic' by the end of the nineteenth century became a natural expression of homosocial conditioning. In a society whose power structure enforced homosocial bonding, homosocial panic was the automatic censor of homosexual desire. Unsurprisingly, the Wilde trials produced a wave of homophobia. Homosexual panic reinforced and in part defined the development of male heterosexuality in particular. The Criminal Amendment Act criminalised practising homosexuals, but homosexual panic was the interior psychological force by which the heterosexual policed himself. Sedgwick's celebrated essay 'The Beast in the Closet' applies these ideas in a reading of the suppressed homosexuality of James's story of 1902 'The Beast in the Jungle'.[9] At the outset of her criticism she remarks: 'There has so far seemed no reason, or little reason, why what I have been calling "male homosexual panic" could not just as descriptively have been called "male heterosexual panic" – or, simply, "male social panic".' Kaja Silverman, drawing on the work of Laplanche and Pontalis, investigates what she terms the Jamesian 'phantasmatic', defined as 'an unconscious phantasy or group of related phantasies which underlie dreams, symptoms, acting out, repetitive behaviour, and daydreams'. Silverman suggests that we should be prepared to read the authorial 'phantasmatic' against the biographical author 'when it is appropriate to do so, against the class, race, gender or historical moment of the biographical author *against* the phantasmatic'. For Silverman the Jamesian 'phantasmatic' encloses 'homosexuality within heterosexuality, and heterosexuality within homosexuality'.[10] The theoretical approaches of Sedgwick and Silverman, in combination with the dialectical approach suggested above, may be taken further. What of the option of female heterosexual panic? Or, at one stride, we may reconsider the displacements and inversion of author to narrator in *The Turn of the Screw* as male to female, homo to heterosexual panic. Such a 'phantasmatic' accommodates homo-heterosexual panic and legitimises the effeminate in the rhetoric of narratology. Support for this may be found in the fictional androgynous cross-dressing of author to character, and to some extent in James's life.

In *The Turn of the Screw* Miles is referred to by the narrator as an 'angel'. 'Angel' was the name James's mother gave him which was echoed derisively by his brother William in mockery of his effeminacy.[11] Henry's homoerotic attachment to his slightly older brother remained the fundamental emotional bond of his life. Girlhood, particularly in James's fiction between 1895 and 1900, has a particular biographical significance: 'His precocious little females grow a little older in each book, as if they were a single child whose life experience is being traced from the cradle to coming-of-age – as if indeed these books were the single book of little Henry James of Washington Square' (Edel, p. 480).

In appraising James's emotional development from childhood to maturity, there is insufficient evidence to be certain of his sexuality, probably because that sexuality itself was rather uncertain. The evidence is negative. There are no grounds for assuming that any of his friendships, male or female, had an active sexual content. Arguably the reverse in fact; James's fastidious sensibility might well have led him to regard the heterosexual act with dismay and the homosexual act with horror. After encountering the ostentatious dandyism of Wilde's high camp in America, James referred to him as 'an unclean beast' (Edel, p. 273). In the course of the Wilde trials the corruption of homosexuality was seen specifically in the association of Wilde with youth. He was regarded as corrupting others. In fact, in Mr Justice Wills's summing up before sentence was given, this found expression along with the word anticipated in James's letter to Gosse: 'you, Wilde, have been the centre of a circle of extensive corruption of the most hideous kind among young men'.[12] For James, social and aesthetic propriety should determine the invisibility of sexual demeanour. Vulgarity was the overt dividing line between the acceptable and the unacceptable, the speakable and the unspeakable. The latter could only be adumbrated as 'the hideous obscure'. What is most surprising about James's letter concerning Wilde is that it is more or less the only one.[13] In the weeks that follow, with all the rumours, facts and misrepresentations of the trial flooding London with one of the most sensational cases of the century, to his correspondents James seems like the Master of Bly; he seemingly turns his back on it.

As writer James parallels this by never spelling out what is the precise nature of the apparent evil in *The Turn of the Screw*. In the Preface he puts it this way:

> Only make the reader's general vision of evil intense enough, I said to
> myself ... and his own experience, his own imagination, his own
> sympathy (with the children) and horror (of their false friends), will
> supply him quite sufficiently with all the particulars. Make him *think*
> the evil, make him think it for himself.[14]

But in a way this partly backfires since, to many late twentieth-
century readers, the evil seems largely to derive both from the governess's mind and from the controlling author (James), who put it
there and hinted at it in such matters as the exclusive visibility of
the apparitions. A further complication is that the reliance on a
willing suspension of disbelief in metaphysical evil is considerably
less strong now than it was in the 1890s and this gives rise to a deconstructive scepticism. James's fictive spell can only work fully on
an imagination that is still prepared to associate sex with sin and
evil, corruption and damnation. Such an imagination accepts that
corruption of the children began before the deaths of Miss Jessel
and Quint and that their ghostly return is either to continue this or
demoniacally claim their souls. One hundred years of causality
having been explained in psychological rather than metaphysical
terms puts the stress rather on a naturalistic explanation that
suggests an altogether radical re-reading.

If one looks at the facts of Miss Jessel and Peter Quint's relationship from the relatively uncensored viewpoint of the 1990s, quite
another perspective emerges. Jessel and Quint, let us assume, were
lovers. On the evidence of Mrs Grose, Quint had had amorous relationships with other females of the household at one time or
another. What we have here are two forms of Victorian transgression – sexual and social. As valet, Peter Quint was a 'base menial'
(p. 64), and Miss Jessel's social inferior. In the Wilde trials the pros-
ecution repeatedly drew attention to the fact of Wilde's association
with young men from a lower class, as if that were necessarily incriminating in itself (like Quint, one of Wilde's associates was a
valet).[15] Sex outside marriage was regarded as sinful. From this
point of view, Miss Jessel can be regarded as either heroic or
foolish. Turning from the frigid social and sexual norms of
Victorian society, she gave all for love – status, income and respectability – since such an affair could hardly have remained
secret. Quint risked losing his job but, as he was playing it fast and
loose in his master's waistcoats already, this was on the cards
anyway.

Within Christian culture carnality has always been linked to the Fall and the Victorian demonisation of sexual transgression is reflected in the story. Within that culture, the reader is to imagine that Miss Jessel and Quint's liaison was perverted and degrading and this sense was passed on to the children. 'Make him think the evil', and in the present period, in which child abuse has become prominent in the press, the imagination might be prompted by the horror of debased orgies of the hetero or homosexual kind which might include the children. But there is an innocent alternative. In L. P. Hartley's *The Go Between* (1953), set in the Edwardian period, the boy Leo seeks to find out about the nature of love from Ted Burgess, a young farmer who is the secret lover of the upper-class Marian. In James's early story 'Gabrielle de Bergerac', the teacher of the aristocratic young Chevalier, and chaste lover of his sister, explains to his charge the basis of democracy in 'humanity, justice and tolerance', and a little later the inevitability of passion, joy and suffering in the beauty of love between men and women.[16] On a less rarefied, romantic plane, at various stages of youth, children want to know initially where babies come from, and eventually how to have sex.

If all the evil is in the imagination of the governess, then perhaps Peter Quint, in his rambles with Miles and out of sympathy for the fatherless situation of the boy, simply took it on himself to explain the facts of life which were eagerly passed on to selected schoolfellows and immediately got Miles expelled. But carnal knowledge has to be evil in this late Victorian world. Of all the commentators on the ghosts, it would appear that only one has speculated on the possibility of their not being evil as the governess insists. Elizabeth Schultz points out how Miss Jessel and Quint are associated with freedom and the natural world, and speculates that their returning as apparitions 'might have extended the children's experience beyond the borders of Bly, beyond the realm of the simplistic romantic fantasy and the Victorian sensibility with which the governess sought to wall them in'.[17] Though Donal O'Gorman with great detail presents a Christian reading of evil and demonic possession in the apparitions and the governess, at one point he concedes that 'ghosts, terrifying though they may be, are generally believed to return upon some laudable errand: to right some wrong, to cry vengeance on a murderer, to reveal the location of hidden treasure, and so forth'.[18] From this point of view, the ghosts might have returned to rescue the children from the 'evil' of the governess who embodies the evil of a perverse society which criminalises and demonises sex. Thus the struggle between good and evil is much more complex than the contemporary stigmatisation of Oscar Wilde as a perverse and evil scapegoat. The forces of good and evil in *The Turn of the Screw* seem to contain their opposites, just as Miss Jessel and Quint are perceived at different times as of 'extraordinary beauty' (p. 59) and 'handsome' (p. 47). Comparably, the simple polarity of the fallen Wilde and the upright James is compromised by common homosexuality. From one point of view, *The Turn of the Screw* defends Victorian values in its demonisation of transgression; from another it subverts those values by demonstrating the origin of evil in society itself, as represented by the governess. This is the case unless one regards the misogynistic representation of a female hysteric as James's final gesture of homosexual panic and homosocial solidarity. The psychomachy between good and evil takes place inside James himself, within the buried levels of innocence and guilt in the disparity between his artistic and social self-presentation and the 'hideous obscure' of homosexuality. This shocking disparity had been exposed to all Victorian society in Wilde's trial. Wilde spoke movingly from the dock on 'the love that dare not speak its name',[19] but the reality of mutual masturbation and fellatio jarred somewhat with Hellenic spirituality – 'the Oscar Wilde horrors' as James referred to it.[20]

Correspondingly, the 'normal' world of *The Turn of the Screw* polarises sexuality and asexuality. Wherever you turn, love is unfulfilled, absent or denied, and virginity is equated with barrenness: Douglas and the governess; the governess and the master. Everyone is childless; Miles and Flora's parents are dead; Douglas dies and the governess dies. At Bly, though manservants are mentioned, there is no sense of generation and the conventionally titled 'Mrs' Grose is a spinster whose infertility is symbolised by illiteracy; she can neither write nor continue her name. The governess is horrified by sex, a horror legitimised by cultural codes of transgression. Normality is a world of sterility and death. 'It was as if ... all the rest of the scene had been stricken with death' (p. 36). But this is already implicit without Quint's first appearance. James believes he is well hidden behind conventional Gothic atmospherics, particularly in the sequence of the first encounter with Quint, after which the subsequent description of the handsome, hatless redhead confirms that he is not so much the master's dead valet, but the devil himself, as Renner discusses.[21] And the devil is the master of doubleness. Yet again that doubleness can be found in society itself.

In summarising past and present research into the Victorian social order in fact and fiction, T. J. Lustig focuses on the governess figure: 'The role of the governess epitomises nineteenth-century anxieties concerning social and sexual borders. Simultaneously *both* one thing and the other and *neither* one thing nor the other, the governess is the liminal figure par excellence'; that is, she is 'not a relation, not a guest, not a mistress, not a servant – but something made up of all'. That 'something' could go from one extreme to another, from gentlewoman preserver of moral proprieties and social distinction – to mistress, to prostitute. Indeed, Lustig points out that James's own French governess 'had been exposed as an "adventuress"'.[22] Clearly, Miss Jessel and the governess represent these polarities. But the doubleness is deepened when we recognise that the liminal position of the governess reflects James's inner homosexual self in relation to his integrated social being. In contrast, it appears that Quint is the heterosexual transgressor tainted with possible demonic homosexual corruption, like Wilde. *The Echo* newspaper summarises, in effect, the onslaught of the cheap press which we know James read: in a word – Wilde was 'damned'.[23] Wilde in prison dwelt on the angel of his damnation, Lord Alfred Douglas, while James, about to reside at Lamb House, dwelt on the story of damnation told by 'Douglas'. In the middle of the Quint–Jessel–governess triangle is another 'Angel': James himself, recreated as Miles. Attention to the permutations of history, art and sexuality brings us closer to the 'hideous obscure'.

James as author creates a fiction and resurrects his childhood prepubescent self, the 'Angel' of the past, when James was ten years old and encountered the villainous Peter Quin in Tom Taylor's story 'Temptation', published in a New York journal.[24] But James can't rescue himself from his subsequent history – in the form of the ineluctable onset of sexuality. In order to attempt to do so, he partly re-enters his effeminate early self by cross-dressing as the virginal governess. Analogously, the governess seeks to freeze history, by perpetuating the Victorian aestheticisation of childhood as a preserved artefact of ideal beauty. Miles and Flora are to be shielded from all forms of sexuality. Peter Quint and Miss Jessel therefore have a dualistic function: their heterosexual transgression is both the inversion of James's homosexual containment – the sexual freedom he knows he can never allow himself – and the social condemnation of corruption. The dualism re-enacts what took place in the Wilde trials, when the dramatist was persecuted for the sexual conduct experienced by a considerable number of his ex-public school persecutors, his upper-class peers.

The life-denying constrictions of Victorian morality are proleptically symbolised in Miles, the youthful James, who is doomed to homo and heterosexual self-denial. Homosexual panic and heterosexual phobia merge in a marriage of death.

> We continued silent while the maid was with us – as silent, it whimsically occurred to me, as some young couple who, on their wedding journey, at the inn, feel shy in the presence of the waiter. He turned round only when the waiter had left us. 'Well – so we're alone!' … I caught him, yes, I held him – it may be imagined with what passion …
>
> (pp. 128, 138)

It may indeed. Throughout the Wilde trials it was continually demonstrated that, beneath all the aesthetic language of poetry, art and beauty, there was squalor, sordidness and ugliness. This is found in the development of *The Turn of the Screw*. In particular, the governess inadvertently suggests a comparison between Bly and Miles's school in the same paragraph – 'the romance of the nursery and the poetry of the schoolroom' with 'the little horrid, unclean school-world' (p. 40) – in language reminiscent of James's censure of Wilde elsewhere, as we have seen. More generally, the beauty of the children is testified to throughout the early pages of the tale. Flora is 'beatific', of 'angelic beauty', like 'one of Raphael's holy infants' (pp. 24–5), and so on. Similarly, around Miles is the 'fragrance of purity' and 'something divine' (p. 32). But the divine gets reversed with the sense of corruption without and within after the apparitions' appearance, and Miles becomes a 'fiend' as much as 'angel' (p. 65). In the above context, when describing her work with the children, the governess anticipates this duality in a slip that is a major fissure in the text – if, that is, a Shakespearian allusion can be considered a 'slip': 'so how could work not be charming that presented itself as a daily beauty?' (p. 40). This is from *Othello*, when Iago says of Cassio: 'He has a daily beauty in his life, / That makes me ugly' (V.i.19–20). There is no way of knowing whether the echo by James is conscious or subliminal, but perhaps, as it has been overlooked in a text regularly scrutinised for allusions, this indicates the latter?

Othello, like *The Turn of the Screw*, is a text heavily patterned by allusions to heaven and hell, angel and devil. The governess's words damn her out of her own mouth, since the allusion aligns her with the 'ugliness' of Iago who is bent on consigning Othello from heaven to hell, from romantic love to damnation. As Iago insists on love as carnality, so the governess insists on Quint and Jessel's love as iniquitous. In this Iago allusion we see how, just as Bly is not 'a castle of romance' but 'big' and 'ugly' (p. 27), so the governess, outwardly the respectable guardian revealed in the full length mirror 'for the first time' (p. 24), reflects an internal ugliness in the mirror of her allusive language. Such a transformation is perceived in Flora as the governess projects her own condition: 'her incomparable childish beauty had suddenly failed ... she was literally, she was hideously hard; she had turned common and almost ugly' (p. 116). The 'hideous obscure' is as much within as without, as it was in Henry James on the opposite side of the 'gulf of obscenity' to his homosexual *Doppelgänger* Oscar Wilde.

'Hideous' is a key term in James's story and it was a word directed at Wilde in the period of the trials. Towards the close of the story, with Flora removed from Bly, the governess knows that she has to confront Miles. She says revealingly, 'what I had to deal with was, revoltingly, against nature' (p. 127), which, from a conservative point of view, ambivalently suggests homosexuality as much, if not more than, the demonic. This is the 'hideous obscure' she refers to a few lines later: 'How ... could I make a reference ['to what had occurred'] without a new plunge into the hideous obscure?' The effect of the ghosts is early summed up in the same word for both, 'horror' (p. 57), just as James had encapsulated 'the Oscar Wilde horrors', as we have seen. A little later the governess's language anticipates the above: 'I find that I really hang back; but I must take my horrid plunge. In going on with the record of what was hideous at Bly I not only challenge the most liberal faith ...' (p. 69); just as the 'hideous' conduct of Wilde in male brothels challenged the most liberal of Victorian faiths. James's letter to Gosse on Wilde's arrest, with its 'horribility' and 'hideous', anticipates the governess's words and Mr Justice Wills's final speech sentencing Wilde. Perhaps James himself was in part echoing the *Daily Telegraph* of 6 April 1895, commenting on the acquittal of Wilde's antagonist the Marquess of Queensbury for libel, which was immediately followed by Wilde's own arrest: even the report of the case had inflicted 'moral damage of the most hideous and repulsive kind'.[25]

In the period between Wilde's arrest and the publication of James's tale, the 'hideous' remained 'obscure', since: 'The official

Court shorthand-writers and compilers of the *Central Criminal Court Sessions Papers*, who might have been expected to present the facts objectively, declined to print the proceedings of any of the trials on the grounds that the details disclosed by them were "unfit for publication".'[26] The governess's paradoxical comment on the children's undisclosed discussion reads like this contemporary situation: 'They say things that, if we heard them, would simply appal us' (p. 110). Nevertheless, the 'hideous' was made even more so by newspaper gossip, rumour and misrepresentation of the 'damned' Wilde. However, the liberal faith of James retained a sense of Wilde's fate as, though 'a very squalid tragedy', it was 'still a tragedy' (Edel, p. 437).[27] Conversely, when the liberal faith of the governess is put to the test, she will not allow herself to be overcome by 'terror' on this third encounter with Quint, because 'the thing was as human and hideous as a real interview: hideous just because it *was* human' (p. 71). The governess's self-controlled judgement here echoes the end of James's letter to Gosse on Wilde's fall as 'this hideous human history'.

When Peter Quint appears for the last time, it is as 'the hideous author of our woe – the white face of damnation', at which the governess feels 'a sick swim at the drop of my victory' (p. 137). Comparably, in the opening lines of James's letter, we find the 'hideously atrociously dramatic ... a sickening horribility'. Yet the lines of James's story reveal even more in the compound Miltonic echo of *Paradise Lost*. Robert Heilman has drawn attention to the Edenic quality of Bly and linked the sense of damnation to Milton's poem of Good and Evil, but without examining this rather heavily resonant line.[28] Some, or all, of the following contexts are invoked: 'Author of all ill' (2.381); 'Author of evil' (6.262); 'all our woe' (1.3; 2.872; 9.645); 'on me, sole cause to thee of all this our woe' (10.935). Satan is 'author' and our 'woe' is the Fall, so the reference reinforces the conventional allusion to sin and damnation. The 'hideous author' for the mid 1890s, an author moreover associated with evil and corruption, would have loomed large as the 'hideous' Oscar Wilde, paralleling the 'hideous ruin', the 'hideous change' and the 'hideous fall' of Milton's Lucifer (*Paradise Lost*, 1.46, 313: 2.177). Similarly, when the apparition of Miss Jessel is discovered in the schoolroom in the act of writing, this 'most horrible of women' is seen as 'my vile predecessor. Dishonoured and tragic' (p. 97). Wilde was James's 'vile' predecessor on stage. 'Dishonoured and tragic' also describes his fate; as James insisted, 'squalid' but 'still a tragedy', and he repeated in a letter to his brother: 'His fall is hideously tragic.'[29] Quint's last appearance is first announced as 'like a sentinel before a prison'. On his arrest, Wilde had been pictured by the press as 'pacing up and down his cell at night like a caged beast'.[30] James dictated *The Turn of the Screw* after Wilde's release from prison in 1897, having just committed himself to a new residence, Lamb House at Rye. Leon Edel speculates that the house 'symbolised the world of his childhood, the place where he had been least free'.[31] Now, James in imagination having returned to the prison house of childhood, Miles is both 'shut in or shut out' (p. 129). James qualifies the governess's initial simile: 'I have likened it to a sentinel, but its slow wheel, for a moment, was rather the prowl of a baffled beast' (p. 134). In the topical context outlined above, the word 'baffled' takes on its aristocratic meaning of 'to subject to public disgrace or infamy'.[32] Wilde the disgraced ex-prisoner, the 'unclean beast', returns to haunt James.

At the end of James's story 'The Beast in the Jungle' (1902) the hero acknowledges that 'He saw the Jungle of his life and saw the lurking Beast'. As we have seen, the Beast had been lurking for many years.

This essay is published here for the first time.

NOTES

[Ronald Knowles, in this new essay, takes a historical-biographical approach to the issue of sexual politics in James and perceives a network of allusions both in and surrounding *The Turn of the Screw* to the persona, and the case, of Oscar Wilde. Sexual anxiety and problems of identity are seen to interact with class tensions, personal and family history, and contemporary events: in equal measure within and beyond the text. Social and sexual dualism induced a sequence of role reversals, in his fiction as in his life, which left Henry James himself a haunted figure. His personal ghost, in contrast to the supernatural revenants of his fictional tale, betokens a spectre of a different order: namely 'homosexual panic'. Ed.]

1. 'The Turn of the Screw', in *The Complete Tales of Henry James*, vol. 10 (London, 1964), p. 18. Hereafter page numbers are given in the text.

2. *The Art of the Novel: Critical Prefaces by Henry James*, ed. Richard P. Blackmur (New York, 1962), p. 171.

3. For an appraisal of the governess as representing the late nineteenth-century understanding of the female hysteric, see Stanley Renner, '"Red hair, very red, close-curling": Sexual Hysteria, Physiognomical Bogeymen, and the "Ghosts" in *The Turn of the Screw*', in Henry James, *The Turn of the Screw*, ed. Peter G. Beidler (Boston, 1995), pp. 223–41. For an argument on the governess as satanically possessed, see Donal O'Gorman, 'Henry James's Reading of *The Turn of the Screw*: Parts II and III', *The Henry James Review*, 1 (1980), 228–56.

4. See Hans-Joachim Lang, 'The Turns in *The Turn of the Screw*', *Jahrbuch für Amerikastudien*, 9 (1964), 110–28; May L. Ryburn, '*The Turn of the Screw* and *Amelia*: A Source for Quint?', *Studies in Short Fiction*, 16 (1979), 235–7; Alice Hall Petry, 'Jamesian Parody, *Jane Eyre*, and *The Turn of the Screw*', *Modern Language Studies*, 13 (1983), 61–78.

5. Leon Edel, *Henry James. A Life* (New York, 1985), pp. 425–47; hereafter page numbers from this biography are given in the text, under the abbreviation 'Edel'.

6. *The Complete Notebooks of Henry James*, ed. Leon Edel and Lyall H. Powers (New York, 1987), p. 109.

7. *Henry James Letters*, vol. 4, ed. Leon Edel (Cambridge, MA and London, 1984), pp. 9–10.

8. Fred Kaplan, *Henry James: The Imagination of Genius. A Biography* (London, 1993), p. 414. For a contemporary reading by F. W. H. Myers, in terms of lesbianism and pederasty in the corruption of children, see Peter G. Beidler, 'The Governess and the Ghosts', *PMLA*, 100 (1985), 96–7.

9. Eve Kosofsky Sedgwick, *Epistemology of the Closet* (New York and London, 1991), pp. 182–212.

10. Kaja Silverman, 'Too Early/Too Late: Subjectivity and the Primal Scene in Henry James', *Novel*, 21 (1988), 153, 165. J. Laplanche and J. B. Pontalis, *The Language of Psychoanalysis*, trans. Donald Nicholson Smith (New York, 1973), is cited on p. 153.

11. Leon Edel, *Henry James: The Treacherous Years* (London, 1969), p. 199; and Edel, *Henry James. A Life*, p. 245.

12. H. Montgomery Hyde, *Famous Trials 7: Oscar Wilde* (Harmondsworth, 1962), p. 272.

13. See Edel, *The Treacherous Years*, pp. 120, 130.

14. *The Art of the Novel*, p. 176.

15. Hyde, *Famous Trials*, p. 249.

16. *The Tales of Henry James*, vol. 1, ed. Maqbool Aziz (Oxford, 1973), pp. 398, 403.

17. Elizabeth Schultz, '"The Pity and the Sanctity of Terror": The Humanity of the Ghosts in *The Turn of the Screw'*, *Markham Review*, 9 (1980), 67–71.

18. O'Gorman (see note 3 above), p. 239.

19. Hyde, *Famous Trials*, p. 201.

20. Edel, *The Treacherous Years*, p. 130.

21. See Renner (note 3 above).

22. T. J. Lustig, *Henry James and the Ghostly* (Cambridge, 1994), pp. 150, 108.

23. Sheridan Morley, *Oscar Wilde* (London, 1976), p. 120.

24. Leon Edel and Adeline Tintner, 'The Private Life of Peter Quin[t]: Origins of *The Turn of the Screw'*, *The Henry James Review*, 7 (1985), 2.

25. Hyde, *Famous Trials*, p. 17.

26. Ibid., p. 20. Because of law and censorship, only in Montgomery Hyde's book of 1962 is the full evidence given and made easily available. Otherwise it appears that only exceptionally, in *The Trial of Oscar Wilde*, ed. Charles Grolleau (privately printed for Charles Carrington, Paris, 1906), was the evidence given – a source acknowledged by Hyde.

27. Wilde eventually read *The Turn of the Screw*, considering it 'a most wonderful, lurid, poisonous little tale like an Elizabethan tragedy': Richard Ellmann, 'A Late Victorian Love Affair', *The New York Review of Books*, 24, 13 (4 August 1977), 7.

28. Robert Heilman, '*The Turn of the Screw* as Poem', in *A Casebook on Henry James's 'The Turn of the Screw'* (New York, 1959), pp. 182–3.

29. Edel, *The Treacherous Years*, p. 200.

30. Hyde, *Famous Trials*, p. 164.

31. Edel, *The Treacherous Years*, p. 200.

32. *OED*, vol. 1.

9

Unsquaring the Squared Route of *What Maisie Knew*

BARBARA ECKSTEIN

In her essay '*What Maisie Knew*: Portrait of the Artist as a Young Girl', Juliet Mitchell provocatively implies a sort of cross-dressing on the part of Henry James. She writes, 'First as the child Maisie, then as the man, Henry James looks through a glass dimly in order that the reflection should be "sharp" and "quiet".'[1] The young girl Maisie becomes, through her learned vision, the man, the artist, Henry James. 'James's description of Maisie's initiation at the deepest level is profoundly bound up with his method for the whole novel, her progress so much its progress, her art his art.'[2] To arrive at the conclusion that her title promises, Mitchell pursues two perspectives through which James sees in the novel: Maisie's, 'straight' and seemingly 'innocent', and Mrs Wix's, 'crooked' and apparently 'pornographic'. Although Maisie's initiation is indeed bound up with the method of the novel, one might better describe that method through the relationship of James, or rather his narrator – who is, after all, present from the very beginning of the novel as Mrs Wix is not – to Maisie. This relationship is not one in which Maisie becomes James: or he, her – except perhaps in the sense that they flatter one another. For Maisie's childhood does not equip her to be an artist, at least not yet, not at thirteen, as far as the novel takes us. In the end it is not true that '[Maisie's] knowledge is pure, her freedom complete'.[3] And yet the development of James's, or rather his third-person narrator's, relationship with Maisie is the method, the progress, of the novel.

The method of the novel is also parody, particularly self-parody.[4] For as the novel proceeds and increasing numbers of Maisie's disreputable guardians square off against one another, and as James more obviously associates the symmetry of 'squaring' with immorality, James's impulses toward formalist symmetry become objects of his own attack. Maisie serves the squaring of her guardians both within the fictional world and narrative form. But the exploitation of her character in both realms finally reveals itself. Though James very early shows the squaring-off of one parent against another to be selfish manipulation, he much more slowly discloses the difficulties with a morality intended to square things – discloses it as though he, or his narrator, learns the limitations of ethical and aesthetic symmetry as we do and Maisie tries to. One would not want to deny James either his mastery or his ability to discover meaning through his writing. As Derrida explains in *Writing and Difference*, 'To write is to know that what has not yet been produced within literality has no other dwelling place, does not await us as prescription in some *topos ouranios*, or some divine understanding. Meaning must await being said or written in order to inhabit itself, and in order to become, by differing from itself, what it is: meaning.'[5] The way in which James's method in *What Maisie Knew* differs from itself I am calling parody, but it is also becoming, that is, finding meaning, especially moral meaning, when certainty – in Derrida's analyses always finally metaphysical certainty – no longer provides it.

An unquestioning identification of James in the preface (1908) with the narrator in the novel (1897) would certainly be a mistake, for the persona of the prefaces is as slippery a self as Nabokov in interviews. As Leo Bersani points out, the voice of the prefaces often misleads.[6] To confound the reader, to entice: these are likely intentions of the prefaces. In addition, as Carren Osna Kaston has noticed, *What Maisie Knew* begins with a documentary, 'anesthetised tone – an assured, cool, legal precision which shows disdain for the immorality of Maisie's parents'.[7] 'The litigation had seemed interminable and had in fact been complicated; but by the decision on the appeal the judgement of the divorce-court was confirmed as to the assignment of the child.'[8] This voice bridging James's and Maisie's worlds produces an effect comparable to that of the James-like narrator in the frame of *The Turn of the Screw*

(1898). So it may at least be said that the non-fictional voice of the preface and the narrative voice of the novel are separate yet not distinct entities. The ambiguity of their difference allows James a full play of possibilities between the two poles: precise, third-person narration in a symmetrical form and indistinct, third/first-person narration in a parody of symmetrical form. The degree to which writer controls subject is at issue.

In the preface James explains the relationship between his narration and his protagonist this way: 'Small children have many more perceptions than they have terms to translate them; ... [therefore] we inevitably note this [Maisie's perceptions] in figures that are not yet at her command and that are nevertheless required.'[9] James takes on this role of spokesperson through a third-person narrator who has every appearance of omniscience. Edel states that the 1890s were, in fact, a period, for James, of refining the author's omniscience. Edel explains, however, that this refinement proceeded by probing the unconscious memory, a murky bog of desires and motivations.[10] So, if Edel is right on both counts, James set himself on a search for the knowledge least likely unequivocally to show itself. The omniscience to be achieved by a narrator on such a search is not that of a God behind the Cloud of Unknowing but that of a mortal within the same linguistic world of unknown desires as the novel's characters – though they too, child protagonists like Maisie in particular, 'drive to attain omniscience in a world of negligent and terrifying adults'.[11]

The narrator and Maisie both encounter numerous obstacles to their omniscience, whether or not either ever quite acknowledges them. 'Oh, I know', Maisie says on the novel's last page as she has on many a page before. She says it the way children do when they know exactly what you mean or when they haven't the least idea. As Dennis Foster observes, what Maisie knows are the linguistic structures of knowledge but without the content of experience.[12] Like most children, and many adults, Maisie expresses understanding to conceal confusion. And indeed clear articulation creates every appearance of order.

Of course the narrator knows a good bit more about experience than Maisie. He also has a considerably more sophisticated command of the structures of knowledge (i.e., language) than she. His omniscience, as the preface describes it, controls nearly half the novel. But at the mid-point of the novel there are some shifts in the narration to first-person plural and, surprisingly, then to first-person singular. Nothing in the preface directly explains the cause or intent of this first-person narration at points in the novel when the language of objectivity would seem especially important to establish the credibility of Maisie's sudden escalated growth and the narrator's ability to put it into words. D. W. Jefferson lamely suggests the limited use of 'I' is a 'slip'.[13] Merla Wolk argues that the narrator, not Mrs Wix and Sir Claude, as Mitchell has it, is the good mother Maisie lacked.[14] The use of 'I', then, marks the point at which the symbiotic mother–child relationship is replaced by acknowledgement that the child is a separate individual. Wolk convinces me that the narrator is the most motherly of the adults in Maisie's fictional milieu, but the 'mother's' willingness to relinquish her hold on Maisie I question.

The simultaneous shift in James's means of composition also pertains to his shift in narration of *What Maisie Knew*. Because of a rheumatic wrist, in the middle of *What Maisie Knew* James finally had to give up manual writing for dictation to a secretary. According to Edel, James's friends swore they could tell the exact chapter at which James switched to dictation by the change in his style.[15] To change the means of production does affect the producer, the product, and its meaning.

The use of first-person narration, plural and singular, was no slip. When James writes, 'We have already learned that [Maisie] had come to like people's liking her to "know"' (*WM*, pp. 144–5) or 'our young lady', he engages in a gentle rhetorical coercion, a conventional call for the reader's complicity. Furthermore, this convention marks a chink in the narrator's wall of confidence; through this chink the narrator draws the reader into the text to corroborate his expression of and affection for Maisie. But more important still are the uses of 'I'. They place the narrator in the text as a character who need no longer, indeed can no longer, maintain his posture as flawless articulator of Maisie's experience.

Though the preface makes no mention of the first-person narration, it does single out for comment the two dramatic instances in the novel that precede, perhaps even precipitate, the use of 'I': Maisie's encounters with the Countess and with the Captain. The preface argues that 'Maisie makes them [these and all adults] portentous by the play of her good faith.' But more intriguing than the argument is the focus on the Countess and the Captain, the judgement of these characters by the voice of the preface, and their relation to the use of 'I'. The preface declares 'the facts involved are that ... the friend [the Countess] to whom [Beale] introduces his daughter is deplorable' whereas it describes Ida's lover as 'the encouraging, the appealing "Captain"'.[16] But the dramatic scenes of the novel do not bear out these judgements.

The Captain has received a great deal of good press from others besides the James of the preface, but he does not altogether deserve it.[17] James touts him as 'the kindly, friendly, ugly gentleman who ... positively answers to [Maisie] for her mother as no one has ever answered'.[18] But the dialogue discloses instead Maisie's great desire to hear such a defence and the Captain's uncertainty about commitment as well as his ignorance of Ida's history. Maisie asks,

> 'You *do* love her?'
> 'My dear child –!' The Captain wanted words.
> 'Then don't do it only for just a little.'
> 'A little?'
> 'Like all the others.'
> 'All the others?' – he stood staring.
> (*WM*, p. 155)

Even though the Captain does finally offer Maisie some reassurance in the ambiguous words 'Oh I'm in for it!' the dialogue demonstrates that Maisie, the narrator, and apparently the voice of the preface all know about the Captain what they want to know, not what he reveals to be true. The sordid drama of Maisie's life exists in defiance of her innocence and of her narrator/author's confidence in the powers of her 'good faith'.

This dramatic scene in chapter sixteen is followed by the first use of narrative 'I' in chapter seventeen. 'This was the second source – I have just alluded to the first – of the child's consciousness of something that, very hopefully, she described to herself as a new phase; ... that she had small remembrance at present of a third [person] illustrates, I am afraid, a temporary oblivion of Mrs Wix' (*WM*, pp. 162–3). That both uses of 'I' are asides suggests they are dispensable and, therefore, deliberate. The first notes the narrator's control of the arrangement of the rhetoric; the second, of the 'moral sense'. He seems to imply that no dramatic scenes should belie his word as Maisie's spokesperson. With the asides, the narrator sidles into the fictional world thus insisting on and undermining his control. He shows his hand to win the game but in so doing becomes only another of the players.

Another dramatic scene, this one with the Countess, further challenges the narrator's control by providing Maisie an opportunity to be more perceptive than innocent. Though this scene is too long to quote in its entirety, it warrants careful attention. For in it Maisie is not innocent. Indeed she, in part, judges the Countess by her exotic appearance with a small-mindedness she has learned from her mother, Mrs Beale, and all the other adults in their world. In addition, the narrator describes Maisie as thinking the Captain nicer than the Countess because of 'Maisie's minor appreciation of ladies' (*WM*, p. 194). Despite these obstacles to Maisie's vision of the Countess, whom she dearly wants to get away from, she can nevertheless distinguish the genuine feeling of the Countess from the fleeting shame of her father who is deserting her. 'The great pain of the thing was that she could see the Countess liked her enough to wish to be liked in return. ... Yes, the Countess wanted her and the Countess was wounded and chilled, and she couldn't help it' (*WM*, p. 195). 'Then she understood as well as if [her father] had spoken it that what he wanted, hang it, was that she should let him off with all the honours – with all the appearance of virtue and sacrifice on his side' (*WM*, p. 187). When the Countess gives Maisie the sovereigns, the reader knows no other adult has given Maisie something for nothing. The penniless Beale says to Maisie, 'Make your stepmother pay' for the taxi, but the Countess, with experience and generosity, cries out. 'Stepmothers *don't* pay! ... No stepmother ever paid in her life!' and she flings more than enough sovereigns in the taxi to pay Maisie's way (*WM*, p. 197).

In the chapter following this exchange, the narrator abruptly shifts again into first-person narration, declaring, 'It was granted her at this time to arrive at divinations so ample that I shall have no room for the goal if I attempt to trace the stages' (*WM*, p. 202). Although this statement bestows maturation on Maisie and accelerates the narrative, it also appears to withhold from the reader more dramatic scenes, like that with the Countess, that might reveal in Maisie values the narrator does not abide, values that will keep him from his goal, the saving of Maisie's moral sense in his terms. He seems to loosen his hold on the character but, in doing so, more overtly makes himself known. James's use of 'I' shows that in order to appear thoroughly capable of assigning words to knowledge, the narrator (like Maisie) must silence what he does not know or cannot control. But it also unveils the narrator as a subject himself. 'I may not even answer for it. ... I shall never get you to believe' (*WM*, p. 205).

Two further points from the preface also speak to the ambivalence of narrative control in the novel. First we read in the preface that 'For satisfaction of the mind ... the small expanding consciousness would have to be saved ... saved ... rather than coarsened, blurred, sterilised, by ignorance and pain.'[19] 'Saved' is the crucial word here. Mrs Wix's desire to save Maisie and Sir Claude by the use of her strict 'moral sense' is the object of much irony within the novel. For example, in France, in the context of Mrs Wix's repeated declaration that she now 'understands' and 'admires' 'kind' Ida, Mrs Wix also declares to Maisie and Sir Claude, 'It's to keep you decent that I'm here and that I've done everything I have done. It's to save you' (*WM*, p. 248). The use of the word 'save' in the preface cannot escape these ironic associations. The confidence in the voice of the preface that moral sense and control, if not manipulation, are required to save a character in or out of fiction calls into question that very possibility. Many critics of *What Maisie Knew* have been quite convinced that Maisie is saved – by art, that is – and, in fact, that she has learned to be an artist because she sees and wonders (e.g. Edel, Kaston, Mitchell, Wolk). But is it Maisie who is saved by art or James and the reader? The author and reader can appreciate the artfulness of the novel. But as we close the book with satisfaction Maisie is left in her world with no secure income; a negligible education; no learned or demonstrated skills in writing, painting, music or any other endeavour; and a guardian/governess, Mrs Wix, who knows less than she. It is difficult to believe that the ability to see and wonder in itself equips her to be an artist – even one without financial security. Use of the word 'save', not only within the context of the novel but also within the James canon, casts considerable doubt on the process of saving. In *The Turn of the Screw*, of the same period as *What Maisie Knew*, the governess's repressed desires, which manifest themselves in a compulsion to save the children, end with the tragic death of Miles. That James himself desires to save his young characters – most especially females – from moral disarray is evident earlier in *The Portrait of a Lady* and elsewhere. But *The Turn of the Screw* and *What Maisie Knew* reveal considerable scepticism about saving and about the sort of assumed omniscience it requires.

Second, in addition to the assertions that he will be Maisie's spokesperson and her saviour, the voice of the preface entices us with one other curious remark: 'I at once recognised that my light vessel of consciousness [the child] ... couldn't be with verisimilitude a rude little boy.'[20] That James seems to identify with the supposed artistic potential in Maisie makes the choice of a girl child all the more intriguing.[21] The choice of a girl suggests James saw something of what Freud eschews and Carol Gilligan formulates nearly a century later: the process of moral maturation of girls as distinguished from that of boys.[22] James may well have had in mind his own difficult gender position as an American male artist when he made a germane observation, which Elizabeth Allen culls from his notebooks, about 'the growing divorce between the American woman (with her comparative leisure, culture, grace, social instincts, artistic ambitions) and the American male immersed in the ferocity of business with no time for any but the most sordid interests, purely commercial, professional, democratic and political'.[23] Nevertheless, in *What Maisie Knew* James's prescient feminism confines its observations of the girl to an 'early age', and the three *women* of the novel are not at all sympathetically drawn. As Mitchell says of Maisie after she fails Mrs Wix's moral test, 'as far as the women in the novel are concerned, she will never be one of them'.[24] And yet, as far as it goes, James's description of Maisie's moral growth could be added to Gilligan's case studies.

In brief, Gilligan describes the moral development of a boy, destined for the public sphere (commerce/law), as a process of separation not only from his mother but from all people in order to learn objective judgement according to law or principle. In the final, postconventional stage of moral maturity, the well-developed boy should judge objectively according to his own principles, his own sense of equity, which may or may not be inside the laws of government and society. Miles, in *The Turn of the Screw*, is a boy learning to separate from relationships, as his uncle has done, to prepare himself for his place in the public sphere. Until he is thoroughly terrified, his articulation, especially in comparison to that of the governess, is highly controlled. The danger of success in this moral maturation process is an inability to sustain relationships.

A girl, according to Gilligan, does not learn to separate; she learns instead to maintain relationships over and above the rules of a game or established objective principle. Responsibility to relationships is the primary value. She makes her judgements contextually – as many have noted Maisie does.[25] Success in this process is, in part, a learned ability to see all sides – though this may have the appearance of equivocation. Contextual judgements result in neither controlled articulation nor symmetrical clarity. The danger of this process is excessive self-abnegation.

Compared to the fate allotted Isabel Archer in 1881, the fate of Maisie in 1897 is less rigidly codified. Isabel, to the detriment of her character's credibility, cleaves to the rules, her marriage contract, despite the strength and significance of her relationship with Ralph Touchett. James, ultimately, does not subject Maisie to such narrative and moral control. Maisie experiences the full confusion of her relationships, beyond the symmetry of moral and narrative formalism.

The danger of self-abnegation, however, still lurks in the novel though James offers no evidence that he sees it. For he does not consider the plight of Maisie as novice to womanhood, a state for which, in *What Maisie Knew*, he shows no compassion. Mrs Beale and Mrs Wix, both lacking money and even first names of their own, desperately pursue their relationships with children and men. To avoid near destitution, Mrs Beale relies on her beauty; Mrs Wix, on pure dogged devotion. (Much more sympathetically drawn, Sir Claude is a man – without a surname – caught between the male world of money, in which he is ineffectual, and the female world of relationships, in which he is 'clawed' by desperate women.) Maisie, also, is in danger of self-abnegation at the end of the novel when she sticks by Mrs Wix, who knows nothing to teach the child. Maisie may well not be 'free' as Sir Claude and readers of the novel declare she is.[26] James's decision to write of a girl child for whom relationships and responsibilities ultimately override rules and independence allows him to explore the limits of his own (and others') moral and narrative rules. But he does not fully consider the dangers inherent in these feminine priorities.

Indeed Maisie arrives at her self-abnegating and contextual decision by default, only after her first set of parents withdraw, her age and experience increase her perception, and her narrator/guardian reveals his weakening grasp. Most important, Maisie judges contextually only after her attempts to act according to the symmetrical codes of 'justice' provided by the guardians fail. She imitates what she has seen and heard as long as she can. With increasing frequency as the novel progresses, Maisie and Mrs Wix, Mrs Beale and Sir Claude discuss how to 'save', 'free', or 'square' one another. All three states are sought through some sort of equity of symmetry; *squared* particularly suggests such mathematical justice. '"Oh I'll square her!" [Sir Claude] cried. ... "Then *everyone* will be squared!" [Maisie] peacefully said' (*WM*, p. 134). 'Mrs Beale had thrown out a partial light in telling her how it had turned out that nobody had been squared. Maisie wished at any rate that somebody *would* be squared' (*WM*, pp. 165–6). If each of Maisie's parents seems to desert each of her step-parents, then the latter will be squared and therefore will be free to be with one another and with Maisie, who has saved them before and can save them again from the appearance of an indiscreet liaison. In this scenario Mrs Wix must be excluded because she destroys the symmetry. In that venerable lady's mind, once Sir Claude is squared by the desertion of Ida, he is free to live with her and Maisie saved from the immorality of his relationship with Mrs Beale. These attempts at squared relationships do not free or save any of the characters, including Maisie, who at first thinks the most squared thing to do is for the four of them to live together: 'Why shouldn't we be four?' (*WM*, p. 271). Instead their squaring efforts call into question the need for a 'proper symmetry' – relational, moral, or aesthetic. James recollects 'promptly thinking [on hearing the germ of *What Maisie Knew*] that for a proper symmetry the second parent should marry too'[27] – thus the beginnings of a formal impulse that the novel drives to a logical extreme where it destroys itself.

The form of the novel is bracketed by two examples of symmetrical justice that apply apparently objective, mathematical principles to a dilemma of responsibility in relationships. The first expression of justice in the novel is the legal custody decision about Maisie. 'She was divided in two and the portions tossed impartially to the disputants. They would take her, in rotation, for six months at a time' (*WM*, p. 4). In his most Swiftian tone, the narrator shows his disapproval of such an arrangement. Maisie is to be a shuttlecock batted back and forth by her parents' mutual hatred. Symmetry does not provide an adequate ethical or relational solution.

This legal judgement sets the pattern for a novel in which there is a great deal of symmetry (dual marriages, dual governesses, dual separations, dual desertions) both in the form of the novel and in the psychodrama it creates. But the narrator's irony consistently disapproves of symmetry as an ethical solution to relationships even as it is embraced as an aesthetic solution to the demands of the plot. This ambivalence about symmetry becomes further deconstructed when Maisie finally gets her opportunity to act as subject, to solve the dilemma and end the novel with symmetry.

When she proposes to Sir Claude that she will sacrifice Mrs Wix if he will sacrifice Mrs Beale, she is practising the rules of 'squaring' in use all around her. 'She turned with an effort to Mrs Wix. "I didn't refuse to give you up. I said I would if he'd give up –!" "Give up Mrs Beale?" burst from Mrs Wix' (*WM*, p. 356). Maisie even suggests that she and Sir Claude wait at the old rampart until Mrs Wix and Mrs Beale leave them – exactly the passive evasion of responsibility practised by Mrs Beale and Sir Claude in their separations from Beale and Ida. Maisie is, nevertheless, widely praised for the wisdom of her offer: first by Sir Claude, who speaks of it 'with a relish as intense now as if some lovely work of art or of nature had been set down among them' (*WM*, p. 356) – note the leap from moral decision to work of art – and then by critics who admire its ability to cement commitment with mutual sacrifice.[28]

Given not only the passive irresponsibility of the offer but also the context of a novel that ridicules symmetry as a legal and personal solution to moral responsibilities in relationships, the efficacy of the offer diminishes. The offer does demonstrate that Maisie has mastered the principles of squaring practised by her guardians in the fictional world and the aesthetic principle of symmetry practised by her guardian, the narrator (even the author), outside the fictional world. She is a precocious child who has learned what is available to be learned. But the context of the novel and its appendage, the preface, demonstrate an ultimate awareness of limits to the value of narrative control and ethical or aesthetic symmetry. Responsible decisions about relationships among people, whose desires reside in unconscious memory, cannot be achieved by subtracting one governess from each side of the equation any more than they can be achieved by dividing one small child in half, as the original custody decision did.

When Maisie's offer unravels in the arguments between Mrs Beale and Mrs Wix – subjects in their own right, after all – the novel returns to where it began: a battle of hatred between two adults whose conflicting sexual desires are projected into a struggle over Maisie. Mrs Beale even asserts, 'We take our stand on the law' (*WM*, p. 361). But the law is at best a source of order, not necessarily of morality. And by now even Mrs Wix knows there are no legal statutes to resolve this dilemma. Why then does James choose Mrs Wix over Mrs Beale and Sir Claude as guardian for Maisie?

As Mitchell asserts, Mrs Wix is one of James's nastiest characterisations.[29] She is small-minded in every imaginable sense of that word. And yet Mrs Wix is preferable in that Maisie's going with her underscores the real difficulties with Maisie's symmetrical proposal. Maisie has some responsibility for her relationship with the pathetic Mrs Wix that, in a world of contextual ethics, will not allow her to discard the woman. Whatever desires the characters, the narrator, James, or the reader have for measurable fairness, a safe harbour, are necessarily thwarted by the complexity of the relationships. Maisie is trapped in a contextual ethical conundrum; she does not ascend into artistry. She is not free. 'You're free – you're free', Sir Claude declares and pushes Maisie, placing her in 'the centre of the room ... *not knowing which way to turn*' (*WM*, p. 356; italics added). James and the reader have the comfort of artful, if not symmetrical, closure for the novel, but even we do not have the comfort of moral certitude. Only a child could say at the novel's closing moment 'Oh I know'. To the reader James has demonstrated that this final statement signifies only a desire, though a courageous desire, to maintain order and to silence confusion perhaps until such time as leisure and education will permit an artistic expression that explores moral uncertainty, a time beyond the form of the plot.

A late twentieth-century reader's anachronism makes more salient James's parody of narrative control in *What Maisie Knew*. But Richard Ellmann might excuse my anachronism as well as his own when he argues that one who has read Beckett cannot read Yeats, Wilde, or Joyce as though he had not.[30] I cannot read James as though I have not read Nabokov; specifically, I cannot read *What Maisie Knew* as though I have not read *Lolita*. Lolita is surely a burlesque of *What Maisie Knew* and also an exercise in slippery self-parody.[31] It ridicules James's art, denies his influence, and imitates his narrative techniques. Nabokov makes overt the struggle between the effete European man and the precocious, nubile girl. He makes overt his narrator's desire to save the girl's childhood – for his own self-serving, and in Humbert Humbert's case decidedly sexual, desires. *All* the sexual desire that lurks in *What Maisie Knew* Nabokov parades before the reader, mocking James's reticence. Nabokov teases the reader with the relationship between narrator (Humbert Humbert) and author in *Lolita* as James does in *What Maisie Knew*. All the questions of control, manipulation, attraction, and moral certitude and salvation that define the relationship between Maisie and her narrator/author, Nabokov addresses in the relationship between Lolita and her Humbert/author.

But Nabokov also follows Lolita into adulthood as only zealous readers of James have done with Maisie. Ironically, what Nabokov finds – Nabokov, who strenuously asserts his authorial omniscience and the primacy of art – is the loving, pregnant, adolescent wife of poor, young Richard Schiller. Dolores Haze Schiller is nothing Humbert Humbert would have her be. She is not saved from ageing by art, nor has she become an artist. In Dolores Haze Schiller, James's, or rather his critics', worst fears are realised. Her freedom has entrapped her. Art again walks right up and bangs its wilful head on the stubborn disarray of life.

From *The Henry James Review*, 9:3 (1988), 177–87.

NOTES

[Barbara Eckstein begins her essay by taking issue with those critics who see Maisie at the end of the novel as free. Indeed, reading *What Maisie Knew* anachronistically, through Nabokov's *Lolita*, she throws doubt on the power of Maisie's knowledge to make her an artist, moral decisions not equating with a work of art. Departing from the 'either/or' of Maisie's innocence or corruption, she examines the 'how' of Maisie's knowledge. In an essay which begins to unravel the strands of narratorial control in the novel, she separates out the non-fictional voice of the preface from that of the third-person narrator and of Maisie, James's 'ironic centre', in a descending hierarchy of linguistic capability: James of the prefaces, his narrator, Maisie. Eckstein deconstructs two of the dramatic scenes in the novel to undermine both narratorial and preface voice. She examines the implications of James's choice of a girl as his central consciousness, reading Maisie's development against recent feminist psychology, which suggests that girls make contextual ethical judgements as opposed to the objective ones of boys. The symmetry of art and the limits of language – whether that of Maisie or of James – in the face of life is shown to be in question. Ed.]

1. Juliet Mitchell, '*What Maisie Knew*: Portrait of the Artist as a Young Girl', in *The Air of Reality: New Essays on Henry James*, ed. John Goode (London, 1972), p. 189.

2. Ibid., p. 177.

3. Ibid., p. 187.

4. *What Maisie Knew* is in its inception very likely a parody as well of moral education novels written and read by women. Towards both James took a tutelary and formidably critical position: see Randall

Craig, '"Read[ing] the Unspoken into the Spoken": Interpreting *What Maisie Knew*', *The Henry James Review*, 2 (1981), 204–12; and Mary Emily Parsons Edwards, 'I. Henry James and the Woman Novelist: The Double Standard in the Tales and Essays. II. Collaborative Learning: Small, Student-Centred Discussion Groups in the English Classroom', *DA*, 40 (1978), 833A (University of Virginia). Also, *What Maisie Knew* follows the plot described by Baym as the tale told and retold by American women writers between 1820 and 1870: 'It is the story of a young girl who is deprived of the supports she had rightly or wrongly depended on to sustain her throughout life and is faced with the necessity of winning her own way in the world': Nina Baym, *Women's Fiction: A Guide to Novels by and About Women in America, 1820–1870* (Ithaca, NY, 1978), p. 11.

5. Jacques Derrida, *Writing and Difference*, trans. Alan Bass (Chicago, 1978), p. 11.

6. Leo Bersani, 'The Jamesian Lie', *Partisan Review*, 36 (1969), 53–79 (53).

7. Carren Osna Kasten, 'Houses of Fiction in *What Maisie Knew*', *Criticism*, 18 (1976), 27–42 (29).

8. Henry James, *What Maisie Knew* (New York, 1936), p. 3; page references in the text are from this edition.

9. *The Novels and Tales of Henry James*, vol. 11 (New York, 1908), p. x (hereafter 'Preface').

10. Leon Edel, *Henry James: The Treacherous Years, 1895–1901* (Philadelphia, 1969), p. 14.

11. Ibid., p. 262.

12. Dennis Foster, 'Maisie Supposed to Know: Amo(u)ral Analysis', *The Henry James Review*, 5 (1984), 207–16 (209).

13. D. W. Jefferson, *Henry James and the Modern Reader* (London, 1964), p. 137.

14. Merla Wolk, 'Narration and Nurture in *What Maisie Knew*', *The Henry James Review*, 4 (1983), 196–206.

15. Edel, *The Treacherous Years*, p. 176.

16. Preface, pp. xii–xiii.

17. Edward Wagenknecht, *Eve and Henry James: Portraits of Women and Girls in His Fiction* (Norman, OK, 1978); M. A. Williams, 'The Drama of Maisie's Vision', *The Henry James Review*, 2 (1980), 36–48.

18. Preface, p. xiv.

19. Ibid., pp. vi–vii.

20. Ibid., p. viii.

21. Edel, *The Treacherous Years*, pp. 263–4.

22. Carol Gilligan, *In a Different Voice: Psychological Theory and Women's Development* (Cambridge, MA, 1982).

23. Elizabeth Allen, *A Woman's Place in the Novels of Henry James* (London, 1984); Henry James, *Notebooks*, ed. F. O. Matthieson and Kenneth B. Murdock (New York, 1961), p. 129.

24. Mitchell, 'Portrait of the Artist', p. 187.

25. Foster, 'Maisie Supposed to Know', p. 209; Craig, 'Reading the Unspoken', p. 206.

26. Allen, *A Woman's Place*, and Armstrong (see n. 28 below) focus on the significance of Maisie's struggle for freedom. Allen more unequivocally agrees with Sir Claude that Maisie is ultimately free. Despite a recognition of the ambiguity of the knowledge Maisie acquires, Juliet Mitchell declares her completely free.

27. Preface, p. v.

28. Allen, *A Woman's Place*, p. 133; Paul B. Armstrong, 'How Maisie Knows: The Phenomenology of James's Moral Vision', *Texas Studies in Language and Literature*, 20 (1978), 517–37 (531).

29. Mitchell, 'Portrait of the Artist', p. 184.

30. Richard Ellmann, 'Nayman of Noland', *The New York Review of Books* (24 April 1986), 27–8, 34–7 (35).

31. Others have made the same connection. Wagenknecht quotes Putt, who describes Maisie as being in her 'pre-Lolita days' (p. 128). And in discussing the influence of James on Nabokov – which the latter denied – Robert Gregory suggests Quilty, Humbert's rival for Lolita, is James, Nabokov's rival. 'That is Quilty's crime – and, I would suggest, James's crime: he came upon Maisie before Nabokov came upon Lolita; he wooed and captured her' – Robert Gregory, 'Porpoise-iveness without Porpoise: Why Nabokov Called James a Fish', *The Henry James Review*, 4 (1984), 52–9 (54).

10

Undoing The Oedipal Family in *What Maisie Knew*

JULIE RIVKIN

The connection between family structure and narrative structure is an old one, at least as old as the story of Oedipus. Indeed, recent narrative theory, following upon Freud, retells the story of Oedipus as the story of narrative. Roland Barthes muses, 'Doesn't every narrative lead back to Oedipus? Isn't storytelling always a way of searching for one's origins, speaking one's conflicts with the Law, entering into the dialectic of tenderness and hatred?'[1] 'The pleasure of the text', Barthes says in his book of that title, 'is ... an Oedipal pleasure (to denude, to know, to learn the origin and the end), if it is true that every narrative (every unveiling of the truth) is a staging of the (absent, hidden, or hypostatised) father – which would explain the solidarity of narrative forms, of family structures, and of prohibitions of nudity.'[2] As another critic comments, 'Barthes's principal metaphor for narrative sequence, for the origination and engendering of story, is paternity, or the son's search for the father. The author seeks patriarchal authority, and narrative sequence embodies that search.'[3] In this formulation, the telos of narrative is the discovery of origins; identity is fixed when paternity is discovered. The unveiling of the secret is the confirmation of both the closure of narrative and the authority of its narrator.

The apparent appropriateness of this oedipal model of narrative to the works of Henry James is suggested by a formulation of

Tzvetan Todorov about the operation of Jamesian narrative. Reading 'The Figure in the Carpet' as James's masterplot, Todorov uncovers the following ghost in James's narrative machine: 'The Jamesian narrative is always based on *the quest for an absolute and absent cause*. ... The secret of Jamesian narrative is precisely the existence of an essential secret, of something not named, of an absent and superpowerful force which sets the whole present machinery of the narrative in motion.'[4] For 'cause' read 'father', and we have a formulation very similar to Barthes's. The search for a secret origin – or originating secret – gets the Jamesian narrative going and makes the desire for knowledge the impetus that moves the narrative forward. If the father has been elevated and abstracted to the status of an 'absent and superpowerful force' in Todorov's account, narrative still finds its end or goal in its origin and thus the metaphor for its own structure in the structure of the family.

In the light of this oedipal or familial model of narrative, what are we to make of a novel like *What Maisie Knew*, which makes no secret – and no issue – of paternity, begins with a divorce, traces the development of a daughter rather than a son, and presents the multiplication and dispersal of parental figures? Maisie Farange moves from bearing messages of hatred back and forth between her warring parents to sanctioning the adulterous relation between her charming step-parents to finally, at the novel's end, leaving even the stepfamily behind and going off with her old governess. The movement from natural parents to step-parents to the extrafamilial figure of governess follows a narrative logic that can scarcely be said to honour the oedipal model. If anything, the course of Maisie's own parents' lives establishes a pattern of departure from the familial centre – though each remarries after the divorce, these remarriages scarcely remake the family. Her father is chronically absent and finally determines to disappear for good by going to America (with a woman who will support him); her mother reappears always in the company of a new gentleman. The substitution of mates shows no sign of conclusion, for even after Maisie has left her mother's custody, her governess lets slip that the infamous Ida on her last appearance had yet another fellow in tow.[5]

If the family structure ostensibly provides a metaphor for the narrative structure, what narrative structure would be engendered by such disruptions of the familial? A narrative that shows so little regard for cleaving to a paternal source is unlikely to be concerned with unveiling an originary secret. Of particular consequence here is

James's choice of a young girl as his authorial delegate. Since the oedipal scheme is shaped by a son's quest for a father, what significance is there in the fact that this is the narrative of a daughter rather than a son?[6] James addresses this question briefly but significantly in his preface:

> All this would be to say, I at once recognised, that my light vessel of consciousness, swaying in such a draught, couldn't be with verisimilitude a rude little boy: since, beyond the fact that little boys are never so 'present', the sensibility of the female young is indubitably, for early youth, the greater, and my plan would call, on the part of my protagonist, for 'no end' of sensibility.[7]

What James refers to here as a 'draught' is a complex familial situation of divorce, remarriage, and infidelity, and his conviction that this is more likely to 'sway' a young girl than a young boy indicates a link between the dissolution of the patriarchal family plot and the development of the sensibility of the young girl. The connection between the family's and the daughter's fate, I will argue, is not arbitrary. To know from the place of the daughter, as vexed as the effort might be, constitutes a challenge to the oedipal model of narrative and to the patriarchal model of family authority, a challenge articulated both in the novel's plot and in its peculiarly ironic narrative strategy.

Both plot and narrative should, according to the oedipal theory, be oriented toward the full disclosure of a hidden truth, but in *Maisie* both are rendered problematic by the use of a daughter as authorial delegate. The story of a young girl who survives for the most part outside the traditional family seems to require an endless series of substitute parents, all pointing to an ideal parent who could never be located within the universe of the novel, while the narrative of this 'quest' can never, by virtue of its own ironic logic, attain a conclusion that would place the young girl within the realm of truth. The 'proper third person' of my title refers both to the hypothetical parental figure and to the grammatical term for the narrative strategy that 'adopts' Maisie's point of view but not her voice. If the natural family is shown to be lacking and in need of supplementation, so also is the 'natural' narrative stance of third-person narration, which is modified and made ironic in this case by its reliance on so improper a delegate. The narrative strategy replaces the oedipal quest with an irresolvably ironic differential between narrator and delegate that precludes any full or final revelation of truth. The instability of narrative knowledge that the novel enacts matches the dispersal of parental authority within the family; Maisie's 'no end of sensibility' must in some respects be 'no end of narrative'.

If the patriarchal family and the oedipal model of narrative operate according to a hierarchy that makes paternal truth primary and narrative representation secondary, the father's authority supreme and the daughter's desires irrelevant, the model that emerges in James's narrative works to invert these principles. Rather than establish the legitimacy and authority of the family, the plot proffers a series of compensations that constantly rearrange the patriarchal family structure. Maisie's parents separate and then relinquish their roles to step-parents who themselves require compensation. And Maisie herself actively inverts the role she is assigned in the oedipal scenario. As daughter and delegate, she should serve as a mere passive recorder of the fluctuating family scene, but instead she comes to participate in and, indeed, to originate the unions and separations among the adults responsible for her welfare. Moreover, rather than unveil a truth that is the culmination of the novel, the narrative departs from the oedipal scenario by creating an irony that ultimately undermines the power of narrative to reveal knowledge and to display truth.

However, just as the oedipal family could be put in question only by being summoned forth as the model at risk, so also the oedipal narrative model of culminating knowledge can only be left behind by being established as the target of narrative irony. Indeed, the novel provides such a powerful critique of the traditional oedipal narrative precisely because the ghost of that structure is so present throughout. For example, there could be no more compelling account of the epistemological programme of oedipal narrative than this passage in which Maisie envisions her story:

> She judged that if her whole history ... had been the successive stages of her knowledge, so the very climax of the concatenation would, in the same view, be the stage at which the knowledge should overflow. As she was condemned to know more and more, how could it logically stop before she should know Most? It came to her in fact as they sat there on the sands that she was distinctly on the road to know Everything. She had not had governesses for nothing: what in the world had she ever done but learn and learn and learn? She looked at the pink sky with a placid foreboding that she soon should have learnt All.[8]

Were it not for the irony, we might see Maisie as she sees herself: the protagonist of a classic oedipal narrative. Irony both invokes and destabilises that ideal, comically suggesting the oedipal goals – 'Everything', 'All' – while indicating that the process by which 'completion' is achieved is in fact interminable – 'to know more and more', 'learn and learn and learn', 'the very climax of the concatenation would ... be the stage at which the knowledge should overflow'.

Although the patriarchal family is still clearly the crucial site for engaging the relations between epistemology and ethics, narration and source, representation and truth, delegation and originating authority, it can scarcely be said to provide a standard of narrative truth and ethical propriety. The novel's critical questions – What *did* Maisie know? Is Maisie's relationship with her stepfather, Sir Claude, incestuous? What is the ethical force of Maisie's final decision to abandon him? – must be reconsidered in the light of the familial structure that is actually developed in *What Maisie Knew*, a structure based not on the propriety of origins or the authority of paternity, but upon a dynamic of substitution that, like Maisie's ever-expanding family, introduces indeterminacy into the traditional oedipal family. Similarly, although *Maisie* invites consideration as a traditional novel of education whose goal is the attainment of a level of knowledge that closes the gap between ironic narrator and naïve character, the novel's narrative irony makes such knowledge unattainable and situates it permanently in the future. The only knowledge, the only closure, the novel can offer is the uncertain perspective of further knowledge to be had, further narratives to be undertaken. Consequently, the traditional critical questions regarding James's narrative strategy – particularly his choice of centres of consciousness or delegates – must be re-examined in light of an irony that seems to work as much against the narrative as in its service.

I

The process of substitution that governs Maisie's family is set in motion in the novel's prologue, in the account of the divorce and custody settlement designed to provide Maisie with a proper home. With an irony that will only grow more telling as the tale continues, the first sentence of the novel records a settlement that is supposed to terminate Maisie's case: 'The litigation had seemed in-terminable and had in fact been complicated; but by the decision on the appeal the judgement of the divorce-court was confirmed as to the assignment of the child' (11, p. 3). The compensatory func-tion of the law in relation to the natural family is only emphasised here by the compensatory character of the law's own procedure – not only does the law intervene to make up for a deficiency in the natural family, but the appeal intervenes in compensation for a deficiency in the original judgement. As the paragraph continues, the deficiencies in both the judgement and the appeal become more strikingly evident: if custody was originally granted to Maisie's father rather than to her mother, it was only because the same shortcomings were judged more pernicious in a woman than in a man. Both parents are 'bespattered from head to foot' but 'the bril-liancy of a lady's complexion (and this lady's, in court, was im-mensely remarked) might be more regarded as showing the spots' (11, p. 3). And if the appeal altered that decision to grant Maisie's mother partial custody, it did so less to restore justice than to com-pensate for Maisie's father's theft of money provided by the mother for the child's care. The law's compensatory strategies might be designed to restore a wholeness and a home, a standard of propriety that Maisie's parents had lost sight of, but each addi-tional compensatory action on the part of the court serves only to mark a further detour from justice.

The apparent equity of the final arrangement – that Maisie is as-signed to both parents, to be transferred between them at six-month intervals – is less a fair balance than a compounding of errors, and suggests that each time she is transferred she will be used again by her parents to right the balance, compensate for the perceived injus-tice of the court. Far from terminating Maisie's case, the law's inter-vention in the structure of the family only serves to invite further interventions, future reckonings on either side designed finally (if futilely) to rectify the balance. Indeed, the novel itself is an ironic testament to the unsettling impact of the court's settlement. The judgement that initiates Maisie's tale, rather than constitute an oedipal origin for her narrative, propels it toward a series of seem-ingly interminable recapitulations of the initial fault. Thus, what compensates for a lack of propriety at the origin, a judgement in settlement of claims, is itself an origin of impropriety.

The allusion to the judgement of Solomon in the next paragraph of the prologue might seem to counter the alleged impropriety of

the court's judgement by grounding Maisie's case in a noble precedent. Solomon, after all, also judged that a child be 'divided in two
and the portions tossed impartially to the disputants' (11, p. 4). But
this recommendation was never enacted, for the true parent revealed herself by her willingness to relinquish the child whole rather
than possess the child by halves. Solomon's judgement depended on
the necessary connection between natural bond and ethical response; the *true* mother acts for the good of the child, and law
follows from this ethical response. The effect of the allusion to
Solomon is actually to expose how far Maisie's judgement is from
the one it supposedly resembles. The law's compensatory strategies
not only compound the errors they are designed to remedy but also
discredit the natural family itself, which offers no foundation from
which to develop a corrective.[9]

Those present who find Maisie's judgement problematic – and it
does seem 'odd justice in the light of those who still blinked in the
fierce light projected from the tribunal' (11, p. 4) – propose not a
return to the 'natural' in the manner of Solomon but a turn away
from the natural parents to a more appropriate substitute: 'What
was to have been expected on the evidence was the nomination, *in
loco parentis*, of some proper third person' (11, p. 4). The paradox
of this recommendation is clear: not only is the 'proper' parental
figure one who would substitute for the natural parents, but that
figure would be most properly parental by being least like the
proper or natural parents. How is one then to determine who might
be a proper figure to serve *in loco parentis* when the natural parents
have ceased to serve as a standard of parental propriety? Although
various of Maisie's caretakers will make a case for the 'propriety' of
their claims, their connection to the natural parents is always a
dubious authorisation of their appropriateness. The assertion of
Maisie's stepmother, Mrs Beale, is a case in point. Speaking of
herself and Maisie's stepfather, Sir Claude, she insists: 'I'm your
mother now, Maisie. And he's your father. ... We're representative,
you know, of Mr Farange and his former wife. ... We take our
stand on the law' (11, p. 361). The comedy of this claim might
derive from the implication of Mrs Beale's chiasmus that Mrs Beale
is 'mother' to Maisie by representing Maisie's father, and Sir
Claude is 'father' to Maisie by representing Maisie's mother, but its
failure to convince derives from their very status as representatives.
Further, the invocation of law, though it intends to remind us that
the figures they represent are legally Maisie's custodians, only

returns us to the impropriety of the original judgement that made them that. Rather than restoring the family by compensating for and replacing the parents who have failed, the step-parents' attempt to occupy the parental place only extends the chain of compensatory familial arrangements that the divorce initiated. The apparently 'interminable' litigation has not really ended; instead, it has developed into a logic of surrogation that augments the imbalance it is designed to remedy. For this reason, the multiplication of parental figures can never be a sufficient compensation: as the narrator observes of Maisie, 'With two fathers, two mothers and two homes, six protections in all, she shouldn't know "wherever" to go' (11, p. 99). Unlike the homelessness of the orphan, Maisie's condition of deprivation is based on an apparent abundance. According to the paradoxical economy that governs these compensatory relations, the more the initial fault is supplemented, the more evident that fault becomes.

II

The law that governs (while ungoverning) Maisie's family life is similar to the one that regulates James's compositional logic. In particular, the dynamic of compensation or delegation appears in the novel's preface as a tracing of effects that escape their causes, or of progeny that escape the authorising intention of their source, to become the originators of a different course of narrative development. The preface opens with a version of the compositional story that stresses the novel's excessive development: '*What Maisie Knew* is at least a tree that spreads beyond any provision its small germ might on a first handling have appeared likely to make for it' (*AN*, p. 140). The image that appears later in the preface to represent the novel's development expresses an even stronger sense of effects that escape their causes: 'Once "out", like a house-dog of a temper above confinement, it defies the mere whistle, it roams, it hunts, it seeks out and "sees" life; it can be brought back but by hand and then only to take its futile thrashing' (*AN*, p. 144). This refusal of his subject to be mastered by its author can also be seen as the primary issue of the novel. What James calls 'the red dramatic spark that glowed at the core of my vision ... the *full* ironic truth' (*AN*, p. 142) is that his protagonist's development might so escape the control of her parents as to make her not only benefit from what might appear to damage her but also originate what she might appear only to suffer passively. As James puts it:

> Not less than the chance of misery and of a degraded state, the chance of happiness and of an improved state might be here involved for the child, round about whom the complexity of life would thus turn to fineness, to richness. ... Instead of simply submitting to the inherited tie and the imposed complication, of suffering from them, our little wonder-working agent would create, without design, quite fresh elements of this order – contribute, that is, to the formation of a fresh tie, from which it would then (and for all the world as if through a small demonic foresight) proceed to derive great profit.
>
> (AN, pp. 141–2)

The child, who is supposed to derive her identity from her parents and therefore to be damaged by their deviations from proper parenthood, can instead 'derive profit' from this situation to the degree that she can serve as an origin herself. In creating a relation between her step-parents, as James puts it, 'the child become[s] a centre and pretext for a fresh system of misbehaviour, a system moreover of a nature to spread and ramify' (AN, p. 143). As the image of the misbehaving pet used for the compositional story should suggest, this 'system of misbehaviour', particularly with its tendency 'to spread and ramify', resembles the novel's own representational system. Maisie creates the parental (or the source) out of step-parent surrogates; similarly the delegate (as 'wonder-working agent') creates the authority from which it supposedly derives. This metaleptic reversal of causes and effects, of originals and derivatives, authors and delegates, is what James calls 'the "full" irony, ... the promising theme into which the hint I had originally picked up would logically flower' (AN, p. 143).

What James refers to as 'the "full" irony' is essentially a logic of plot and plot composition. Not included is narrative or epistemological irony, the irony for which *Maisie* is famous. The novel is concerned, after all, with what Maisie *knew*, not with what she did. By making Maisie his authorial delegate, James would seem to offer direct access to her knowledge. But, as James's discussion of his representational strategy in the preface makes clear, one can only know what Maisie knew through the agency of a parental narrator who, in order to be one with Maisie, must be quite different from her. The discussion bears a curious resemblance to the problem the novel traces at length – that of finding an appropriate custodial figure for the child – but in the preface it is a problem of narrative strategy rather than of family experience.

In the preface James traces out the following narrative problem: even though it is the child's story that he wishes to tell, the child's vision of the complex alignments and rearrangements in the adult world that makes for interest, James still finds himself at a loss when he considers relying on the child alone for an account of the events taking place around her. If he restricts the picture to what she 'might be conceived to have *understood*', there will be 'great gaps and voids' and the narrative will lose 'clearness of sense' (*AN*, p. 145). Instead of relying on what she understands, then, James will 'stretch the matter to what my wondering witness materially and inevitably *saw*; a great deal of which quantity she either wouldn't understand at all or would quite misunderstand' (*AN*, p. 145). Extending his narrative beyond his character's understanding is the first step, but not the only one; were he to confine himself to her terms for that experience, he would still be too restricted. Although Maisie's terms 'play their part', as he puts it, 'our own commentary constantly attends and amplifies' (*AN*, p. 146). Since 'small children have many more perceptions than they have terms to translate them' (*AN*, p. 145), the narrator must be a translator, providing 'vocabulary' for the child's rich if unexpressed 'vision'.

In other words, in the account of his narrative strategy, James demonstrates why he must use the third rather than the first person, although his goal is to present Maisie's point of view. Or, to be fair, since James rarely used the first person, his account shows why he cannot use the third-person narration in which the character's terms match the narrator's – *le style indirect libre*. Instead, the narrative strategy imposed on him is necessarily an ironic one; the narrator 'knows' more than the child whose experience he presents, and the narrator uses terms that are beyond the vocabulary of the child. The irony structured into James's third-person narrative stance is striking, but so too is something that might seem out of keeping with the irony – his characterisation of the narrator. As attendant of the child – amplifier of her experience and translator of her perceptions – the narrator sounds very much like a caretaker. Is it possible that James's narrator is the 'proper third person' called for at the trial, the figure who can serve *in loco parentis*?

There is something attractive about this suggestion, no doubt because it makes the telling of Maisie's tale an act of justice that compensates for the deprivations she suffers in her actual experience. There would be someone looking out for her interests, after all – not her parents or her step-parents or her governess, but her *narrator*.[10] But a parental narrator would not be able to escape the problems that afflict the other parental figures within the novel. Since the role that the narrator plays is predominantly an epistemological one – making knowable Maisie's situation and her correct or deluded perception of it – it is as an epistemological issue that this inability to represent the parent manifests itself. If the narrator were a true parent – that is, the father in the oedipal model – he would be a standard of truth. And, although Maisie herself might wander in error, she would be accompanied by a figure who could take the measure of her deviations from the truth. Some things she would understand and other things she would misunderstand, but the narrator would never confuse the two; the reader would always know 'what Maisie knew'. This is probably what Wayne Booth calls 'stable irony'.[11] But anyone who, after reading the novel, feels inclined to put a question mark rather than a period after the title – what, after all, *did* Maisie know? – would question the notion of a stable irony as well.

The differential in knowledge that James requires in order to make Maisie's story comprehensible cannot help but baffle the very comprehension it seeks to produce. Although the narrator's function is to represent Maisie's experience, supply 'terms' for her 'perceptions', how can her perceptions be distinguished from the terms used to represent them? In 'amplifying' Maisie's consciousness for us, he makes it impossible for us to distinguish the borders between Maisie's knowledge and his own: how then can we know what Maisie knew? Is there also a 'proper third', a standard or criterion of judgement or distinction, lacking in this case as well? Rather than distinguishing between Maisie's understanding and her misunderstanding, the narrator's intervention only obscures the distinction. James gives us an image for the difficulty when he speaks of how he renders Maisie's activity of spirit 'in figures that are not yet at her command and that are nevertheless required whenever those aspects about her and those parts of her experience that she understands darken off into others that she rather tormentedly misses' (*AN*, p. 146). If understanding 'darkens off' into misunderstanding, is it always possible to know the difference? Rather than provide a parental base from which to measure the misunderstanding of the child and the misbehaviour of the adults, the narrative strategy dramatises the epistemological indeterminacy it might be seen as attempting to alleviate. Instead of following the oedipal narrative model, in which the son moves toward the truth in the discovery of the secret of origins, *What Maisie Knew* disperses the secret through a narrative irony that precludes distinguishing between parent and child, paternal narrator and pre-sentient daughter. Indeed, rather than arguing that we only know 'what Maisie knew' through the agency of her narrator, it might be more accurate to argue that we only know what the narrator 'knew' through the agency of his compositional surrogate, his wayward daughter. Irony puts everyone, it seems, in a potentially dependent position – not *in loco parentis* but *in loco filiae*.[12]

III

If the narrator depends as much upon a daughter for representation as that daughter depends upon him, what does this do to the authority of Oedipus as a model both for narrative and for family life? The confusion of knowledge fostered by the narrative irony inherent in James's compositional strategy in *Maisie* is no less a confusion of the oedipal sexual scenario. For if the border between narrator and narrated is broken down, so too are the borders between genders. While the oedipal scenario functions primarily to mark the boundary of prohibition (incestuous desire and the threat of castration) that defines and assures male sexual identity, the ironic logic of James's novel erodes such boundaries. It is no accident, then, that the novel arrives finally at a situation in which incest itself, that ultimate marker of the transgression of sexual, generational, and familial categories, becomes indeterminate. In rewriting the father–daughter relation, James is pursuing the logic of his own narrative strategy, but alternatively we could say that his narrative strategy is a consequence of his attempt to know from the place of the daughter.

The novel's complex critique of the oedipal scenario begins where Maisie's education does, in her father's home. There, in keeping with the oedipal model that defines female identity as lacking, the first thing Maisie comes to learn is a sense of her own deficiency. The gentleman friends of her father, who tease and play with her and make her light their cigarettes, reproach her for having legs like 'toothpicks'. The word sticks in Maisie's mind and contributes to 'her feeling from this time that she was deficient in something that would meet the general desire' (11, p. 10). What Maisie takes as the 'general desire' is, of course, only the 'gentlemen's' desire – a substitution that indicates how the social order that makes small girls feel deficient manages to disguise its own patriarchal origins. Maisie's deficiency is further specified: 'She found out what it was: it was a congenital tendency to the production of a substance to which Moddle, her nurse, gave a short ugly name, a name painfully associated at dinner with the part of the joint that she didn't like' (11, p. 10). Although Maisie learns the word, the reader does not; but the circumlocution that substitutes for it is far more suggestive than any direct revelation. Though the 'ugly name' Maisie learns is ostensibly different from the 'ugly name' we have been taught to use in designating that sense of lack girls acquire in the oedipal stage, that sense of oedipal lack is nonetheless implied in the word she does learn.[13] However, the text departs from the oedipal scenario in refusing to fix Maisie's sense of lack to a determinate referent. If Maisie is missing something that would meet male desire, we may be incorrect to sense an allusion to an absent male part. Perhaps the daughter is not 'woman' enough to meet the gentlemen's desire. In keeping with such expectations, students of mine have suggested the word must be 'fat' and that the circumlocution obliges the reader to undergo a process of discovery analogous to Maisie's own, so that we share her experience of comprehension when we arrive at the word 'obviously' intended. But I would claim that the effect is the reverse. Rather than presenting 'knowledge' as the safe arrival at the right answer, the circumlocution introduces a multiplicity of associations that cannot simply be dismissed with the naming of an innocuous word to fill in the blank. Instead of letting the reader supply the referent and delimit Maisie's sense of lack, the narrator's circumlocution works to extend that sense of lack by virtue of its own indeterminacy of reference.

Moreover, circumlocution defines Maisie's being in a larger sense, her role in the exchanges between her divorced parents. The unspoken word that names Maisie's lack naturally reminds the reader of another linguistic suppression linked with Maisie's sense of deficiency – she is not allowed to read the letters sent her by her mother. Watching her father chuck her mother's unopened letters to her into the fire, and able to read only the monogram on the envelope, Maisie suffers 'a scared anticipation of fatigue, a guilty sense of not rising to the occasion' (11, p. 10). The image of impotence – of 'not rising to the occasion' – returns us to the oedipal associations of that unnamed lack, particularly since this is a daughter's failure *vis-à-vis* her mother. But here again there is an ambiguity; rather than the father's love for the mother giving the daughter a sense of inadequacy, as in the classic oedipal scenario, it is the father's hatred of the mother that leaves Maisie feeling guilty. Yet she also feels a 'charm of ... violence' (11, p. 10) in her father's treatment of these letters; perhaps their meaning is more readily discerned in her father's treatment of them as 'dangerous missiles' than in any knowledge that might come from acquainting herself with their contents.

Maisie's sense of inadequacy is distinct enough – and confusing enough – to lead her to compare it with her memory of her earlier experience. Moddle, Maisie's nurse, a figure whose name suggests not only 'ma' and 'coddle' but also 'model', only presented Maisie with a desire that could be met – that she not play too far from her nurse. Like the 'model' that she is, this mother figure is associated with proximity and resemblance; the only thing she questions is distance between herself and the child. This Edenic memory of an unbroken continuity between mother figure and child (in Kensington Gardens) conforms to a psychoanalytic account of the pre-oedipal stage, in which the daughter has no strong sense of a boundary between self and other and consequently no sense of personal inadequacy. [14] But once the father has introduced a sense of difference, Maisie's Moddle cannot alter it: 'They still went to the Gardens, but there was a difference even there; she was impelled perpetually to look at the legs of other children and ask her nurse if *they* were toothpicks' (10, p. 17). Conforming to the 'model' is no longer enough to protect Maisie from a sense of inadequacy; indeed Moddle herself responds to Maisie in such a way as to confirm Maisie's worst fears: 'Oh my dear, you'll not find such another pair as your own' (10, p. 11). Again this new stage of experience would appear to fit the psychoanalytic model – the oedipal stage is marked by the daughter's discovery of the father, and with it the discovery of separateness, sexual difference, and lack.

However, Moddle's phrase – 'You'll not find such another pair as your own' – should also bring to mind a referent other than Maisie's ignominious 'toothpicks', a referent that alters the psychoanalytic reading just advanced. Perhaps the 'pair' that marks Maisie as different from the other children is not a part of her body but a part of her family – her parents. Indeed, as the novel progresses the word 'pair' will come to refer almost exclusively to her parents – and never in flattering terms (as in the ironic exclamation from Maisie's stepmother: 'They're a pretty pair of parents!' 11, p. 59). The sentence that follows Moddle's utterance confirms this association by tracing Maisie's own intuition: 'It seemed to have to do with something else that Moddle often said; "You'll feel the strain – that's where it is; and you'll feel it still worse, you know"' (11, p. 11). The 'strain' and the 'pair' are linked in Maisie's mind, and even if she feels it for the moment as something wrong with her legs – 'that's where it is' Moddle had said – the other meanings traced here also leave their mark. Indeed Maisie's sense of her identity as deficiency and difference is inscribed upon her body by the patriarchal order, but it would be hard to determine whether the inscription is of oedipal lack, parental conflict, desire, fear, or something worse.

The greatest irony in this presentation of Maisie's first consciousness of her new condition comes in the sentence that sums it up. Since Moddle has told her that what she is feeling – and will feel worse – is 'the strain', 'from the first Maisie not only felt it, but knew she felt it' (11, p. 11). The statement is comic – or pathetic – or both. That this sense of deficiency and difference should not only be experienced by Maisie but be called 'knowledge' might be the hardest lesson of Maisie's early education. At issue here is not 'what Maisie knows' but what it means for Maisie to 'know' – how knowledge is conceived and constructed. In spite of the irony that separates the reader from Maisie, the irony that makes this incident amusing to the reader and troubling for Maisie, there are parallels between how the process of signification works for the reader and how Maisie's perceptions are constituted as 'knowledge'. In particular, meaning comes not in the tracing of a referent but in the tracing of circumlocutionary effects. For example, Maisie's sense that 'her features had somehow become prominent' because 'they were so perpetually nipped by the gentlemen who came to see her father' (11, p. 10) does not make us wish to measure Maisie's features for physical growth (knowledge as reference) but leads us to see Maisie's growth as a function of how she is perceived (knowledge as effect). The reader comes to 'know' Maisie not by replacing circumlocution with substance (the word 'fat' in this case) but by seeing how there is no knowledge outside of circumlocution.

If circumlocution signals both Maisie's adherence to and her departure from the oedipal model of sexual identity, her linguistic behaviour as a medium of communication between her divorced parents will have the same duality. While it at first confirms her place in an oedipal scenario, it eventually becomes a means of escaping from that scenario. Since the divorce of Maisie's parents afflicts the very circumstances of meaning, Maisie's movements between the two households are linguistic as well as emotional crises. Moddle tries to calm Maisie's anxiety about her first crossing by creating what amounts to a sense of linguistic continuity. In fact, she literally gives Maisie words to hold on to:

> [Her fear] would have darkened all the days if the ingenious Moddle hadn't written on a paper in very big easy words ever so many pleasures that she would enjoy at the other house. These promises ranged from 'a mother's fond love' to 'a nice poached egg to your tea', ... [and] at the supreme hour, ... by Moddle's direction, the paper was thrust away in her pocket and there clenched in her fist.
>
> (11, p. 12)

But these are not the only words that Maisie bears as she crosses the gulf. Asked by her mother whether her father has any message for her, Maisie dutifully repeats, 'He said I was to tell you, from him, ... that you're a nasty horrid pig!' (11, p. 13).

The fate of these two communications suggests the difficulty Maisie experiences as a mediating term between two opposing sources of meaning. Maisie can carry, concealed but read, the words that promise a linguistic consistency and familial harmony (word of a loving mother from the realm of a loving father), while she transmits without interpreting the words that mark the opposition between the two parents. Maisie's mother cannot be both 'fond and loving' and 'a nasty horrid pig', but for the moment Maisie does not attempt to match the words she's been given to bear; she simply lets the message she carries pass through her. This practice suits her parents, who are content to use her to deliver their venomous messages. Maisie's mother's response to her father's insult is not literally reproduced, but we learn that it is a 'missive that dropped into her memory with the dry rattle of a letter falling into a pillar-box. Like the letter it was, as part of the contents of a well-stuffed post-bag, delivered in due course at the right address' (11, p. 14). In this image Maisie is a courier, ensuring at once that letters are delivered and that they remain, by her at least, unread. To that extent, she is the perfectly oedipal signifier, beholden exclusively to her source, undeviating in her representation of it.[15]

If, in the first phase of Maisie's development, difference – sexual difference, the difference between her parents – was inscribed on her own body, in this next phase Maisie survives the radical opposition between the two homes and thus preserves intelligibility by not letting difference make a mark. As an unresisting medium of exchange, she seems for the moment saved from the radical divergence of the meanings she represents; her meaning exists only for the senders and receivers of messages, her parents. And when this unwitting strategy ceases to work, it is not because Maisie has begun to read the messages themselves but because she has learned to read their effects. She 'puzzle[s] out with imperfect signs, but with a prodigious spirit, that she had been a centre of hatred and a messenger of insult, and that everything was bad because she had been employed to make it so' (11, p. 15). And because she has learned to read her parents, they will cease being able to read her. Inverting the oedipal scenario, Maisie's response shows that knowledge of the source need not prescribe loyalty to its authority but can instead permit a self-empowering departure from its prescriptions.

As in the first phase when Maisie's sense of deficiency was a displacement of her parents' offence, Maisie's sense of self-blame in this situation also displaces responsibility from her parents. But in considering herself unduly responsible ('everything was bad because she had been employed to make it so') she also opens the possibility of her own agency. 'Her parted lips locked themselves with the determination to be employed no longer' (11, p. 15). The 'parted lips', like the 'post bag', are images of female receptivity, associated with that sense of 'congenital deficiency' that marked Maisie's first experience of her 'difference'. Her resistance turns the image of lack (physical inadequacy, reading disability) into an image of power; the empty mailbag becomes an inner space to which she lays claim. Characteristically this gesture is misunderstood, but it is a misunderstanding that Maisie promotes and from which she benefits:

> The theory of her stupidity, eventually embraced by her parents, corresponded with a great date in her small still life: the complete vision, private but final, of the strange office she filled. It was literally a moral revolution and accomplished in the depths of her nature. The stiff dolls on the dusky shelves began to move their arms and legs; old forms and phrases began to have a sense that frightened her. She had a new feeling, the feeling of danger; on which a new remedy rose to meet it, the idea of an inner self or, in other words, of concealment.
>
> (11, p. 15)

Maisie has used one form of difference to create another: where previously she survived the difference between her parents' opposing meanings by refusing to comprehend them, she now discovers the possibility of a difference between what she sees and what she shows. What Maisie discovers, in other words, is irony. And her pleasures are those of the ironist: 'She spoiled their fun, but she practically added to her own. She saw more and more; she saw too much' (11, pp. 15–16).

The discovery of this possibility of resistance is linked to the replacement of Moddle by Miss Overmore, as Maisie shifts her relation to parental language from copying to overcoming. Moddle is now associated in her mind with various lapses, lapses connected significantly with her physical being and her linguistic competence. Maisie remembers primarily her 'hungry disappearances from the nursery and distressful lapses in the alphabet', in particular with regard to 'the important letter haitch' (11, p. 16). If the characteristic of the 'haitch' in Cockney speech – and I assume this is what Maisie notes – is to be present when it ought to be absent and absent when it ought to be present, we could find no fuller demonstration of Maisie's desire now to differ from her model.

But if one leaves behind the oedipal model of narration, in which signs owe their meaning to a 'parental' authority of original truth or correct knowledge or decisive judgement, in favour of an ironic model in which there will always be a difference between sign and meaning, how can one know – and by that token, be – any one thing, securely and properly? The situation is about to become more complex, as the following exchange between Maisie and Miss Overmore should suggest. Told by her mother that she's to let her father know 'that he lies and he knows he lies' (11, p. 17), Maisie consults her governess on the truth of this accusation. Miss Overmore, caught in the act of darning a sock, blushes. She 'then pricked again at her muffled hand so hard that Maisie wondered how she could bear it' (11, pp. 17–18):

> It was then that her companion addressed her in the unmistakeable language of a pair of eyes of deep dark grey. 'I can't say No', they replied as distinctly as possible; 'I can't say No, because I'm afraid of your mamma, don't you see? Yet how can I say Yes after your papa has been so kind to me, talking to me so long the other day, smiling and flashing his beautiful teeth at me the time we met him in the Park, the time when, rejoicing at the sight of us, he left the gentleman he was with and turned and walked with us, stayed with us for half

an hour?' Somehow in the light of Miss Overmore's lovely eyes that
incident came back to Maisie with a charm it hadn't had at the time,
and this in spite of the fact that after it was over her governess had
never but once alluded to it.

(11, p. 18)

What Maisie learns from this question is not whether her father or
her mother lies – or indeed whether they know they lie – but how
the very conceptions of 'truth' and 'knowledge' seem to mean differently in the 'unmistakeable language' of Miss Overmore's grey eyes.
Indeed this language does not behave as language does in the oedipal
model, in which signs derive their meaning from a mastering truth at
the origin. Rather, 'truth' in Miss Overmore's language seems to be
determined on the basis of its effects. If Miss Overmore cannot say
either 'yes' or 'no' to Maisie's question, thereby fixing one parent as
a speaker of truth and the other as a liar, it is because she cannot
choose between the effects of either determination of truth. As a
poor but beautiful young woman trying to make her way up in the
world, Miss Overmore does not know whether her own best interests lie in loyalty to her present employer, Maisie's mother, or her
future employer and possibly more, Maisie's father. If fear keeps her
from defaming Maisie's mother, hope and desire keep her from
corroborating the mother's claim and defaming Maisie's father.

The similarity of Miss Overmore's position to Maisie's own – for
both are young and female and dependent upon two warring adults
for their maintenance – makes her response instructive. Although
Miss Overmore apparently refrains from judgement, her silent communication has an insurrectionary force, for it frees 'truth' from
parental authority, placing it instead in the hands of those whom, in
the oedipal model, it was supposed to master. If Maisie has been
made something of a semiotic servant by her parents, it is fitting
that she should learn survival from a servant. Maisie's ability to
feign stupidity works to baffle her parents' use of her as an emissary
of hatred, but when she ceases to serve this need, she must reconceive the nature of her function. The little revolution in this case
consists as much in learning to manipulate signs to generate effects
(without consideration for their proper meaning) – putting the
daughterly servant before the paternal master – as in learning that
one can be, quite improperly, two different things at once, or any
number of things, for that matter. To be a self is, for Maisie, to be
potentially any number of selves.

Miss Overmore is the occasion of this unfixing of identity, but it is a lesson that extends beyond the present case. For example, as Maisie's parents' strategy for mutual revenge evolves from wrenching Maisie away to refusing to come claim her, Maisie quickly learns a new identity that makes her presence necessary. Told by Miss Overmore, now living with her father, that 'a lady couldn't stay with a gentleman that way without some awfully proper reason' (11, p. 32), she also learns that 'a long legged stick of a tomboy' is an awfully proper reason. Maisie immediately tries out this 'proper reason' in another context, reforming other identities to fit her new self-definition. That is, if this identity makes a place for her in her father's house, it should do the same in her mother's. When Miss Overmore tells her that her mother is travelling with a gentleman 'whom, to be painfully plain on it, she had – well, "picked up"' (11, p. 39), Maisie sees a place for herself. 'If she should go to her mother', she proposes to Miss Overmore, 'perhaps the gentleman might become her tutor' (11, p. 40).

> 'The gentleman?' The proposition was complicated enough to make Miss Overmore stare.
> 'The one who's with mamma. Mightn't that make it right – as right as your being my governess makes it for you to be with papa?'
> Miss Overmore considered; she coloured a little; then she embraced her ingenious friend. 'You're too sweet! I'm a *real* governess.'
> 'And couldn't he be a real tutor?'
> 'Of course not. He's ignorant and bad.'
> 'Bad –?' Maisie echoed with wonder.
> Her companion gave a queer little laugh at her tone. 'He's ever so much younger – 'But that was all.
> 'Younger than you?'
> Miss Overmore laughed again; it was the first time Maisie had seen her approach so nearly to a giggle. 'Younger than – no matter whom.'
> (11, p. 40)

What Maisie appears to have learned, and to a degree that startles the woman who has taught her, is that the identities of the people around her are not fixed but are determined by the relations in which they are engaged. If Maisie's governess can become her stepmother and her mother can become 'her ladyship', there would seem to be no reason why her mother's gentleman friend might not become her tutor. Although Miss Overmore might insist, for example, that she is a 'real' governess, Maisie is actually more accurate when she sees that tutors, like governesses, are not 'real' but can be made or unmade to fit the occasion. Identity is not an essence, something inherited at birth and fixed until death, but a construct always susceptible to reconstruction.[16]

This discovery should explain why *Maisie* could not fit the oedipal model of narrative, the model with which we began. If identity in *Maisie* is always an effect of representations and always subject to reconstruction, clearly a genealogical model like the oedipal one, which privileges the determining influence of origins, of fathers, and of fixed truths, could not provide Maisie with an answer to the question of who she is. Maisie's mode of coming to knowledge – a mode that is entirely contextual and relational – only appears to differ from the way knowledge and truth are constituted in the adult world. In fact, her behaviour exposes the hidden workings of that world, for the adults construct their identities in the same way that Maisie comes to learn of them. While they pretend to have 'real' identities, they are in fact determined by the sites they occupy, the relations they inhabit, and the representations they make of themselves. Who is old and who is young? Who is a governess and who is a lord? These distinctions are not absolute but conventional, and Maisie reveals the source of their identity to be no more authoritative than the source of her knowledge.[17] [...]

In commenting on the novel's conclusion in the preface, James notes the impact of Maisie's fate on his own ironic narrative strategy:

> She wonders ... to the end, to the death – the death of her childhood, properly speaking; after which (with the inevitable shift, sooner or later, of her point of view) her situation will change and become another affair, subject to other measurements and with a new centre altogether. The particular reaction that will have led her to that point, and that it has been of an exquisite interest to study in her, will have spent itself; there will be another scale, another perspective, another horizon.
>
> (*AN*, 146–7)

The 'death of her childhood' is also the end of a certain narrative strategy and the evocation of another 'point of view'. As Maisie comes of age, narrative irony becomes not only unnecessary but inappropriate. This alone does not distinguish *Maisie* from other novels of education: they too conclude with the exhaustion of an ironic narrative strategy – in particular when, by the story's close, the ironic distance between narrator and character is dissolved and the character comes to share the perspective of the narrator. Indeed, the closing of that ironic separation marks such novels of education as oedipal narratives; the character comes to learn the 'truth' that the narrator possessed all along and thus to share the paternal authority once exercised only by the narrator. In *What Maisie Knew*, however, the effect is quite distinct. The reduction of the difference between narrator and character merely underscores its irreducibility. The ironic strategy is exhausted not because Maisie comes to share the perspective of her narrator but because, as the neophyte becomes master of her own life, she has passed outside the terms of the narrative altogether. The narrator would himself have to undergo an education analogous to Maisie's – one that would lead him to adopt 'another perspective' and speak from 'a new centre' – in order to continue as her narrative guardian.

No doubt James's insight into the insurmountable alterity of his character at the end of the novel has something to do with the fact that she is a daughter become a young woman, at least in fictional terms. But it also has to do with the nature of irony and especially with that peculiar habit irony has of turning against itself. At the end of the novel, the irony governing the narrative is effectively reversed, while also being irreversibly proliferated. For the plot and the narrative strategy insist that Maisie assume a position of knowledge (the 'inevitable shift ... of her point of view') that can no longer be treated ironically, making the novel impossible to narrate in the form in which, up until this point, it has been narrated. Indeed, this shift effectively submits the narrator to an irony resembling that to which he has hitherto submitted his young charge. It is for this reason, perhaps, that the novel ends with a picture of puzzlement over Maisie's knowledge and an implicit suggestion that, in order to do this knowledge justice, some other narrative would be needed. Such a narrative would require – in the words of the preface – some other 'scale', some other 'horizon' to encompass Maisie's new point of view.

The narrative, therefore, is subject to the same logic that governs the undoing of oedipal family relations. Just as the ideal of the proper surrogate parent – or proper third person – is shaped by the model of an original parent, so too the ideal of a perfectly parental narrator – or proper third person – is based on the ideal of a disinterested *pater fabulae* who stands outside the fictional world, transcending it and in that transcendence fully mastering it. However, in the same way that the proper parent's need for surrogation shows him to be deficient, an inappropriate model for familial propriety, the transcendental narrator's dependency on a delegate to accomplish his ends and confirm his ironic mastery shows him to be insufficient and renders his narrative incomplete. The narrator, like Maisie, can never know, or narrate, 'All'. Consequently, rather than exhaust irony, the ending of *What Maisie Knew* merely compounds it. The novel ends not with what the oedipal model promises and what Maisie herself envisioned as the culmination of her story – a knowledge of 'Everything' – but instead with the conclusive impossibility of ever ascertaining, or narrating, 'what Maisie knew'.

From Julie Rivkin, *False Positions: The Representational Logics of Henry James's Fiction* (Stanford, CA, 1996) pp. 123–45, 160–2, 209–11.

NOTES

[Julie Rivkin's feminist reading of *What Maisie Knew*, excerpted from the substantial chapter in her recent book, brings together Freudian psychoanalysis and the narrativity of Roland Barthes, both of which have as their masterplot that familial narrative *par excellence*, the story of Oedipus. Noting the appropriateness of Barthes' oedipal theory of narrative (the search for a father) to Todorov's theory of the Jamesian narrative telos (the search for a cause), Rivkin examines the implications for this story of a daughter, not a son, who, inverting Oedipus, to begin with has three father figures: Beale, Sir Claude and her narrator, 'the proper third person', whom she will eventually abandon. Rivkin uses the text to interrogate Freudian psychoanalytical theory of gender identity and Barthes' theory of narrative. Unlike the classical protagonist of the educational novel, who comes to share the perspective of the paternal truth, the truth of the *pater fabulae*, *What Maisie Knew* famously ends in uncertainty, the gap between narrator/father and character/daughter unclosable. Rivkin sees a parallel between the proper surrogate parent for Maisie and the perfectly parental narrator: the one exposing the inadequacy of Maisie's original parent, the other the inadequacy of the *pater fabulae*. Moving outside the oedipal model of narrative, where the son comes to share the truth of the father and signs owe their meaning to parental authority, Maisie inhabits the ironic space where truth is freed from this authority and identity is seen to be a construct. Rivkin shows that writing from the place of a daughter disrupts the oedipal narrative model, throws into question the patriarchal family and exposes the *pater fabulae*, who – like Maisie – can never know or narrate all. Ed.]

1. Roland Barthes, *The Pleasure of the Text*, trans. Richard Howard (New York, 1975), p. 47.

2. Ibid., p. 10.

3. Dianne Sadoff, 'Storytelling and the Figure of the Father in *Little Dorrit*', *PMLA*, 95 (1980), 234–45 (235). Other critics who have done important work on the relation between patriarchal familial structure and narrative structure include Peter Brooks, in his *Reading for the Plot* (New York, 1984); Edward Said, in *Beginnings: Intention and Method* (Baltimore, MD, 1975); and Patricia Drechsel Tobin, in *Time and the Novel* (Princeton, NJ, 1978). For powerful feminist critiques of the oedipal theory of narrative, I am indebted to Teresa de Lauretis's 'Desire in Narrative', in her *Alice Doesn't: Feminism, Semiotics, Cinema* (Bloomington, IN, 1984) and Susan Winnett's 'Coming Unstrung', *PMLA*, 105, 3 (1990), 505–18.

4. Tzvetan Todorov, *The Poetics of Prose*, trans. Richard Howard (Ithaca, NY, 1977), p. 145.

5. James's selection of a daughter of divorced parents as his delegate is of historical as well as literary interest given the actual transformations under way in the patriarchal family during the era preceding the composition of *Maisie*. The Divorce and Matrimonial Causes Act of 1857, along with the Married Women's Property Act of 1882 and the Guardianship of Infants Act of 1886, marked at least three major areas of change in the structure of the family. By making divorce more widely available (formerly divorce required an Act of Parliament), by granting married women legal status and the right to own property, and by allowing the welfare of the child and the rights of the mother to be considered in child custody cases (before 1870 the father always retained custody of the child), these three legal reforms altered what had previously been a thoroughly patriarchal institution. These changes received enormous publicity, not only through the efforts of highly visible figures like Caroline Norton (who agitated for the Property Act), but also through an increasingly active press that tended to report on the divorce trials of the upper classes in sordid detail. The number of divorces rose from 4 in 1856 to around 200 in 1860 to over 550 by 1900, and the decade of the 1880s witnessed some of the most prominent – and most scandalous – divorce trials of the century.

   The divorce statistics are from Allen Horstman's *Victorian Divorce* (London, 1985), p. 110. For further discussion of Victorian divorce see Horstman; John Eekalaar and Mavis Maclean, *Maintenance After Divorce* (Oxford, 1986), pp. 1–31; O. L. McGregor, Louis Blom-Cooper and Colin Gibson, *Separated Spouses: A Study of the Matrimonial Jurisdiction of Magistrates Courts* (London, 1970), pp. 14–22. For a discussion of the Married Women's Property Act see Lee Holcombe, *Wives and Property: Reform of the Married Women's Property Act* (Toronto, 1983). The new laws about child custody are treated in Susan Maidment, *Child Custody and Divorce: The Law in Social Context* (London, 1984), pp. 89–131.

Not surprisingly, given the publicity divorce was receiving, it became an increasingly acceptable and even popular literary subject. Marcia Jacobson, in her *Henry James and the Mass Market* (Tuscaloosa, AL, 1983), p. 102, situates *What Maisie Knew* in the following literary context: 'Divorce novels began appearing in America in the eighties and in England in the nineties, as Howell's *A Modern Instance* (1882) and Hardy's *Jude the Obscure* (1896) remind us. Particularly relevant to James's novel is the fact that, between 1892 and 1895, the years in which *Maisie* was taking shape and James was most attentive to the English stage, every major English playwright was writing "problem plays" about the Marriage Question. ... These plays appeared in rapid succession: Oscar Wilde's *Lady Windermere's Fan* (1892) and *A Woman of No Importance* (1893), Arthur Wing Pinero's *The Second Mrs Tanqueray* (1893), *The Notorious Mrs Ebbsmith* (1895), and *The Benefit of the Doubt* (1895), and Henry Arthur Jones's *The Case of the Rebellious Susan* (1894) and *The Masqueraders*.'

6. I am grateful to J. Hillis Miller for raising this issue.

7. Henry James, *The Art of the Novel: Critical Prefaces*, ed. Richard P. Blackmur (New York, 1934), pp. 143–4. Subsequent page references are given in the text, abbreviated as *AN*.

8. *The Novels and Tales of Henry James*, vol. 11 (New York, 1908), p. 281. Subsequent references are indicated in the text by volume and page number.

9. John Carlos Rowe has observed how James's legal families strain the notion of the natural family, and in a reading of *The Spoils of Poynton* he discusses some of the reasons for that tension: '*The Spoils of Poynton* calls our attention to the unnaturalness of such legalities as sustain a classed and patriarchal society and to the disorientations of history that are required to sustain some idea of the orderly transmission of authority from one generation of men to the next': Rowe, *Theoretical Dimensions of Henry James* (Madison, WI, 1984), p. 100.

10. Merla Wolk argues for the maternal function of the narrator in her 'Narration and Nurture in *What Maisie Knew*', *The Henry James Review*, 4:3 (1983), 196–206.

11. Wayne Booth, *A Rhetoric of Irony* (Chicago, 1974), pp. 1–86.

12. My discussion of the problem of making Maisie's knowledge accessible is indebted to Neil Hertz's excellent article about *What Maisie Knew* and Freud's case history of Dora, 'Dora's Secrets, Freud's Techniques', *Diacritics*, 13:1 (1983), 65–76. Noting what he describes as 'the confusion of tongues between an author and his young

surrogate' (p. 67), Hertz suggests a parallel between James's difficulties in giving voice to Maisie's story without contaminating it and Freud's difficulties in narrating the case of his young female analysand. The issue here, according to Hertz, is less one of transference than of identification – both male analyst and male author being unable to distinguish themselves sufficiently from the young girl whose story they are supposed to represent.

13. The Jamesian text departs from the oedipal scenario in much the way that Derrida departs from Lacan on this same issue: rather than essentialising lack of castration, Derrida refuses 'the metaphysical gesture (albeit a negative one) of making absence, the lack, the hole, a transcendent principle': Alan Bass, in Jacques Derrida, *Margins of Philosophy*, trans. Alan Bass (Chicago, 1982), p. 6n.

14. I am basing my account of the daughter's pre-oedipal stage and of the bond between mother and child on Nancy Chodorow's chapter 'Gender Differences in the Preoedipal Period', in her *The Reproduction of Mothering: Psychoanalysis and the Sociology of Gender* (Berkeley, CA, 1978), pp. 92–110.

15. This discussion of Maisie as the perfect oedipal signifier is implicitly alluding to Jacques Lacan's 'Seminar on *The Purloined Letter*', trans. Jeffrey Mehlman, *Yale French Studies*, 48 (1973), 38–72, in which he writes 'the letter always arrives at its destination' (p. 72).

16. As Miss Overmore's insinuations make plain, age is no more stable than identity, being likewise an entirely relative term. Maisie's reflections on the subject of age make this instability more explicit: 'The only mystification … was the imposing time of life that her elders spoke of as youth. For Sir Claude then Mrs Beale was "young", just as for Mrs Wix Sir Claude was: that was one of the merits for which Mrs Wix most commended him. What therefore was Maisie herself, and, in another relation to the matter, what therefore was mamma? It took her some time to puzzle out with the aid of an experiment or two that it wouldn't do to talk about mamma's youth. She even went so far one day, in the presence of that lady's thick colour and marked lines, as to wonder if it would occur to any one but herself to do so. Yet if she wasn't young then she was old; and this threw an odd light on her having a husband of a different generation. Mr Farange was still older – that Maisie perfectly knew, and it brought her in due course to the perception of how much more, since Mrs Beale was younger than Sir Claude, papa must be older than Mrs Beale. Such discoveries were disconcerting and even a trifle confounding: these persons, it appeared, were not of the age they ought to be' (11, pp. 80–1).

17. Dennis Foster explores similar issues from a Lacanian perspective. See his 'Maisie Supposed to Know: An Amo(u)ral Analysis', *The Henry James Review*, 5 (1984), 207–16.

11

What Maisie Knew and the Improper Third Person

SHEILA TEAHAN

James's preface to *What Maisie Knew* is oddly defensive in tone. James is clearly uneasy about the novel's subject, the dilemma of a young girl surrounded by the adulterous intrigues of her parents and step-parents, and he devotes some attention to anticipating charges of having 'mixed Maisie up' in the novel's erotic quadrangle. As often in the history of James criticism, the preface has proven a self-fulfilling prophecy: critics have tended to repeat the antinomies of James's own ambivalence towards the novel, replaying both the preface's and the text's own internal debate as to whether Maisie is corrupt or innocent, disingenuous or precociously wise – the ambiguity, in short, about how much Maisie knows.

The novel's critics, including James himself, are correct in their intuition that Maisie's equivocal knowledge invites investigation, such as the novel's own repeated probings of her 'moral sense'. But, as I shall argue, James's own doubts about the moral sense of *What Maisie Knew*, and the playing out of these doubts in subsequent criticism, can be attributed to something other than the novel's manifest thematic content. His defensiveness may arise less from its adulterous theme than from a representational strategy that creates the knowledge it appears to reflect, for though the narrator claims merely to report what Maisie knows, he is deeply implicated in the construction of that knowledge. Maisie's ambiguous knowledge and her ultimate scapegoating, the figurative death marked in James' preface as 'the death of her childhood', are themselves produced by the Jamesian representational strategy of the central intelligence, which both brings Maisie into being and sacrifices her in the name of its own antithetical logic.

As its title indicates, *What Maisie Knew* is explicitly concerned with the epistemology of the Jamesian reflective centre. The novel's narrative strategy is one of deliberate self-restriction to Maisie's impressions; as James exhorts himself in his notebook entries, 'make my point of view, my *line*, the consciousness ... of the child ... EVERYTHING TAKES PLACE BEFORE MAISIE'.[1] But because 'children have many more perceptions than they have terms to translate them',[2] this scheme assumes a rhetorical disjunction between narrator and receptive intelligence. If Maisie is an 'infant' (*AN*, p. 145) in the etymological sense of *infans*, speechless or without language, then the 'great gaps and voids' of her verbal capacity must be filled by the narrator himself. Although 'Maisie's terms accordingly play their part', the narrator's 'own commentary constantly attends and amplifies', translating Maisie's perceptions into 'figures that are not yet at her command' (*AN*, pp. 145, 146). The narrator fills out the lacunae of Maisie's linguistic resources and mediates her preverbal consciousness. His relation to her is one of translation or metaphor, through those words' shared etymological meaning of a transference or carrying over.

The ambiguities of this scheme may account for the defensive tone of the preface.[3] In his eagerness to forestall the objection that 'nothing could well be more disgusting than to attribute to Maisie so intimate an "acquaintance" with the gross immoralities surrounding her' (*AN*, p. 149), James acknowledges the rhetorical conundrum pointed to by the novel's title. For given the difficulty of distinguishing the narrator's terms from Maisie's, since she can only know what the narrator tells us she knows, 'what Maisie knew' names a symbiotic narrative relation in which her knowledge depends on its articulation by the adult narrator.[4] And despite James's scruples about 'the "mixing-up" of a child with anything unpleasant' (*AN*, pp. 148–9), the novel's opening figuratively repeats exactly this crime: Maisie's parents pour 'evil' into her 'little gravely-gazing soul as into a boundless receptacle', and the Jamesian vessel of consciousness becomes 'a ready vessel for bitterness, a deep little porcelain cup in which biting acids could be mixed'.[5]

It is Maisie's status as 'ironic centre' that assures her narrative value (*AN*, p. 147). She is the centre not only of the novel's rhetorical scheme as central consciousness, but of its chiasmic adulterous plot, in which she brings together first her father and governess, then the spouses of her divorced parents, in an erotic alliance. She forges 'an extraordinary link between a succession of people' (*Notebooks*, p. 147), bringing together Sir Claude and Mrs Beale and supplying them with a 'jolly good pretext' (*WM*, p. 189), such that they become 'interested and attached, finally passionately so' (*Notebooks*, p. 71). By keeping her father and Miss Overmore 'perfectly proper', Maisie not only provides them with a *locus standi* or 'leg to stand on before the law' but permits James's narrative itself to 'stand beautifully on its feet' (*WM*, pp. 39, 36; *AN*, p. 142). Maisie is ironically complicitous in the novel's adulterous design. Her equivocal role resembles that of the coin with two antithetical faces described in the preface: 'no themes are so human as those that reflect for us, out of the confusion of life, the close connexion of bliss and bale, of the things that help with the things that hurt, so dangling before us for ever that bright hard metal, of so strange an alloy, one face of which is somebody's right and ease and the other somebody's pain and wrong' (*AN*, p. 143). In the manner of this strange alloy, Maisie operates as a two-faced coin that signifies both bliss and bale, right and wrong. Her effect is anomalous and alogical, like a coin stamped with two incompatible values.

In her capacity as 'centre and pretext for a fresh system of misbehaviour, a system moreover of a nature to spread and ramify', Maisie develops the narrative design imaged as a tree in James's preface: 'I recognise ... another instance of the growth of the "great oak" from the little acorn; since "What Maisie Knew" is at least a tree that spreads beyond any provision its small germ might on a first handling have appeared likely to make for it' (*AN*, pp. 143, 140). James counts *What Maisie Knew* among the 'comparative monsters' whose narrative mass exceeds their originating germ (*AN*, p. 98). The novel was to have been a ten thousand word story, and James's notebook entries express incredulity and frustration at the discrepancy between the text and its ostensible germ. In *The Art of the Novel*, 'monstrosity' is associated with narrative's capacity for producing unforeseeable and unaccountable developments; Maisie's 'monstrosity' is representative of the aberrant potential of narrative itself. The plot's evolution is neither foreseen nor accounted for by its origin in Maisie's perceiving consciousness. Even James finds himself entangled in the unforeseeable threads of this narrative web; in the preface, he comically figures himself as pulling at the threads of his narrative 'tangle' in an effort to straighten it out (AN, p. 146).

For the narrator, the characters, and James himself, Maisie's uncanny ability to generate plot developments, such as the affair between her parents' lovers, eludes logical explanation. Thematically, this problem is expressed as the question of whether Maisie possesses an adequate 'moral sense'; tropologically, it is expressed in the novel's figuration of accounting, settlement, and 'squaring' as a debt that Maisie incurs. That Maisie herself is to be held accountable for the settling of the novel's interpersonal equation becomes clear after the chiasmic crossing that brings together her father's new wife and her mother's lover. Mrs Beale's disclosure that 'nobody had been squared' (WM, p. 166) leads to an ironic revelation, Maisie's

> dim apprehension of the unuttered and the unknown. The relation between her step-parents had then a mysterious residuum; this was the first time she really had reflected that except as regards herself it was not a relationship.
>
> (WM, p. 168)

Like the 'residuum of truth' identified in the preface as the end of representation (AN, p. 141), this residuum signifies a 'remainder', the unaccounted for remains of an unbalanced equation or chemical analysis. The alliance between Claude and Mrs Beale, in which Maisie is inadvertently instrumental, leaves a mysterious residuum of fundamental unaccountability.[6]

This chemical imagery is pervasive in James's writings on narrative form. In The Art of the Novel, he figures representation as an 'exquisite chemistry' or 'rare alchemy' of chemical analysis and reduction (AN, pp. 87, 230). The chemical imagery in What Maisie Knew reflects the novel's concern with its formal and epistemological grounding, and the problem of accounting for Maisie's equivocal agency is played out in this system of economic and chemical terminology. Maisie herself is ultimately figured as a mathematical or chemical 'residuum' or remainder that must be erased if the text's narrative economy is to be satisfactorily squared, and the problem of her moral sense is compared to a baffling mathematical problem.

According to the logic of this figurative pattern, the question of Maisie's moral sense would be resolved if she could only be made to understand these figures, in the dual sense of numbers and of tropes. But because of the double-edged causality governing Maisie's knowledge, the attempts by Mrs Wix and Mrs Beale to rectify her lack of schooling only implicate her further in the compromising knowledge against which they mean to inoculate her. An account of Maisie's and Mrs Beale's excursions to hear edifying lectures, themselves a parody of Maisie's antithetical education in the novel as a whole, contains a comic literalisation of the Jamesian vessel of consciousness:

> the walk ... from the station through Glower Street (a pronunciation for which Mrs Beale once laughed at her little friend) [was] a pathway literally strewn with 'subjects'. Maisie imagined herself to pluck them as she went, though they thickened in the great grey rooms where the fountain of knowledge, in the form usually of a high voice that she took at first to be angry, plashed in the stillness of rows of faces thrust out like empty jugs.
>
> (WM, p. 164)

The empty jugs present a humorously literalist image of Maisie as receptive intelligence, and the passage plays ironically on the 'danger of filling too full any supposed and above all any obviously limited vessel of consciousness' (AN, p. 63) intrinsic to the compositional law of the reflector. Precisely this danger is realised in Maisie's relations with Mrs Wix, who reacts to her pupil's inadvertent indiscretions by insisting that she should 'know better' (WM, p. 271). Maisie can meet the requirements of Mrs Wix's morality only by mastering the implications of the 'terms' supplied her by the narrator; that is, by an initiation into the very knowledge that is forbidden her. The vignette thematises the novel's central problem, 'the particular phenomenon that, had [Maisie] felt the need of words for it, she might have called her personal relation to her knowledge' (WM, p. 268). Mrs Wix's disgusted pronouncement that Maisie is 'too unspeakable' names the paradox that follows from the novel's narrative strategy (WM, p. 272). For if what Maisie knows is unspeakable, and what she doesn't know 'ain't worth mentioning' (WM, p. 101), to quote Wix herself, then Maisie's knowledge inhabits the nebulous region between the unspeakable and the unmentionable.

Mrs Wix generates a continuous parody of the novel's narrative strategy. As 'a dim, crooked little reflector' (Notebooks, p. 162), she embodies a comic version of Maisie's role as reflective centre.

Her 'straighteners' concretise a running joke about point of view: intended to correct a 'divergent obliquity of vision', they instead correct the vision of her interlocutors (*WM*, p. 25). Recalling the 'straight and sure advance to the end' James envisions for his plot (*Notebooks,* p.161), her straighteners figure the straight narrative path James associates with the scenic method, and so the coherent linear causality that would counteract the unpredictable deviations and transgressions the plot enacts. But it is finally difficult to distinguish Mrs Wix's flawed perspective from Maisie's own reflective consciousness, 'the last little triangle of cracked glass to which so many fractures had reduced the polished plate of filial superstition' (*WM*, p. 218). Like the plot itself, Maisie's effect as flawed receptive centre threatens to wander into diversions as dangerous as Wix's obliquity of vision.

The pretence that Maisie's preverbal knowledge exists prior to the narrator's figurative translation of it ultimately breaks down, and with it the representational strategy of the central consciousness. Unable to report directly the contents of Maisie's consciousness, the narrator can only articulate his inability to answer for her knowledge and its uncanny effects: 'what there was no effective record of indeed was the small strange pathos on the child's part of an innocence so saturated with knowledge' (*WM*, pp. 182–3). Or:

> Nothing more remarkable had taken place in the first heat of her own departure, no act of perception less to be overtraced by our rough method, than her vision, the rest of that Boulogne day, of the manner in which she figured. I so despair of courting her noiseless mental footsteps here that I must crudely give you my word for its being from this time forward a picture literally present to her.
>
> (*WM*, pp. 280–1)

The metaphor of overtracing implies that the narrator is merely reproducing a perception that exists in Maisie's preverbal consciousness before he names it. But the dependence of Maisie's knowledge on the narrator's figures, and the implications of this dependence given the narrator's own linguistic sophistication, are what is in question here. In fact, one of the oddest features of the passage is the formulation that concludes it: 'I must crudely give you my word for its being from this time forward a picture literally present to her.' In its interplay between literal and figurative ('the manner in which she figured'), the passage interrogates the status of figurative language in the novel as a whole. For if we have access to 'what

Maisie knew' only through the narrator's figures for it, what is the literal term of Maisie's knowledge? In that it exists only in the narrator's mediation, her knowledge has, strictly speaking, no literal term at all. The narrator's relation to Maisie is one of catachresis in the sense of figure without the ground of a literal term.[7]

In violation of the novel's proclaimed narrative strategy of a 'picture restricted' to Maisie's consciousness (AN, p. 145), the representation of her putative knowledge takes the form mainly of first-person narratorial intrusions such as those quoted above. Since Maisie's knowledge is not available without the narrator's mediation, he must repeatedly step in to assure us that her knowledge outstrips even his own verbal resources.[8] But because each turn of events only confirms the unspeakability of what Maisie knows, the novel increasingly resorts to this emergency measure. The narrator, who remains effaced through most of the novel, makes more and more first-person appearances towards the end of the novel, but only to claim that Maisie's knowledge is so prodigious as to resist articulation altogether.

This foregrounding of the narrator's presence is not only rare in James, but also defies his famous strictures against first-person narratorial intrusions. His complaint in the 1883 essay on Trollope reveals what is at stake:

> He took a suicidal satisfaction in reminding the reader that the story he was telling was only, after all, a make-believe. He habitually referred to the work in hand (in the course of that work) as a novel, and to himself as a novelist, and was fond of letting the reader know that this novelist could direct the course of events according to his pleasure ... It is impossible to imagine what a novelist takes himself to be unless he regard himself as an historian and his narrative as a history. It is only as an historian that he has the smallest *locus standi*. As a narrator of fictitious events he is nowhere; to insert into his attempt a backbone of logic, he must relate events that are assumed to be real.[9]

In the guise of rehearsing the *topos* of presenting the novel as history, James posits an antithesis between first-person narration and the very grounds of narrative. The 'terrible *fluidity* of self-revelation', as he terms it in the preface to *The Ambassadors* (AN, p. 321), is held to be antithetical to the backbone or standing place that would ground the novel in something outside itself.[10] The *locus standi* or 'backbone of logic' in *What Maisie Knew* is Maisie

herself, for it is Maisie's case that permits the story 'to stand beautifully on its feet' (*AN*, p. 142).

But Maisie's unspeakability necessitates the narrative intrusions
of the last third of the novel – intrusions that participate in the 'suicidal' element of first-person narrative in Trollope. If Trollope takes
a suicidal satisfaction in calling attention to the artifice of his own
narrative, James involuntarily narrates the collapse of his own *locus
standi*, exposing not only the fictional status of what Maisie knew
but, more radically, its unspeakability: each such intrusion shatters
the illusion of the transparency of the narrator's mediating 'terms'.
The narrator's first-person intrusions may be suicidal, but it is
Maisie who pays for his suicidal bent by 'wondering' to 'the end, to
the death – the death of her childhood', as the preface puts it (*AN*,
p. 146). Despite James's strictures against first-person narrative,
there is a complicitous continuity between the intrusive narrator
and the apparently antithetical strategy of the central consciousness.
The narrator's intrusions, then, are not a cause of epistemological
instability, as the Trollope essay implies, but its effect.

The supersaturation of Maisie's knowledge brings the narrative
itself to an impasse or 'pretty pass' (*WM*, p. 283):

> She judged that if her whole history, for Mrs Wix, had been the suc-
> cessive stages of her knowledge, so the very climax of the concatena-
> tion would, in the same view, be the stage at which the knowledge
> should overflow. As she was condemned to know more and more,
> how could it logically stop before she should know Most? It came to
> her in fact as they sat there on the sands that she was distinctly on
> the road to know Everything. She had not had governesses for
> nothing; what in the world had she ever done but learn and learn
> and learn? She looked at the pink sky with a placid foreboding that
> soon she should have learned All. They lingered in the flushed air till
> at last it turned to grey and she seemed fairly to receive new informa-
> tion from every brush of the breeze. By the time they moved home-
> ward it was as if this inevitability had become for Mrs Wix a long,
> tense cord, twitched by a nervous hand, on which the valued pearls
> of intelligence were to be neatly strung.
>
> (*WM*, pp. 281–2)

This passage traces an ironic epiphany, and the culmination of
Maisie's knowledge is marked by a series of escalating abstractions
('more ... Most ... Everything ... All'), capitalised as if to accentu-
ate its status as a 'merely' linguistic construction. Maisie's acquisi-
tion of knowledge is linked to death through its alignment with a

fatal overflowing of the Jamesian vessel of consciousness. The figure of the twitching of a string of pearls, which resonates with a recurring Jamesian image for the central intelligence, is significant here. *Of In the Cage* (1898), the nearly contemporary novella that literalises the trope of the 'encaged' centre of consciousness (*AN*, p. 321), James remarks: 'the range of wonderment attributed in our tale to the young woman at Cocker's differs little in essence from the speculative thread on which the pearls of Maisie's experience, in this same volume – pearls of so strange an iridescence – are mostly strung. She wonders, putting it simply, very much as Morgan Moreen wonders; and they all wonder, for that matter, very much after the fashion of our portentous little Hyacinth' (*AN*, p. 156). As in *What Maisie Knew*, a connection is made between the lifeline or thread of consciousness and the activity of wondering that leads to death or figurative annihilation; the protagonist of *In the Cage* enjoys a delusional 'consciousness that could end only with death'.[11] Here the snapping of the thread signifies the snapping or breaking of the narrative ground or 'basis' Maisie represents, a 'collapse' like the 'break[ing of] the chain of the girl's own consciousness' in 'A London Life' (*AN*, p. 137).

Moreover, the passage recounting the concatenation of Maisie's knowledge is closely related to certain notebook entries in which James contemplates the scenic method that enabled him to complete the novel: 'I realise – none too soon – that the *scenic* method is my absolute, my imperative, my *only* salvation' (*Notebooks*, p. 167):

> Ah, this *divine* conception of one's little masses and periods in the scenic light – as rounded ACTS; this patient, pious, nobly 'vindictive' application of the scenic philosophy and method – I feel as if it still (and above *all*, YET) had a great deal to give me, and might carry me as far as I dream! God knows how far – into the flushed, dying day.
>
> (*Notebooks*, p. 162)

James's salvific 'flushed dying day' recalls the 'flushed air' intimating the fatal overflow of Maisie's knowledge in the passage discussed above. This resonance points to an odd economy; the recourse to the scenic method that spells Maisie's demise as reflective centre is the vehicle of James's own salvation. Further, James's slip of 'vindictive' for 'vindicating' aligns him with the 'vindictive []' motives ascribed to Maisie's parents in the preface (*AN*, p. 140). The vindictive bent of Maisie's parents is displaced onto

James, or rather onto the rhetorical strategy, at once vindicating and vindictive, that both constructs Maisie's knowledge and pushes that knowledge to its (vindictive) breaking point.

This constellation of figures also recalls a critical passage in 'The Pupil' (1892) which, in a prolepsis of Morgan Moreen's death, figures a similar flushing into knowledge:

> When he tried to figure to himself the morning twilight of childhood, so as to deal with it safely, he saw it was never fixed, never arrested, that ignorance, at the instant he touched it, was already flushing faintly into knowledge, that there was nothing that at a given moment you could say an intelligent child didn't know. It seemed to him that he himself knew too much to imagine Morgan's simplicity and too little to disembroil his tangle.[12]

The position of the tutor Pemberton here is analogous to that of Mrs Wix. He both knows too much to assume Morgan's innocence and too little to straighten, as with Mrs Wix's straighteners, the narrative tangle in which Morgan is implicated. The figure of dis-embroiling a tangle also recalls James's metaphor for his own narrative powers: 'the force for which the straightener of almost any tangle is grateful while he labours, the sense of pulling at threads intrinsically worth it' (*AN*, p. 146). But, like the 'snap of a tension' effected by Mrs Beale's ultimatum to Sir Claude (*WM*, p. 301), such a pulling at threads threatens to snap the narrative lifeline of the centre of consciousness itself. Morgan's fate is an oxymoronic 'morning twilight of childhood' similar to the figurative death foreseen for Maisie in the preface:

> Successfully to resist (to resist, that is, the strain of observation and the assault of experience) what would that be, on the part of so young a person, but to remain fresh, and still fresh, and to have even a freshness to communicate? – the case being with Maisie to the end that she treats her friends to the rich little spectacle of objects embalmed in her wonder. She wonders, in other words, to the end, to the death – the death of her childhood, properly speaking; after which (with the inevitable shift, sooner or later, of her point of view) her situation will change and become another affair, subject to other measurements and with a new centre altogether.
>
> (*AN*, p. 146–7)

This inevitable shift to a 'new centre' coincides not only with the death of Maisie's childhood but with the death of Maisie's point of view itself, with the novel's abandonment of the compositional law of the centre of consciousness.

What Maisie Knew explicitly identifies this shift of centre as a form of death:

> There was literally an instant in which Maisie fully saw – saw madness and desolation, saw ruin and darkness and death.
>
> (*WM*, p. 225)

> She was yet to learn what it could be to recognise in some lapse of a sequence the proof of an extinction, and therefore remained unaware that this momentary pang was a foretaste of the experience of death.
>
> (*WM*, p. 291)

This lapse of a sequence signifies both a lapse in narrative coherence and the extinction of Maisie herself. Her extinction is anticipated as early as the novel's prologue, where the narrator refers to the need for a third party who could have mediated between Maisie and her parents: 'what was to have been expected on the evidence was the nomination, *in loco parentis*, of some proper third person, some re-spectable or at least some presentable friend' (*WM*, p. 4). This third person is realised in the 'good lady' who comes forward, in the same paragraph, to offer Maisie a home, and she delivers 'a grim judgement of the whole point of view' that amounts to 'an epitaph for the tomb of Maisie's childhood' (*WM*, p. 5). But this proper third person fails to mask the complicity between the whole point of view effected by the novel's representational strategy and the third-person discourse of the narrator himself. His relation to Maisie is inherently improper, though James would have it other-wise, when he assures us in the preface that Maisie's death is, after all, only figurative: 'she wonders ... to the death – the death of her childhood, properly speaking'. Instead, the proper third person evoked in the prologue calls attention to the causal connection between the death of Maisie's childhood and the novel's whole point of view.[13]

Paradoxically, James can only ground the narrative in Maisie's knowledge by abandoning indirect discourse altogether for scene, the heavy reliance on dialogue typical of the final chapters. It is the scenic method, finally, that sees James 'out of the wood, at all, of this interminable little *Maisie*' (*Notebooks*, p. 167). Through its re-course to the scenic method, the novel thus virtually abandons the pretence that Maisie's knowledge exists prior to its articulation by the narrator. This contradiction brings the novel to a definitive representational impasse – an impasse dramatised by the reduction of the dialogue to a series of stuttering repetitions: 'She refused – she refused!' 'You're free – you're free', 'I know, I know!' 'She hates you – she hates you', 'leave her, leave her!' and so on. Like the repetitive Mrs Wix, James's text falls into conspicuous 'iteration' (*WM*, p. 261).

What Maisie Knew thus reaches a double impasse. On the one hand, Maisie is confronted with her own unaccountability, which follows from her ineluctable indebtedness to the narrator's figures. On the other, the text reaches the impasse of its inability to articulate what Maisie knew in anything *but* these figures – its inability, that is, to name a knowledge that has no literal name. This double impasse is figured by the text, precisely, *as* a figure:

> The question of the settlement loomed larger to her now: it depended, she had learned, so completely on herself. Her choice, as her friend had called it, was there before her like an impossible sum on a slate, a sum that in spite of her plea for consideration she simply got off from doing while she walked about with him.
>
> (*WM*, p. 341)

This dilemma culminates in Mrs Wix's investigation of Maisie's moral sense:

> 'Haven't I, after all, brought it out?' ... Sir Claude and Mrs Beale stood there like visitors at an 'exam'. She had indeed an instant a whiff of the faint flower Mrs Wix pretended to have plucked and now with such a peremptory hand thrust at her nose. Then it left her, and, as if she were sinking with a slip from a foothold, her arms made a short jerk. What this jerk represented was the spasm within her of something still deeper than a moral sense. She looked at her examiner; she looked at the visitors; she felt the rising of the tears she had kept down at the station. They had nothing – no, distinctly nothing – to do with her moral sense. The only thing was the old flat shameful schoolroom plea. 'I don't know – I don't know.'
>
> 'Then you've lost it.' Mrs Wix seemed to close the book as she fixed the straighteners on Sir Claude. 'You've nipped it in the bud. You've killed it when it had begun to live.'
>
> (*WM*, pp. 353–4)

In keeping with the novel's ironic education plot, the exposure of Maisie's lack of a moral sense is staged as a schoolroom exam. But because her 'schoolroom plea' reverses her programmatic reply up to this point ('Oh I know!'), what results is 'a slip from a foothold', the definitive collapse of Maisie's (and James's) epistemological footing or *locus standi*. This marks the definitive collapse of the novel's foothold in the double sense of epistemological and rhetorical grounding, a fall that, to invoke a master Jamesian trope, lands us in the 'abyss' (*WM*, p. 360).[14]

In a parody of the novel's own settlement, Mrs Wix seems to close the book on James's 'slip of a girl', enforcing a peremptory closure. She not only straightens out Maisie, but fixes her straighteners on Sir Claude. Yet her accusation lets slip the novel's narrative ruse. The usual term in James for glasses is 'nippers'. Lambert Strether's nippers figure his quest for epistemological clarity in *The Ambassadors*; Mr Longdon, the representative of outmoded values in *The Awkward Age*, fixes his double eye-glass on his interlocutors while pondering their moral laxity. Might there be a complicity between Mrs Wix's straighteners and Sir Claude's alleged crime of having nipped in the bud Maisie's moral sense? To straighten Maisie out is to nip her in the bud, thanks to the questionable moral sense of a narrative strategy that requires its heroine to wonder 'to the death of her childhood'.

Maisie's final banishment with Mrs Wix signifies a doubly figurative death – a death that is both figurative in nature and causally linked to Maisie's dependence on the narrator's own terms, figures in both the economic and rhetorical senses, that are 'not yet at her command' (*AN*, p. 146). Such figures remain beyond the mastery of the Jamesian reflective centre, their effects incalculable. Though James would have it that the narrator merely translates Maisie's thoughts, this translation is far from innocent. Like a metaphor, a translation is a transfer or carrying over that creates as well as nominates. James figures the growth of Maisie's knowledge as the progress of a letter whose delivery is perpetually deferred: thus her mother's abuse drops into Maisie's memory 'with the dry rattle of a letter falling into a pillar-box. Like the letter it was, as part of the contents of a well-stuffed post-bag, delivered in due course at the right address' (*WM*, p. 14). If, like a metaphor, a translation is a transfer that never quite delivers, the translation of this preverbal material is both impossible and fatal.

For this reason, it is figurative language itself that finally cannot be accounted for in *What Maisie Knew*. The 'residuum of truth' or 'ironic truth' cryptically identified in James's preface as the source of Maisie's charm as reflective centre (*AN*, pp. 141, 142) may be the residuum of language itself, the figures generated by the continuous ironic distance or disjunction between Maisie and the narrator. By amplifying Maisie's perceptions to an unknowable degree, such figures remain the unknown variable in the novel's narrative equation.[15]

The figurative language on which the centre of consciousness strategy depends is at once a vulnerability and a source of power. According to *The Art of the Novel*, the value of the central intelligence is its very 'appeal to incalculability' (*AN*, p. 329). The Jamesian centre of consciousness creates incalculable effects in the fictions in which it is deployed; it not only reflects but shapes the events of those fictions. For example, the death of Maisie's childhood is 'caused' as much by the representational logic of the central consciousness as by the psychological or intersubjective structures simulated in the novel's realistic plot. Because the narrator's figures prove incompatible with the 'sublime economy' of form (*AN*, p. 120), the novel must sacrifice the representational strategy that generates those figures, as it does Maisie herself. The claim of the centre of consciousness to provide a formal or epistemological centre and ground for narrative proves incompatible with the figures in which it is constructed, an incompatibility reflected by the oxymoron of the ironic centre, as James terms Maisie's narrative function. Her role as a phenomenological or narrative centre cannot be reconciled with her decentring ironic distance from the narrator whose figures attend and amplify, effecting the self-suspension or self-negation characteristic of irony. Maisie's drama as centre of consciousness is thus an allegory of the novel's rhetorical situation and of the compositional law of the central consciousness itself – an allegory whose uncanny consciousness of its own narrative subterfuges perhaps accounts for its peculiar power.

From *Studies in American Fiction*, 21:2 (1993), 127–40.

NOTES

[Sheila Teahan provides a rhetorical, figurative analysis of the narration and language of *What Maisie Knew*, *vis-à-vis* Maisie as 'ironic centre', in an essay subsequently expanded in her book *The Rhetorical Logic of Henry James* (Baton Rouge, LA, 1995). Illustrating how the narrator's relation to Maisie implicates him in the creation of Maisie's knowledge, her knowledge depending on his articulation by figure or metaphor, Teahan focuses on the consequent collapse of the novel's narrative strategy, as the narrator increasingly makes first-person appearances to assure the reader of Maisie's knowledge. James's project is thus rescued by recourse to the scenic method. In her examination of figures, Teahan considers the figuration of Maisie's knowledge by the 'improper third person' of her title, as well as the figurative death of Maisie's childhood proclaimed in James's preface, against similar phenomena in other works ('In the Cage', 'A London Life', and 'The Pupil') in an analysis which connects the problem of the articulation of Maisie's knowledge with the residuum of language itself. The whole may thus be read as an allegory of the duplicity of representation. Ed.]

1. *The Complete Notebooks of Henry James*, ed. Leon Edel and Lyall H. Powers (New York, 1987), pp. 148, 149; page numbers hereafter are given in the text, under the abbreviation *Notebooks*.

2. Henry James, *The Art of the Novel*, ed. R. W. B. Lewis (Boston, 1984), p. 145; page numbers hereafter are given in the text, under the abbreviation *AN*.

3. As Neil Hertz has noted, James's unease about his novel's subject invites comparison to Freud's similar defensiveness in *Dora*; see Hertz, 'Dora's Secrets, Freud's Techniques', in *The End of the Line* (New York, 1985).

4. A number of critics, however, assume that it is possible to distinguish the narrator's language from Maisie's. Donna Przybylowicz, for example, argues that Maisie ultimately acquires mastery of the 'figures' initially in the narrator's control: 'one notes an increase in the use of analogies as Maisie matures and grows more aware and a concomitant reduction in the use of imagery on the narrator's part to describe her inchoate sensations, for she eventually initiates much of the figurative language herself': *Desire and Repression: The Dialectic of Self and Other in the Late Works of Henry James* (Tuscaloosa, AL, 1986), p. 26.

5. *What Maisie Knew*, in *The Novels and Tales of Henry James*, vol. 11 (New York, 1908, and 1936), pp. 14, 5; page numbers are hereafter given in the text, under the abbreviation *WM*.

6. For a Lacanian reading of the 'residuum', see Dennis Foster, 'Maisie Supposed to Know: Amo(u)ral Analysis', *The Henry James Review*, 5 (1984), 207–16 (212). James's terminology of residue and residuum resonates suggestively with Shoshana Felman's reflection on the textual residue inherent to reading: 'the question of a reading's "truth" must be at least complicated and re-thought through another question, which Freud, indeed, has raised, and taught us to articulate: what does such "truth" (or any "truth") leave out? What is *made to miss*? What does it have as its function to overlook? What, precisely,

is its residue, the remainder it does not account for?' See *Literature and Psychoanalysis: The Question of Reading: Otherwise*, ed. Shoshana Felman (Baltimore and London, 1982), p. 117.

7. On catachresis, see J. Hillis Miller, *The Ethics of Reading* (New York, 1987), p. 21.

8. However, many critics have taken the problem of 'what Maisie knew' unironically, assuming that she undergoes moral and epistemological growth over the course of the novel.

9. Henry James, 'Anthony Trollope', in *Essays on Literature, American Writers, English Writers* (New York, 1984), pp. 1330–56 (1343).

10. The interrelated metaphors of *locus standi*, 'logic', 'backbone', 'ground', and so on, belong to an entire set of metaphysical assumptions about unity, linearity, and causality, governing the Western theory of history and of narrative fiction. For an account of how these metaphors have conditioned thinking about the 'realistic' novel, see J. Hillis Miller, 'Narrative and History', *ELH*, 41 (1974), 455–73.

11. Henry James, *In the Cage and Other Stories*, ed. S. Gorley Putt (London, 1972), p. 72.

12. 'The Pupil', *The Novels and Tales of Henry James*, vol. 11, p. 547.

13. Several critics have noticed the connections between the novel's narrative strategy and Maisie's figurative 'death'. Carren Kaston notes that 'James himself uses Maisie in the novel's preface in some of the same ways that her various parents use her in the novel': see *Imagination and Desire in the Novels of Henry James* (New Brunswick, 1984), p. 123. Neil Hertz comments on the preface's 'thematics of sacrifice and compensation', and suggests that 'the figurative death Maisie is said to endure is made to seem the price paid for the remarkable transforming effects of her wonder' (Hertz, 'Dora's Secrets', p. 125). I would argue, however, that the effect of Maisie's 'wonder' is more ironic than redemptive.

14. For a reading of this passage and of the novel that complements mine in many respects, see J. Hillis Miller, *Versions of Pygmalion* (Cambridge, MA, 1990), pp. 23ff. This essay was composed before the appearance of Miller's work, and I have not attempted to revise my own argument in the light of its implications. My reading differs from Miller's especially in its emphasis on the indeterminacy of Maisie's knowledge as a rhetorical construction of the novel's representational strategy itself, whereas Miller emphasises the undecidable nature of the ethical basis of Maisie's actions.

15. The crux of the critical debate about the status of figurative language in the novel is economically summarised by Przybylowicz: 'her ... perceptions ... are presented through a cross-referencing of metaphors,

signifying a preverbal level of comprehension of actions and feelings that are interpreted and created by the narrator' (p. 26). The question is precisely whether the narrator merely interprets ('translates', in James's term) or actually creates her knowledge; the two possibilities imply, respectively, constative and performative theories of language. For other discussions of figurative language in the novel, see Foster, 'Maisie Supposed to Know', Hertz, 'Dora's Secrets' and Miller, *The Ethics of Reading*; also Walter Isle, *Experiments in Form: Henry James's Novels, 1896–1901* (Cambridge, MA, 1968); Kenny Marotta, '*What Maisie Knew*: The Question of Our Speech', *ELH*, 46 (1979), 495–508; and Philip M. Weinstein, *Henry James and the Requirements of the Imagination* (Cambridge, MA, 1971).

Further Reading

MAIN COLLECTED EDITIONS

The Complete Tales of Henry James, ed. Leon Edel, 12 vols (London: Rupert Hart-Davis, 1962–4). This edition reproduces the text of the first book (or periodical) edition.

The Novels and Tales of Henry James, The New York Edition, 26 vols (24 vols New York: Scribner's, 1907–9; 2 vols 1918). This edition incorporates the author's revisions and a series of prefaces.

OTHER GENERAL COLLECTIONS

Henry James Letters, ed. Leon Edel, 4 vols (Cambridge, MA: Belknap Press, 1974–84).

The Critical Muse: Selected Literary Criticism, ed. Roger Gard (Harmondsworth: Penguin, 1987).

The Complete Notebooks of Henry James, ed. Leon Edel and Lyall H. Powers (New York: OUP, 1987).

BIBLIOGRAPHIES

Bradbury, Nicola, *Henry James: Annotated Critical Bibliography* (Brighton: Harvester, 1987).

Edel, Leon and Laurence, Dan H., *A Bibliography of Henry James*, 3rd edition (Oxford: Clarendon Press, 1982).

Funston, Judith E., *Henry James, 1975–1987: A Reference Guide* (Boston: G. K. Hall, 1991).

McColgan, Kristin Pruitt, *Henry James, 1917–1959: A Reference Guide* (Boston: G. K. Hall, 1979).

Scura, Dorothy McInnis, *Henry James, 1960–1974: A Reference Guide* (Boston: G. K. Hall, 1979).

Taylor, Linda J., *Henry James, 1866–1916: A Reference Guide* (Boston: G. K. Hall, 1982).

RECENT OR AVAILABLE INDIVIDUAL EDITIONS

The Turn of the Screw, ed. Robert Kimborough (New York: W. W. Norton, 1966) [text follows New York Edition: includes copious critical apparatus, cited below as Kimbrough (1966)].

The Aspern Papers and The Turn of the Screw, ed. Anthony Curtis (Harmondsworth: Penguin, 1984) [New York Edition].

The Turn of the Screw and Other Stories, ed. T. J. Lustig (Oxford: OUP, 1992) [New York Edition].

The Turn of the Screw, ed. Allan Lloyd Smith (London: Everyman/Dent, 1993) [text unspecified].

The Turn of the Screw, ed. Peter G. Beidler (Boston: Bedford Books/St. Martin's Press, 1995). [New York Edition text: best all-round available edition, including copious and up to date critical apparatus, cited below as Beidler (1995).]

What Maisie Knew, ed. Douglas Jefferson and Douglas Grant (Oxford: OUP, 1966; 1980) [New York Edition].

What Maisie Knew, ed. Paul Theroux, additional notes by Patricia Crick (Harmondsworth: Penguin, 1984) [New York Edition].

What Maisie Knew, ed. Adrian Poole (Oxford: OUP, 1996) [New York Edition].

BIOGRAPHY

Edel, Leon, *Henry James: A Life* (London; Flamingo/HarperCollins, 1996). [An abridged and updated version of Edel's 5-vol. biography, published 1953–72.]

Kaplan, Fred, *Henry James: The Imagination of Genius* (London: Hodder & Stoughton, 1992; London: Sceptre, 1993).

COLLECTIONS OF CRITICAL ESSAYS

Bloom, Harold (ed.), *Henry James's Daisy Miller, The Turn of the Screw and Other Tales* (New York: Chelsea House, 1987).

Edel, Leon (ed.), *Henry James: A Collection of Critical Essays* (Englewood Cliffs, NJ: Prentice-Hall, 1963; reprinted 1987).

Goode, John (ed.), *The Air of Reality: New Essays on Henry James* (London: Methuen, 1972).

Pollak, Vivian R. (ed.), *New Essays on Daisy Miller and The Turn of the Screw* (Cambridge: CUP, 1993).

Tanner, Tony (ed.), *Henry James: Modern Judgements* (London: Macmillan, 1969).

Tompkins, Jane P. (ed.), *Twentieth Century Interpretations of 'The Turn of the Screw' and Other Tales: A Collection of Critical Essays* (Englewood Cliffs, NJ: Prentice-Hall, 1970).

Willen, Gerald (ed.), *A Casebook on Henry James's 'The Turn of the Screw'* (New York: Crowell, 1959; 2nd edition, 1969): text plus large critical anthology [cited below as Willen (1969)].

CONCORDANCES

Bender, Claire E. and Todd K., *A Concordance to Henry James's 'The Turn of the Screw'* (New York and London: Garland, 1988) [based on New York Edition].

Hulpke, Erika and Bender, Todd K., *A Concordance to Henry James's 'What Maisie Knew'* (New York and London: Garland, 1989).

GENERAL LITERARY, THEORETICAL AND CULTURAL STUDIES   These include essential discussion of James texts.

Bayley, John, *The Short Story: Henry James to Elizabeth Bowen* (New York and London: Harvester Wheatsheaf, 1988).

Bersani, Leo, *A Future for Astyanax: Character and Desire in Literature* (Boston: Little, Brown, 1976).

Blanchot, Maurice, *The Sirens' Song*, ed. Gabriel Josipovici, trans. Sacha Rabinivitch (Brighton: Harvester Press, 1982).

Booth, Wayne C., *The Rhetoric of Fiction* (Chicago: U. of Chicago Press, 1961).

Booth, Wayne C., *Critical Understanding: The Powers and Limits of Pluralism* (Chicago and London: U. of Chicago Press, 1979).

Brooke-Rose, Christine, *A Rhetoric of the Unreal: Studies in Narrative and Structure, Especially of the Fantastic* (Cambridge, CUP, 1981; paperback 1983).

Brooks, Peter, *The Melodramatic Imagination: Balzac, Henry James, Melodrama, and the Mode of Excess* (New Haven and London: Yale UP, 1976).

Cavaliero, Glen, *The Supernatural and English Fiction* (Oxford: OUP, 1995).

Caws, Mary Ann, *Reading Frames in Modern Fiction* (Princeton, NJ: Princeton UP, 1985).

Cornwell, Neil, *The Literary Fantastic: From Gothic to Postmodernism* (New York and London: Harvester Wheatsheaf, 1990).

Ellmann, Richard, 'A Late Victorian Love Affair', *New York Review of Books*, 24, 13 (4 August 1977), 6–10.

Gray, Bennison, *The Phenomenon of Literature* (The Hague: Mouton, 1975).

Keating, Peter, *The Haunted Study: A Social History of the English Novel 1875–1914* (London: Fontana, 1991; first published 1989).

Miller, J. Hillis, *Versions of Pygmalion* (Cambridge, MA: Harvard UP, 1990).

Paglia, Camille, *Sexual Personae: Art and Decadence from Nefertiti to Emily Dickinson* (Harmondsworth: Penguin, 1992; first published 1990).

Sedgwick, Eve Kosofsky, *Epistemology of the Closet* (Harmondsworth: Penguin, 1994; first published 1990).

Stanzel, F. K., *A Theory of Narrative*, trans. Charlotte Goedsche (Cambridge: CUP, 1984; paperback 1986; first published in German 1979; 2nd revised edition 1982).

Stock, R. D., *The Flutes of Dionysus: Daemonic Enthrallment in Literature* (Lincoln and London: U. of Nebraska Press).

Todorov, Tzvetan, *The Fantastic: A Structural Approach to a Literary Genre*, trans. Richard Howard (Cleveland and London: Press of Case Western Reserve University, 1973; reprinted Ithaca, NY: 1975; first published in French, 1970).

Todorov, Tzvetan, *The Poetics of Prose*, trans. Richard Howard (Oxford: Blackwell, 1977; first published in French, 1971).

SELECTED GENERAL CRITICISM ON JAMES These studies include useful contributions on *Turn of the Screw* or *What Maisie Knew*.

Banta, Martha, *Henry James and the Occult: The Great Extension* (Bloomington: Indiana UP, 1972).

Beidler, Paul G., *Frames in James: 'The Tragic Muse', 'The Turn of the Screw', 'What Maisie Knew' and 'The Ambassadors'* (Victoria, BC: University of Victoria, 1993).

Bell, Millicent, *Meaning in Henry James* (Cambridge, MA: Harvard UP, 1991).

Bradbury, Nicola, *Henry James: The Later Novels* (Oxford: Clarendon Press, 1979).

Clair, John A., *The Ironic Dimension in the Fiction of Henry James* (Pittsburgh, PA: Duquesene UP, 1965).

Cross, Mary, *Henry James: The Contingencies of Style* (Basingstoke: Macmillan, 1993).

Delbaere-Garant, Jeanne, *Henry James: The Vision of France* (Paris: Société d'Editions 'Les Belles Lettres', 1970).

Egan, Michael, *Henry James: The Ibsen Years* (London: Vision, 1972).

Gale, Robert L., *A Henry James Encyclopedia* (Westport, CT: Greenwood Press, 1989).

Goetz, William R., *Henry James and the Darkest Abyss of Romance* (Baton Rouge and London: Louisiana State UP, 1986).

Hardy, Barbara, *Henry James: The Later Writing* (Plymouth: Northcote House/British Council, 1996).

Hocks, Richard A., *Henry James and Pragmatist Thought: A Study in the Relationship Between the Philosophy of William James and the Literary Art of Henry James* (Chapel Hill: U. of North Carolina Press, 1974).

Hutchinson, Stuart, *Henry James: An American as Modernist* (London/ Totowa, NJ: Vision / Barnes & Noble, 1982 / 1983.

Jolly, Roslyn, *Henry James: History, Narrative, Fiction* (Oxford: Clarendon Press, 1993).

Kaston, Carren, *Imagination and Desire in the Novels of Henry James* (New Brunswick, NJ: Rutgers UP, 1984).

Krook, Dorothea, *The Ordeal of Consciousness in Henry James* (Cambridge: CUP, 1967).

Llewellyn Smith, Virginia, *Henry James and the Real Thing: A Modern Reader's Guide* (Basingstoke: Macmillan, 1994).

Lustig, T. J., *Henry James and the Ghostly* (Cambridge: CUP, 1994).

Mackenzie, Manfred, *Communities of Honor and Love in Henry James* (Cambridge, MA and London: Harvard UP, 1976).

Michaels, Walter Benn, 'Writers Reading: James and Eliot', *Modern Language Notes [MLN]*, 91 (1976), 827–49.

Moon, Heath, 'More Royalist Than the King: the Governess, the Telegraphist, and Mrs Gracedew', *Criticism*, 24 (1982), 16–35.

Poole, Adrian, *Henry James* (New York and London: Harvester Wheatsheaf, 1991).

Purdy, Strother B., *The Hole in the Fabric: Science, Contemporary Literature and Henry James* (Pittsburgh, PA: U. of Pittsburgh Press, 1977).

Rimmon, Shlomith, *The Concept of Ambiguity – the Example of James* (Chicago and London: U. of Chicago Press, 1977).

Rivkin, Julie, *False Positions: The Representational Logics of Henry James's Fiction* (Stanford, CA: Stanford UP, 1996).

Rowe, John Carlos, *The Theoretical Dimensions of Henry James* (Madison, WI: U. of Wisconsin Press, 1984).

Samuels, Charles Thomas, *The Ambiguity of Henry James* (Urbana: U. of Illinois Press, 1971).

Shine, Muriel G., *The Fictional Children of Henry James* (Chapel Hill: U. of North Carolina Press, 1968).

Tanner, Tony, *Henry James: I–III* (*I–II*, Harlow, Essex: Longman/British Council, 1979; *III*, Windsor, Berks: Profile Books, 1981).

Teahan, Sheila, *The Rhetorical Logic of Henry James* (Baton Rouge and London: Louisiana State UP, 1995).

Vaid, Krishna Baldev, *Technique in the Tales of Henry James* (Cambridge, MA: Harvard UP, 1964).

Walton, Priscilla L., *The Disruption of the Feminine in Henry James* (Toronto: U. of Toronto Press, 1992).

Ward, J. A., *The Search for Form: Studies in the Structure of James's Fiction* (Chapel Hill: U. of North Carolina Press, 1967).

Williams, Merle A., *Henry James and the Philosophical Novel* (Cambridge: CUP, 1993).

Wilkinson, Myler, 'Henry James and the Ethical Moment', *Henry James Review*, 11, 3 (1990), 153–75.

SELECTED CRITICISM SPECIFICALLY ON *THE TURN OF THE SCREW*   Including the more important individual essays from volumes listed in the 'Collections of Critical Essays' section above.

Aldrich, C. Knight, 'Another Twist to *The Turn of the Screw*', *Modern Fiction Studies*, 13 (1967), 167–78; reprinted in Willen (1969).

Allen, John J., 'The Governess and the Ghosts in *The Turn of the Screw*', *The Henry James Review*, 1:1 (1979), 73–80.

Anderson, Don, '"A Fury of Intention": The Scandal of Henry James's *The Turn of the Screw*', *Sydney Studies in English*, 15 (1989–90), 140–52.

Armstrong, Paul B., 'History and Epistemology: The Example of *The Turn of the Screw*', *New Literary History*, 19 (1987–8), 693–712.

Aswell, E. Duncan, 'Reflections of a Governess: Image and Distortion in *The Turn of the Screw*', *Nineteenth-Century Fiction*, 23 (1968–69), 49–63.

Beidler, Peter G., 'The Governess and the Ghosts', *PMLA*, 100 (1985), 96–7.

Beidler, Peter G., *Ghosts, Demons and Henry James: 'The Turn of the Screw' at the Turn of the Century* (Columbia: U. of Missouri Press, 1989).

Beidler, Peter G., 'Introduction: Biographical and Historical Contexts' and 'A Critical History of *The Turn of the Screw*', in *The Turn of the Screw* (1995) [see above], pp. 3–19 and 127–51 [includes bibliography]. Hereafter Beidler (1995).

Bell, Millicent, '*The Turn of the Screw* and the *Recherche de L'Absolu*', in *Henry James: Fiction as History*, ed. Ian Bell (London: Vision Press, 1984), pp. 65–81.

Bell, Millicent, 'Class, Sex and the Victorian Governess: James's *The Turn of the Screw*', in Pollak (1993), 91–119.

Blackall, Jean Frantz, 'Cruikshank's *Oliver* and "The Turn of the Screw"', *American Literature*, 51 (1979–80), 161–78.

Bohlmeijer, Arno, 'The Intruder: Henry James and "The Turn of the Screw"', *Encounter*, 69:1 (June, 1987), 41–50.

Cargill, Oscar, 'Henry James as Freudian Pioneer', in Willen (1959/1969), first published 1956; revised as '*The Turn of the Screw* and Alice James', *PMLA*, 78 (1963), 238–49; reprinted in Kimbrough (1966), pp. 145–65.

Chase, Dennis, 'The Ambiguity of Innocence: *The Turn of the Screw*', *Extrapolation*, 27 (1986), 197–202.

Chinitz, Lisa G., 'Fairy Tale Turned Ghost Story: James's *The Turn of the Screw*', *The Henry James Review*, 15 (1994), 264–85.

Cohen, Paula Marantz, 'Freud's *Dora* and James's *Turn of the Screw*: Two Treatments of the Female "Case"', *Criticism*, 28:1 (1986), 73–87.

Cook, David A. and Corrigan, Timothy J., 'Narrative Structure in *The Turn of the Screw*: A New Approach to Meaning', *Studies in Short Fiction*, 17 (1980), 55–65.

Costello, Donald P., 'The Structure of *The Turn of the Screw*', *Modern Language Notes*, 75 (1960), 312–21.

Cranfill, Thomas Mabry and Clark, Robert Lanier, Jr, *An Anatomy of the Turn of the Screw* (New York: Gordian Press, 1971; first published Austin, TX, 1965).

Crowl, Susan, 'Aesthetic Allegory in "The Turn of the Screw"', *Novel: A Forum on Fiction*, 4:2 (1971), 107–22.

Eaton, Marcia M., 'James's Turn of the Speech-Act', *British Journal of Aesthetics*, 23 (1983), 333–45.

Edel, Leon, 'The Point of View', in Kimbrough (1966), pp. 228–34; first published 1955.

Edel, Leon and Tintner, Adeline R., 'The Private Life of Peter Quin[t]: Origins of "The Turn of the Screw"', *The Henry James Review*, 7, 1 (1985), 2–4.

Elgar, Viti, 'The Origin and Validation of Interpretive Hypotheses or "The Turn of the Screw": Whose Screws Need Tightening?', *Essays in Poetics*, 4:2 (1979), 37–58.

Enck, John J., 'The Turn of the Screw & The Turn of the Century', in Kimbrough (1966), pp. 259–69.

Faulkner, Howard, 'Text as Pretext in The Turn of the Screw', Studies in Short Fiction, 20 (1983), 87–94.

Felman, Shoshana, 'Turning the Screw of Interpretation', in Literature and Psychoanalysis: The Question of Reading: Otherwise, ed. Shoshana Felman (Baltimore and London: Johns Hopkins UP, 1982), pp. 94–207; first published Yale French Studies, 55–6 (1977), same pagination. Excerpt reprinted as '"The grasp with which I recovered him": A Child is Killed in The Turn of the Screw', in Beidler (1995), 193–206.

Freundlieb, Dieter, 'Explaining Interpretation: The Case of Henry James's The Turn of the Screw', Poetics Today, 5:1, (1984), 79–95.

Goddard, Harold C., 'A Pre-Freudian Reading of The Turn of the Screw', in Kimbrough (1966), pp. 181–209; also in Willen (1959/69); written early 1920s and first published 1957.

Hallab, Mary Y., 'The Governess and the Demon Lover: The Return of a Fairy Tale', The Henry James Review, 8, 2 (1987), 104–15.

Halttunen, Karen, '"Through the Cracked and Fragmented Self": William James and The Turn of the Screw', American Quarterly, 40 (1988), 472–90.

Heilman, Robert, 'The Turn of the Screw as Poem', in Kimbrough (1966), pp. 214–28; also in Willen (1969), pp. 174–88; first published 1948.

Heller, Terry, The Turn of the Screw: Bewildered Vision (Boston: Twayne, 1989).

Higson, Andrew, 'Gothic Fantasy as Art Cinema: The Secret of Female Desire in The Innocents', in Gothick Origins and Innovations, ed. Allan Lloyd Smith and Victor Sage (Amsterdam and Atlanta, GA: Rodopi, 1994), pp. 204–17.

Hill, Robert W., Jr, 'A Counterclockwise Turn in James's "The Turn of the Screw"', Twentieth-Century Literature, 27 (1981), 53–71.

Kauffman, Linda S., 'The Author of Our Woe: Virtue Recorded in The Turn of the Screw', Nineteenth-Century Fiction, 36, 2 (1981), 176–92; revised in her Discourses of Desire: Gender, Genre and Epistolary Fictions (Ithaca and London, Cornell UP, 1986), pp. 203–39.

Kenton, Edna, 'Henry James to the Ruminant Reader: The Turn of the Screw', in Willen (1969), 102–14; first published 1924.

Killoran, Helen, 'The Governess, Mrs Grose and "the Poison of an Influence" in The Turn of the Screw', Modern Language Studies, 23 (1993), 13–24.

Kirby, David, The Portrait of a Lady and The Turn of the Screw (Basingstoke and London: Macmillan, 1991).

Krook, Dorothea, 'Intentions and Intentions: The Problem of Intention and Henry James's "The Turn of the Screw"', in The Theory of the Novel: New Essays, ed. John Halperin (New York: OUP, 1974), pp. 353–72.

Lind, Sidney E., '"The Turn of the Screw": The Torment of Critics', Centennial Review, 14 (1970), 225–40.

Lloyd Smith, Allan, 'A Word Kept Back in The Turn of the Screw', in Creepers: British Horror and Fantasy in the Twentieth Century, ed. Clive Bloom (London: Pluto Press, 1993), pp. 47–63.

Macleod, Norman, 'Stylistics and the Ghost Story: Punctuation, Revisions, and Meaning in *The Turn of the Screw*', in *Edinburgh Studies in the English Language*, ed. John M. Anderson and Norman Macleod (Edinburgh: John Donald, 1988), pp. 133–55.

McElroy, John Harmon, 'The Mysteries at Bly', *Arizona Quarterly*, 37 (1981), 214–36.

McMaster, Graham, 'Henry James and India: A Historical Reading of *The Turn of the Screw*', *Clio*, 18 (1988), 23–40.

McMaster, Juliet, '"The Full Image of a Repetition" in *The Turn of the Screw*', *Studies in Short Fiction*, 6 (1968–9), 377–82.

McWhirter, David, 'In the "Other House" of Fiction: Writing, Authority, and Femininity in *The Turn of the Screw*', in Pollak (1993), 121–48.

Mahbobah, Albaraq, 'Hysteria, Rhetoric, and the Politics of Reversal in Henry James's *The Turn of the Screw*', *The Henry James Review*, 17 (1996), 149–61.

Mansell, Darrel, 'The Ghost of the Language in *The Turn of the Screw*', *Modern Language Quarterly*, 46 (1985), 48–63.

Matheson, Terence J., 'Did the Governess Smother Miles? A Note on James's *The Turn of the Screw*', *Studies in Short Fiction*, 19 (1982), 172–5.

Mazzella, Anthony J., 'An Answer to the Mystery of *The Turn of the Screw*', *Studies in Short Fiction*, 17 (1980), 327–33.

Miall, David S., 'Designed Horror: James's Vision of Evil in *The Turn of the Screw*', *Nineteenth-Century Fiction*, 39 (1984–5), 305–27.

Milne, Fred, L., 'Atmosphere as Triggering Device in *The Turn of the Screw*', *Studies in Short Fiction*, 18 (1981), 293–9.

Murphy, Brenda, 'The Problem of Validity in the Critical Controversy over *The Turn of the Screw*', *Research Studies*, 47:3 (1979), 191–201.

Murphy, Kevin, 'The Unfixable Text: Bewilderment of Vision in *The Turn of the Screw*', *Texas Studies in Literature and Language*, 20:4 (1978), 538–51.

Nardin, Jane, '*The Turn of the Screw*: The Victorian Background', *Mosaic*, 12, 1 (1978), 131–42.

O'Gorman, Donal, 'Henry James's Reading of *The Turn of the Screw*', *The Henry James Review*, 1 (1980), 125–38 and 228–56.

Pecora, Vincent P., 'Reflection Rendered: James's *The Turn of the Screw*', in his *Self and Form in Modern Narrative* (Baltimore and London: Johns Hopkins UP, 1989), pp. 176–213.

Petry, Alice Hall, 'Jamesian Parody, *Jane Eyre*, and "The Turn of the Screw"', *Modern Language Studies*, 13 (1983), 61–78.

Renaux, Sigrid, *The Turn of the Screw: A Semiotic Reading* (New York: Peter Lang, 1993).

Renner, Stanley, 'Sexual Hysteria, Physiognomical Bogeymen, and the "Ghosts" in *The Turn of the Screw*', *Nineteenth-Century Literature*, 43 (1988), 175–94; revised version in Beidler (1995), 223–41.

Robbins, Bruce, 'Shooting Off James's Blanks: Theory, Politics and *The Turn of the Screw*', *The Henry James Review*, 5, 3 (1984), 192–9.

Robbins, Bruce, '"They don't much count, do they?": The Unfinished History of *The Turn of the Screw*', in Beidler (1995), 283–96.

Roellinger, Francis X., 'Psychical Research and "The Turn of the Screw"', in Kimbrough (1966), pp. 132–45; first published 1949.

Rubin, Louis D., 'One More Turn of the Screw', *Modern Fiction Studies*, 9 (1963–4), 314–28; reprinted in Willen (1969).

Rust, Richard Dilworth, 'Liminality in *The Turn of the Screw*', *Studies in Short Fiction*, 25 (1988), 441–6.

Ryburn, May L., '*The Turn of the Screw* and *Amelia*: A Source for Quint?', *Studies in Short Fiction*, 16 (1979), 235–7.

Schrero, Elliot M., 'Exposure in *The Turn of the Screw*', *Modern Philology*, 78 (1980–1), 261–74.

Schultz, Elizabeth, '"The Pity and the Sanctity of Terror": The Humanity of the Ghosts in "The Turn of the Screw"', *Markham Review*, 9 (1980), 67–71.

Scott, James B., 'How the Screw is Turned: James's *Amusette*', *University of Mississippi Studies in English*, 4 (1983), 112–31.

Sheppard, E. A., *Henry James and 'The Turn of the Screw'* (Auckland and Oxford: Auckland UP and Oxford UP, 1974).

Siebers, Tobin, 'Hesitation, History and Reading: Henry James's *The Turn of the Screw*', *Texas Studies in Language and Literature*, 25 (1983), 558–72.

Siegel, Eli, *James and the Children: A Consideration of Henry James's 'The Turn of the Screw'* (New York: Definition Press, 1968).

Siegel, Paul, '"Miss Jessel": Mirror Image of the Governess', *Literature and Psychology*, 18 (1968), 30–8.

Silver, John, 'A Note on the Freudian Reading of *The Turn of the Screw*', in Kimbrough (1966), pp. 239–43; first published 1957.

Solomon, Eric, 'The Return of the Screw', in Kimbrough (1966), pp. 237–45; first published 1964.

Spilka, Mark, 'Turning the Freudian Screw: How Not to Do It', in Kimbrough (1966), pp. 245–53; first published 1963.

Taylor, Michael J. H., 'A Note on the First Narrator of "The Turn of the Screw"', *American Literature*, 53:4 (1982), 717–22.

Tuveson, Ernest, '*The Turn of the Screw*: A Palimpsest', *English Studies in Literature*, 12 (1972), 783–800.

Walton, Priscilla L., '"What then on earth was I?": Feminine Subjectivity and *The Turn of the Screw*', in Beidler (1995), 253–67.

West, Muriel, 'The Death of Miles in *The Turn of the Screw*', in Willen (1969), pp. 338–49; first published 1964.

Wilson, Edmund, 'The Ambiguity of Henry James', in his *The Triple Thinkers* (Harmondsworth: Penguin, 1962, pp. 102–50); reprinted with 1959 postscript in Willen (1959/69); first published 1933–4; revised 1938 and 1952.

SELECTED CRITICISM SPECIFICALLY ON *WHAT MAISIE KNEW*

Armstrong, Paul B., 'The Phenomenology of James's Moral Vision', *Texas Studies in Literature and Language*, 20:4 (1978), 517–37.

Brown, Christopher, 'The Rhetoric of Closure in *What Maisie Knew*', *Style*, 20:1 (1986), 58–65.

Colt, Rosemary M., 'Innocence Unleashed: The Power of the Single Child', in *The Significance of Sibling Relationships in Literature*, ed. JoAnna Stephens Mink and Janet Doubler Ward (Bowling Green, OH: Bowling Green State University Popular Press, 1993), pp. 11–22.

Craig, Randall, '"Read[ing] the Unspoken into the Spoken": Interpreting *What Maisie Knew*', *The Henry James Review*, 2, 3 (1981), 204–12.

Everett, Barbara, 'Henry James's Children', in *Children and Their Books: A Celebration of the Work of Iona and Peter Opie*, ed. Gillian Avery and Julia Briggs (Oxford: Clarendon Press, 1989), pp. 317–35.

Foster, Dennis, 'Maisie Supposed to Know: Amo(u)ral Analysis', *The Henry James Review*, 5: 3 (1984), 207–16.

Galbraith, Mary, 'What Everybody Knew Versus What Maisie Knew: The Change in Epistemological Perspective from the Prologue to the Opening of Chapter 1 in *What Maisie Knew*', *Style*, 23: 2 (1989), 197–212.

Havey, Jonathan, 'Kleinian Developmental Narrative and James' *What Maisie Knew*', *University of Hartford Studies in Literature*, 23:1 (1991), 34–47.

Heller, Lee E., 'The Paradox of Individual Triumph: Instrumentality and the Family in *What Maisie Knew*', *South Atlantic Review*, 53:4 (1988), 77–85.

Kaufman, Marjorie, 'Beside Maisie on that Bench in Boulogne', *The Henry James Review*, 15 (1994), 257–63.

Leavis, F. R., 'What Maisie Knew', in his *Anna Karenina and other Essays* (London: Chatto & Windus, 1967), pp. 75–91; first published 1950.

Lowe, James, 'Color in *What Maisie Knew*: An Expression of Authorial Presence', *The Henry James Review*, 9: 3 (1988), 188–98.

McCall, Dan, 'What Maisie Saw', *The Henry James Review*, 16 (1995), 48–52.

Marotta, Kenny, '*What Maisie Knew*: The Question of Our Speech', *ELH*, 46 (1979), 495–508.

Mitchell, Juliet, '*What Maisie Knew*: Portrait of the Artist as a Young Girl', in Goode (1972), 168–89.

Munich, Adrienne Auslander, 'What Lily Knew: Virginity in the 1890s', in *Virginal Sexuality and Textuality in Victorian Literature*, ed. Lloyd Davis (Albany: State U. of New York Press, 1993), pp. 143–57.

Smith, Geoffrey D., 'How Maisie Knows: The Behavioral Path to Knowledge', *Studies in the Novel*, 15: 3 (1983), 224–36.

Williams, M. A., 'The Drama of Maisie's Vision', *The Henry James Review*, 2: 1 (1980), 36–48.

Wolk, Merla, 'Narration and Nurture in *What Maisie Knew*', *The Henry James Review*, 4: 3 (1983), 196–206.

Notes on Contributors

Marianne DeKoven is Professor of English and Director of the Institute for Research on Women at Rutgers University. She is the author of *Rich and Strange: Gender, History, Modernism* (Princeton, NJ, 1991) and *A Different Language: Gertrude Stein's Experimental Writing* (Madison, WI, 1983). Her current book project concerns the political and cultural movements of the 1960s, particularly feminism, in relation to the transition to postmodernism.

Barbara Eckstein is Associate Professor of English at the University of Iowa. The author of *The Language of Fiction in a World of Pain*, she is currently at work on two projects in the period after World War II. One is a comparativist study of Japanese American, African American, and American Indian oral histories and how they negotiate post-war relocation, racial policies and access to full US citizenship. The other uses the tools of cultural geography, the suggestions of African American fiction, and social history to study how post-war federal integration policies have been implemented or, more often, elided in three specific locations.

Shoshana Felman is Thomas E. Donnelley Professor of French and Comparative Literature at Yale University. She is the author of *The Literary Speech Act: Don Juan with Austin, or Seduction in Two Languages* (Ithaca, NY, 1984); *Writing and Madness: Literature/Philosophy/Psychoanalysis* (Ithaca, NY, 1985); *Jacques Lacan and the Adventure of Insight: Psychoanalysis in Contemporary Culture* (Cambridge, MA, 1987); *Testimony: Crises of Witnessing in Literature. Psychoanalysis and History* (New York and London, 1992, in collaboration with Dori Laub, MD); and *What Does a Woman Want? Reading and Sexual Difference* (Baltimore, MD, 1993).

Ronald Knowles is Senior Lecturer in English at the University of Reading. His recent books include *Henry IV Parts I & II* ('The Critics Debate', 1992), *Understanding Harold Pinter* (Columbia, SC, 1995), and *Gulliver's Travels: The Politics of Satire* ('Twayne's Masterwork Studies', 1996). He is currently editing *Henry VI Part II* for the Arden Shakespeare (3rd series).

T. J. Lustig is Lecturer in American Studies at Keele University. He is the author of *Henry James and the Ghostly* (Cambridge, 1994) and editor of The World's Classics edition of *The Turn of the Screw and Other Stories* (Oxford, 1992). He has also published a novel, *Doubled Up* (1990) and is currently working on an interdisciplinary study of contemporary American cultural issues.

Beth Newman is Associate Professor of English at Southern Methodist University, Dallas, Texas. She has published essays on nineteenth-century fiction in *PMLA, ELH, Novel* and *Criticism* and is completing a book, *The Fictive Gaze: Sexual Politics and Visual Relations in Nineteenth-century British Fiction*.

John H. Pearson is Associate Professor and Chair of the Department of English at Stetson University, DeLand, Florida. His recent work includes *The Prefaces of Henry James: Framing the Modern Reader* (1997) and articles on semiotics, autobiography, non-fiction prose and gender studies in literature. He is currently working on nineteenth-century aesthetics in the work of Henry James and Constance Fenimore Woolson.

Julie Rivkin is Associate Professor of English at Connecticut College. She is the author of *False Positions: The Representational Logics of Henry James's Fiction* (Stanford, CA, 1996), as well as articles on Henry James and other writers, in *PMLA, Contemporary Literature, The Henry James Review* and elsewhere. She is editing, with Michael Ryan, *Literary Theory: An Anthology* (Oxford, 1997).

John Carlos Rowe is Professor in the Department of English and Comparative Literature, at the University of California, Irvine. His books include *Henry Adams and Henry James* (1976), *Through the Custom-House: Nineteenth-Century American Fiction and Modern Theory* (1982), *The Theoretical Dimensions of Henry James* (1984), *At Emerson's Tomb: The Politics of Classic American Literature* (1997), and *The Other Henry James* (in press). He has edited (with Rick Berg) *The Vietnam War and American Culture* (1991), and *New Essays on the Education of Henry Adams* (1996). He is currently completing *Culture and United States Imperialism*.

Ronald Schleifer is Professor of English at the University of Oklahoma. He is editor of *Genre* and co-editor of 'The Oklahoma Project for Discourse and Theory'. His recent books include *Rhetoric and Death: The Language of Modernism and Postmodern Discourse Theory*, and *Culture and Cognition: The Boundaries of Literary and Scientific Inquiry* (co-authored with Robert Con Davis and Nancy Mergler). He is co-editor (with Robert Con Davis) of *Contemporary Literary Criticism* (now in its fourth edition).

Sheila Teahan is Associate Professor of English at Michigan State University, where she specialises in nineteenth-century American literature. She is the author of *The Rhetorical Logic of Henry James* (Baton Rouge, LA, 1995) and has published articles in *Arizona Quarterly, The Henry James Review* and *Studies in American Fiction*.

Index